The All-Party Oireachtas Committee was established on 3 July 1996. Its terms of reference are:

> *In order to provide focus to the place and relevance of the Constitution and to establish those areas where Constitutional change may be desirable or necessary, the All-Party Committee will undertake a full review of the Constitution. In undertaking this review, the All-Party Committee will have regard to the following:*
>
> *a   the Report of the Constitution Review Group*
>
> *b   certain constitutional matters, ie Articles 2 and 3, the Right to Bail, Cabinet Confidentiality and Votes for Emigrants which are the subject of separate consideration by the Government*
>
> *c   participation in the All-Party Committee would involve no obligation to support any recommendations which might be made, even if made unanimously*
>
> *d   members of the All-Party Committee, either as individuals or as Party representatives, would not be regarded as committed in any way to support such recommendations*
>
> *e   members of the All-Party Committee shall keep their respective Party Leaders informed from time to time of the progress of the Committee's work*
>
> *f   none of the parties, in Government or Opposition, would be precluded from dealing with matters within the All-Party Committee's terms of reference while it is sitting, and*
>
> *g   whether there might be a single draft of non-controversial amendments to the Constitution to deal with technical matters.*

The committee comprises nine TDs and two senators:

> Austin Currie, TD, Minister of State
> Síle de Valera, TD
> Frances Fitzgerald, TD
> Senator Ann Gallagher
> Brian Lenihan, TD
> Kathleen Lynch, TD
> Derek McDowell, TD
> Michael McDowell, TD
> Willie O'Dea, TD
> Jim O'Keeffe, TD
> Senator Michael O'Kennedy.

The secretariat is provided by the Institute of Public Administration:

> Jim O'Donnell, *secretary*
> John Conlon, *assistant secretary.*

At its first meeting on 5 July 1996 the committee elected Jim O'Keeffe, TD, as chairman. At its second meeting on 25 July 1996 it elected Senator Michael O'Kennedy as vice-chairman.

While no constitutional issue is excluded from the committee's remit, it is not a body with exclusive concern for constitutional amendments: the Government, as the executive, is free to make constitutional proposals at any time; and indeed in November 1996 it successfully proposed that Article 40.4 be amended to allow changes in the legislation on bail. Moreover, any political party represented in the Dáil may also take a constitutional initiative at any time.

Contents

Jim O'Keeffe TD, chairman of the All-Party Oireachtas Committee on the Constitution

Foreword

In its programme *A Government of Renewal* the government undertook to establish an All-Party Oireachtas Committee to carry out a review of the Constitution and make recommendations where constitutional change might be necessary or desirable. As a preliminary step, in April 1995 it established a committee of experts drawn from the areas of public administration, economics, education, law, political science and sociology – with lawyers being predominant – under the chairmanship of Dr T K Whitaker. The *Report of the Constitution Review Group* was published on 3 July 1996 and on the same day the All-Party Oireachtas Committee on the Constitution was established.

The Committee set to work immediately. It had available to it the comprehensive 700-page report of the Constitution Review Group. In addition, there were seventeen sets of documents compiled by the Constitution Review Group as background briefing for each of the chapters of its report. The Committee also had access to the submissions made by people and organisations to the Constitution Review Group.

To help us to orient ourselves on this material we invited Dr Whitaker to address us on the strategic issues dealt with in his report. It proved to be a valuable and rewarding experience and I was pleased in thanking Dr Whitaker to acknowledge the successful publication of the *Report of the Constitution Review Group* as one of his greatest services to the state. We also had the benefit of a number of meetings with Gerard Hogan, BL, FTCD, whose exceptional input to the work of the Constitution Review Group has been recognised.

Submissions

The first major step taken by the Committee was to invite the public to make written submissions on the recommendations of the Constitution Review Group or on any other constitutional issues they wished to place before us. During the period November 1996 to February 1997, we met with the representatives of the organisations which, in addition to making written submissions, wished to make supplementary oral presentations.

Function

Concomitantly the Committee sought to clarify its function. It examined the history of constitutional reviews, a series which began with the establishment by the Taoiseach Seán Lemass of an Oireachtas committee on the Constitution in August 1966. We found that the results, in terms of amendments made on foot of the reviews, have been meagre. The Committee then examined the referendum – the instrument of change – to ensure that it was apt for so complex a task as carrying out a large number of constitutional changes within a reasonable period. We concluded that it was, provided financial arrangements were put in place for funding referenda, following the Supreme Court judgment in the *McKenna* case. We then looked at how amendments should be managed. We found there were two major approaches. The 'Big Bang' approach would involve putting all the changes together in one compendious proposal to the people. It would run the risk, however, of bringing the whole endeavour to a negative conclusion if enough people were repelled by one or a number of amendments to such an extent as to reject the whole proposal. The other approach – the one favoured by the committee – was to draw up a programme of amendments.

From its preliminary examination, then, the Committee came to see its task as drawing up a programme of amendments which, implemented over five years, would renew the Constitution in such a way as to meet the needs, and carry the aspirations, of the present and the coming generation. No state with the referendum procedure for changing its constitution has succeeded in implementing such a programme. The enterprise is a pioneering one that will search out our psychological resources.

The Committee appreciates that success in the enterprise requires two things – a commitment from the party leaders in the Oireachtas to sustain the work over any changes of administration and the engagement, over the period, of the people in public discussion and consideration of the proposals for amendment. In the matter of constitutional change, one of the glories of our Constitution is that while it is politicians who propose it is the people who dispose.

Procedure

The Committee has decided to proceed by way of issuing progress reports which will bring forward periodically parts of its programme of proposed amendments. This first progress report, therefore, in addition to setting forth the framework within which the Committee has approached its work, contains seven distinct elements of its programme of proposed amendments under the headings:

- The Power to Dissolve Dáil Éireann
- Constitutionality of Bills and laws
- Local Government
- The Electoral and Ethics Commission
- The Ombudsman
- 'Woman in the home' and gender-inclusive language in the Constitution
- Omnibus Proposal: Technical/Minor Amendments.

Second progress report
The Committee has also moved towards completion of its progress report. It will deal with Seanad Éireann.

Acknowledgements

I am very grateful to my colleagues on the Committee, and especially to Senator Michael O'Kennedy, the vice-chairman, for their sustained work, which involves considerable reading, study and consultation outside of, and in addition to, formal meetings. The committee has held fifteen meetings in the ten months since it was established – a meeting every fortnight if one excludes the July–August period.

The secretariat to the Constitution Review Group was provided by the Institute of Public Administration whose Assistant Director General, Jim O'Donnell, acted as secretary. His writing, editing and publishing skills helped to ensure that their massive report appeared in the year allotted for its writing and production. Our Committee greatly appreciates the value of the arrangement which has allowed the knowledge and experience that he and the assistant secretary, John Conlon of the Department of Finance, gained on that project to be transferred to the service of our Committee.

The work of a Committee such as ours greatly depends upon the quality of the research put into developing the database that underpins it. In this regard I would like to commend particularly John Conlon. For the organisation of meetings and the careful production of the text, the Committee expresses its thanks to Jennifer Armstrong and Marie O'Neill (and to Louise Warren who helped earlier). Finally, I would like to thank Tom Turley who at the later stages of the production of this first progress report provided editorial services.

Jim O'Keeffe, TD

Chairman

April 1997

1 Constitutional Reviews

Constitutional Reviews

Introduction

In being charged to make a full review of the Constitution, the All-Party Oireachtas Committee on the Constitution is the latest group to undertake the task of periodic constitutional review initiated by Seán Lemass. In a speech in March 1966 the then Taoiseach suggested that:

> ... the time [has] come for a general review of *Bunreacht na hÉireann*. It is possible that some of the views regarding the procedures and institutional arrangements for applying the democratic principles on which the Constitution is framed, which prevailed thirty years ago, could now be modified in the light of our own experience or that of other countries in the intervening years.

Mr Lemass accepted that the principles of the Constitution continued to have a strong appeal, but he argued that 'the manner in which these principles were expressed and the procedures by which it was decided to apply them might not be as suitable to our present requirements as they were ...'. In any case, the Supreme Court had in some instances interpreted the Constitution 'in a way its drafters had not expected or intended'. He thought there was 'a case for carrying out a general review of the provisions of the Constitution'. In the Dáil a week later, he made it clear that he was thinking of this as a routine operation: such a review ought to be undertaken 'every twenty-five years or so'.

In 1966, an informal Oireachtas Committee charged to review the Constitution was established. It issued an interim report in 1967 – its only report. In 1966, too, the Taoiseach asked the Attorney General to set up a legal committee to review the Constitution in conjunction with, but separately from, the Oireachtas Committee. In 1968, the legal committee produced a draft report and ceased its work.

Constitutional issues in relation to Northern Ireland were addressed by an Inter-Party Committee on the Implications of Irish Unity established in 1972 by the Taoiseach, Jack Lynch. It failed to produce a report by the time it lapsed with the dissolution of the Dáil in February 1973 but its work was continued by the All-Party Committee on Irish Relations established in July of that year by the Taoiseach, Liam Cosgrave. The committee failed to agree recommendations for constitutional change and it lapsed with the dissolution of the Dáil in 1977. In 1981, the Taoiseach, Dr Garret FitzGerald, announced his 'constitutional crusade'. He aimed to eliminate the sectarian and confessional nature of some parts of *Bunreacht na hÉireann* and to replace them with pluralist principles and so allay the suspicions of Unionists. He subsequently established a Constitution Review Body, a group of legal experts under the chairmanship of the Attorney General. This committee lapsed with the fall of the first FitzGerald administration in 1982 without reporting.

In 1983, on his return to power, Dr FitzGerald established, with the support of the other party leaders as well as the leader of the SDLP, the New Ireland Forum. Among the conclusions in its report, published in 1984, was that '... a new Ireland will require a new constitution which will ensure that the needs of all traditions are fully met'.

In 1988, the Progressive Democrats published *Constitution for a New Republic*. The Progressive Democrats were concerned to bring forward a truly republican and pluralist constitution which would be acceptable to all political and religious traditions. Its leader, Desmond O'Malley, TD, said they had put it out for public discussion.

Constitutional issues in regard to Northern Ireland were again addressed by the Forum for Peace and Reconciliation established by the Government in October 1994 following the Downing Street Declaration of 15 December 1993 made jointly by the Taoiseach, Albert Reynolds, and the British Prime Minister, John Major. The Forum had not issued an agreed report on these matters when it adjourned *sine die* in March 1996.

In 1995, the Taoiseach John Bruton, with the concurrence of the other party leaders, established the Constitution Review Group '... to establish those areas where constitutional change may be desirable or necessary, with a view to assisting the All-Party Committee on the Constitution, to be established by the Oireachtas, in its work'. The Review Group had fifteen members selected from different backgrounds – public administration, economics, education, law, political science and sociology – with lawyers being predominant. The Review Group presented its report in 1996. It is the most thorough analysis of the Constitution from the legal, political science, administrative, social and economic perspectives ever made.

A fuller description of these constitutional reviews is given in Appendix I.

Results of reviews

In the thirty-year period since 1966, eighteen proposals to amend the Constitution have been put to the people. Of these, only five, of which three were approved by the people, proceeded directly from the process of constitutional review begun in 1966 (see Appendices II and III). The other thirteen proceeded from politico-economic aspirations related to such issues as accession to the European Communities and ratification of the Treaty on European Union, or from social needs such as the right to remarry and the right to life.

Sources of demands for change

However, also as a result of the various reviews, a clear understanding of the major sources of the demands for constitutional amendment has emerged:

i)   *Northern Ireland* It is appreciated by the parties in the Oireachtas that in the event of a successful conclusion to the moves for peace and reconciliation in Northern Ireland the Constitution will need to be revised. It will need to reflect fully 'the principle of consent in Northern Ireland and demonstrably be such that no territorial claim of right to jurisdiction over Northern Ireland contrary to the will of a majority of its people is asserted, while maintaining the existing birthright of everyone born in either jurisdiction in Ireland to be part, as of right, of the Irish nation' (*A New Framework for Agreement*, para 21). In recognition of the fears of the Unionist community, it needs to provide for a modern, democratic, pluralist society and seek to remove any element in the democratic life and organisation of the state that can be represented as a real and substantial threat to the way of life and ethos of Unionists (see Downing Street Declaration, para 6). It will need to provide for North/South institutions 'to cater adequately for present and future social and economic inter-connections on the island of Ireland, enabling representatives of the main traditions, North and South, to enter agreed dynamic, new, co-operative and constructive relationships' (*A New Framework for Agreement*, para 24). The political parties in the Oireachtas are agreed that Articles 2 and 3 are best dealt with in the context of an overall agreement on Northern Ireland. However, under *A New Framework for Agreement*, the Irish government is committed to do all in its power to ensure that any other obstacles to peace and reconciliation in the Constitution are removed.

ii) *European Union* Article 6 of the Constitution declares that 'all powers of government, legislative, executive and judicial, derive, under God, from the people, whose right it is to designate the rulers of the State and, in final appeal, to decide all questions of national policy, according to the requirements of the common good'. The Constitution was designed for a nation-state. When Ireland decided to become a member of the European Communities, a decision which would cede law-making powers over certain executive functions to the institutions of a supra-national body, the approval of the people had to be sought. This was achieved by an amendment of Article 29 dealing with International Relations. The development of the powers of the European Communities and the transformation of the Communities into the European Union have required further constitutional amendments to this Article.

Given the increasing importance, if not dominant role, that the European Union now plays in regulating our lives, in restricting the scope of the law-making powers of the government and in constraining the Irish courts in their interpretation of the law, it has been suggested that the profound legal and structural changes resulting from Ireland's membership of the EEC/EU are not adequately reflected in Article 29 and that amendments to a number of Articles might present the political reality more truly: that Article 5 of the Constitution describing the nature of the State – 'Ireland is a sovereign, independent, democratic state' – might be aptly amended by inserting after 'Ireland' 'as a member of the European Union', that Article 9 of the Constitution, which deals with the right of citizenship and the political duties of all citizens, that is, 'Fidelity to the nation and loyalty to the State', might be enhanced by incorporating the substance of Article 8 of the Treaty establishing the European Community to reflect more accurately what it now means to be an Irish citizen:

- every person holding the nationality of a Member State shall be a citizen of the Union

- citizens of the Union shall enjoy the rights conferred by this Treaty and shall be subject to the duties imposed thereby.

iii) *International human rights developments* The Constitution, enacted at a time when fascist and communist totalitarianism was savaging the rights of the individual in vast stretches of Europe, contained a ringing assertion of those rights. Following World War II there developed in Western Europe and elsewhere a widespread movement to identify, and find means of legally asserting, a whole range of personal rights – political, social, economic and cultural. These were embodied in a number of important international conventions – the Universal Declaration of Human Rights (1948), the European Convention on Human Rights (1950), the International Covenant on Civil and Political Rights (1966), and the International Covenant on Economic, Social and Cultural Rights (1966) – all of which Ireland has ratified. The rights set forth in these conventions are more numerous than those enumerated in the Irish Constitution. However, the capacity of the Irish courts under the Constitution to identify rights other than those specifically enumerated has progressively extended the constitutional protection afforded to people living in Ireland. Moreover, in regard to some personal rights the level of protection afforded by our Constitution is superior to that provided by the international conventions. There has emerged a need to find the optimal accommodation between the Constitution and the international conventions.

iv) *Socioeconomic change* Bunreacht na hÉireann was designed for a predominantly rural population. In 1936, 65% of the people lived in the countryside or in small villages of a few hundred people. They lived mainly on the land and off the land. There was little industry; commercial activity was underdeveloped and based in the larger towns and cities. In the sixty years since, economic development has transformed the demographic pattern – 60% of the people live in towns of more than 1,500 people, half of them in Dublin and its hinterland. In addition, the development of a world trade in the sixties and the concomitant exposure of society to a global range of ideas and mores through the electronic media has intensified the change in social attitudes and patterns.

Commentators have pointed to the effects of consumerism: the communitarian values which bind people together are squeezed out by the forcefully asserted demands of the individual. Religious spokespersons, too, have found consumerism to be a source of the process of secularisation which seeks to remove religion from the public arena and confine it to the ambit of the private individual.

Sociological studies have documented the phenomenal changes in the rate of marriage formation, the fertility of marriage, the diversity of family units outside of those based on marriage, the levels of marriage breakdown and the numbers of Irish women seeking abortions in Britain. Moreover, disadvantaged groups within society have been progressively reaching a greater self-consciousness.

Socioeconomic ferment is the pulse of politics. People vary in their ideas about the appropriate constitutional responses required from time to time to maintain the stability and health of the whole political system.

v) *Working experience* Sixty years' experience of working under the institutions and procedures provided for in the Constitution has inevitably created an awareness of a range of ways in which the Constitution might be amended to work more satisfactorily. Some such changes would be of a substantive nature, for example, in regard to the procedures surrounding a dissolution of Dáil Éireann, the representative basis of, and electoral system for, Seanad Éireann, and the placing of a time limit on the declaration of a state of emergency. Other such changes would be of a technical character, for example, amendment of Article 28.6.2° to provide for the nomination of a senior minister in the event of a situation arising in which neither the Taoiseach nor the Tánaiste was available to act, amendment of Article 16.7 to deal more precisely with casual vacancies in Dáil Éireann, amendment of Article 26.2.1° to extend the period within which the Supreme Court's judgment must be given in cases where a Bill has been referred by the President for a decision on its constitutionality.

vi) *Outdating of provisions* Some references in the Constitution have become obsolete and therefore should be deleted – for example, Article 29.4.2° which was inserted to allow the State to use the services of the British monarchy for external relations' purposes in the period 1937 to 1948, the words 'or the office of the Executive Council of Saorstát Éireann' in Article 31.2.ii, and possibly some of the Transitory Articles (51-63).

vii) *Inaccuracies* A number of inaccuracies have been noticed in the course of the various reviews, for example, the words 'and on the system of proportional representation' in Article 12.2.3°, the occasional lack of correspondence between the Irish and English texts (thus in the English version of Article 12.4.1° the word 'completed' needs to be substituted for 'reached') and the use of 'Oireachtas' rather than 'Each House of the Oireachtas' in the English version of Article 15.7.

Conventional wisdom

The various constitutional reviews have also produced insights into how the task of reviewing the Constitution should be approached:

i) *Inclusiveness* Most constitutions have come into being as a result of revolution, defeat in war or the breakdown of a political system. A new constitution seeks to gather the people around a new political vision. It usually embodies assertions of difference between the new state and the old. Consequently it tends to be exclusive in some respects. Since a constitution, if it is to endure, must perform the great political function of binding people together in peace, anyone who seeks to review a constitution should attend carefully to the possibility of making it more inclusive. The Fifth Amendment of our Constitution (1972), a product of the 1967 review, deleted the provision relating to the special position of the Roman Catholic Church, and advanced inclusiveness in relation to religions.

ii) *Clarity and simplicity* A constitution should be accessible to the ordinary person. It should aim to be as clear and simple as possible. It should enunciate principles and leave to legislation the detailing of the processes through which the principles are to be expressed.

iii) *Strategic issues* The apparatus of a modern state is extensive and complex. Every year, parts of the system are changed in functions and structures to respond to current political, economic or social needs. A constitution should not concern itself to describe the whole apparatus of the state. It should concentrate on the state's strategic components – those important stabilising structures (in our case, the Oireachtas, the Government, the courts) which are subject only to occasional change.

iv) *Transient concerns* A constitution should deal with the perennial concerns of society. If it provides for transient concerns it becomes, with the passage of time, loaded with redundant provisions. In this respect our Constitution is admirably restrained. The use of vocational bodies in respect of Seanad Éireann, being based on the *passé* corporativist ideas of the 1930s, is the only striking example of a transient concern finding its way into the text.

v) *Minimalism* A good constitution develops organically, maintaining an overall balance in its provisions between the rights of the community and the rights of the individual, between providing for public order and personal liberty, between the powers it distributes among its major organs. Those reviewing a constitution must engage in an Article by Article audit which will suggest amendments in the existing text and the addition of new Articles. Care must be taken lest such changes affect the overall balance of a constitution in unexpected ways. Tinkering with the constitutional mechanisms may also cause imbalance. The Constitution Review Group quotes the advice it was given in this regard: 'If it ain't broke, don't fix it'.

A good constitution also develops through the interpretation of it by judges in cases brought before them in the courts. The case-law that develops around a constitution produces greater certainty for everyone. It is a certainty bought at considerable accrued expense to the state which usually bears the costs of constitutional challenges (because of the general benefits which flow from such decisions). Unnecessary changes in the Constitution jeopardise this evolved jurisprudence.

For these reasons, those charged with reviewing the Constitution tend to adopt a minimalist approach.

Defining its role

In approaching its task the Committee had the great advantage of having available to it from the outset the report of the Constitution Review Group, chaired by Dr TK Whitaker. This report had surveyed, in so far as it could, the work of the other groups that had engaged in review of the Constitution over the past thirty years; and it had brought to bear its own great resources in terms of knowledge and experience in its thorough review of the Constitution.

The Constitution Review Group concluded that the Constitution has, generally speaking, performed successfully. However, it formulated about a hundred recommendations to bring about desirable change. In addition it recommended that the text of the Constitution should be made gender sensitive – a process which would involve changes in approximately eighty sections and subsections.

The people

The Committee first canvassed the reactions of the people to the recommendations of the Constitution Review Group. It sent a copy of the report to all the individuals who, and organisations which, had made submissions to the Constitution Review Group. It invited all major state bodies and national interest groups to make observations. It placed a notice in the national press at the beginning of August 1996 inviting written submissions and followed this up with a reminder on local radio in September. Some groups who made submissions requested an opportunity to make supplementary oral presentations. The Committee agreed to this and the presentations were made between November 1996 and February 1997.

Seanad Éireann

The Constitution Review Group discussed Seanad Éireann in its report but decided that, in the time available to it, it could not carry out an adequate analysis of that formally important institution of state. It had recommended that 'a separate, comprehensive, independent examination of all issues relating to Seanad Éireann should be conducted'. To get this process under way quickly, the Committee commissioned two eminent political scientists, Mr John Coakley of University College Dublin and Professor Michael Laver of Trinity College Dublin, to produce a study, 'Options for the Future of Seanad Éireann'. This was submitted to the Committee on 5 December 1996. It is a sophisticated analysis based on the Inter-Parliamentary Union's extensive database (and is probably the first systematic use of that invaluable source of information in any country). The Committee also sought the views of serving senators and a number of distinguished former senators. On 30 January 1997 the chairman opened a Seanad debate extending over two days on the role of Seanad Éireann.

Realistic goal

As a result of these steps the Committee had quickly available to it an immense amount of advice, admittedly some conflicting, on the changes that should be recommended. However, the Committee was well aware that the practical results of the reviews over the past thirty years had been meagre. It also found it sobering to look at international experience. Constitutional amendment is relatively infrequent. The oldest written constitution – the American constitution – has been amended only twenty-six times in its two hundred and twenty years of existence. Ireland, which is second to Italy among the member states of the European Union in the number of times it has changed its constitution, has done so only fifteen times. Moreover, the Committee could find no example of a constitution amendable only by referendum which had been the subject of a process of total review. Machiavelli's dictum is clearly potent: 'It should be borne in mind that there is nothing more difficult to handle, more doubtful of success, and more dangerous to carry through than initiating changes in a state's constitution' (*The Prince*).

The fact that the task set for the Committee has never been carried through elsewhere does not mean it cannot be done – it simply underscores the great challenge of the enterprise. It does mean, however, that one must coolly survey the approaches that may lead to success.

The 'Big Bang' approach

One approach would be to embody all the changes agreed by the Committee in a revised text of the Constitution and present it to the people as a single proposal. This in effect was what was done in the case of *Bunreacht na hÉireann* in 1937 – it built on, and extended, the 1922 Constitution. The great advantage of this approach is that it is simple, straightforward and speedy. The Committee felt, however, that it would need the dynamic of a new political departure, such as a settlement in Northern Ireland, to carry forward such a heavily laden proposal. The approach also has the inherent risk that even though the people might generally favour the proposal, a majority of them might variously oppose one or more of the recommendations in it so vehemently as to reject the proposal *in toto*. This would wreck the whole endeavour by bringing it to a completely negative conclusion.

A programme of constitutional renewal

Another approach – the one recommended by the Committee – would be to draw up a programme of constitutional amendments, aimed at renewing the Constitution in all its parts, for implementation over a number of years. The great advantage of this approach is that it would give the people time to reflect on the proposed changes and to make up their minds with due deliberation. Its great disadvantage might be that the sustained political will required of public representatives for success might be sapped by short-term political pressures. The approach also requires the party leaders to concert on the value of the process for it to continue from one administration to another.

From our discussion of the major sources of the demands for constitutional change it is clear that a programme of constitutional renewal would contain a large variety of proposed amendments. Some would be substantive, others would be technical. Some would be controversial, others not. Such a programme poses a challenge to the political will of the people, too. They must embrace the goal of the programme, that is to say, a renewed Constitution contoured to their needs and those of the coming generation (rather than to those of the previous generation). They must also grapple with the negative syndrome that tends to operate in the referendum process as people ask, 'Are all these changes really for the common good or have those proposing them ulterior motives?' Thus, confidence in the process must be developed between the people and their public representatives.

Conclusion

In reflecting on all these issues the Committee considers that:

- it should draw up a programme of constitutional reform to be implemented over a number of years

- it should engage the people from an early stage in discussion of the elements of the programme

- to get this process under way in an orderly and manageable fashion it should publish a series of reports dealing with the various elements of the programme

- it should draw up the programme in such a way that the people can most efficiently deal with it (so as to avoid referendum fatigue)

- the programme should be implemented in such a way that the economies of combining referenda with local, Dáil, Presidential and European Parliament elections are made.

2 The Referendum

The Referendum

The instrument of change

Article 46.1 *Any provision of this Constitution may be amended, whether by way of variation, addition, or repeal, in the manner provided by this Article.*

46.2 *Every proposal for an amendment of this Constitution shall be initiated in Dáil Éireann as a Bill, and shall upon having been passed or deemed to have been passed by both Houses of the Oireachtas, be submitted by Referendum to the decision of the people in accordance with the law for the time being in force relating to the Referendum.*

46.3 *Every such Bill shall be expressed to be 'An Act to amend the Constitution'.*

46.4 *A Bill containing a proposal or proposals for the amendment of this Constitution shall not contain any other proposal.*

46.5 *A Bill containing a proposal for the amendment of this Constitution shall be signed by the President forthwith upon his being satisfied that the provisions of this Article have been complied with in respect thereof and that such proposal has been duly approved by the people in accordance with the provisions of section 1 of Article 47 of this Constitution and shall be duly promulgated by the President as a law.*

{Airteagal 46.5

Aon Bhille ina mbeidh togra chun an Bunreacht seo a leasú ní foláir don Uachtarán a lámh a chur leis láithreach, ar mbeith sásta dó gur comhlíonadh forálacha an Airteagail seo ina thaobh agus gur thoiligh an pobal go cuí leis an togra sin de réir forálacha alt 1 d'Airteagal 47 den Bhunreacht seo, agus ní toláir don Uachtarán é a fhógairt go cuí ina dhlí.}

Article 46 of the Constitution lays down that any provision of the Constitution may be amended by referendum. Reference to the people is a more democratic way of amending a constitution than a decision by parliament – the more common way – however weighted the majority in such cases may need to be. Those constitutions which prescribe the referendum as the instrument for changing them have been classified as 'rigid'. An early concern of the Committee was to establish what degree of flexibility is allowed by the constitutional provisions on the referendum.

Some people maintain that the procedures for the referendum laid down in the Constitution make it uncommonly more difficult to make amendments. The concern centres mainly on Article 46.4 where it states that a Bill can contain 'a proposal or proposals' for amendment of the Constitution. Where a Bill contains more than one proposal it has been suggested that every such proposal must be put separately to the people. It has been argued that this is clear from the terms of Article 46.5, especially the Irish text, and Article 47.1 which states that 'every proposal' is 'held to have been approved by the people' if a majority of the votes cast at a referendum are cast in favour of its enactment into law. On the other hand, it might be argued that these references specifying how a single proposal is approved are merely indicating the conditions that must be met by the class which is designated by the term 'proposal' and do not intend to specify that the process must attend each member of the class separately. This interpretation could, therefore, equally well congrue with the reference to a Bill containing 'a proposal or proposals'.

People who might insist on the narrow definition of the term 'proposal' would presumably be concerned to obviate a situation in which the Oireachtas might seek to have a regressive provision approved by associating it with a popular one in a single proposal. They might also feel that an omnibus proposal, that is to say, one that contains a number of proposals within it, would be unfair where the people were likely to give different answers if the proposals contained in it were put singly. However, since proposals put by the government are publicly debated in the Dáil and their consequences thoroughly explored through the adversarial process there, the fairness or otherwise of proposals is exposed and, because the people have the power to reject proposals, their judgment, in principle, cannot be coerced. Incidentally, while it is clear from Article 46.4 that a Bill can contain 'a proposal or proposals' for amendment of the Constitution, it is not immediately clear what 'any other proposal' means. However, since it stands in opposition to 'a proposal or *proposals*' (emphasis added), it can only do so on the basis of a difference in kind. There are two kinds of proposal that may be contained in a Bill – constitutional and legislative. The term 'a proposal or proposals' explicitly refers to what is constitutional; 'any other proposal' must, therefore, refer to what is legislative. If a Bill

Article 47.1 *Every proposal for an amendment of this Constitution, which is submitted by Referendum to the decision of the people shall, for the purpose of Article 46 of this Constitution, be held to have been approved by the people, if, upon having been so submitted, a majority of the votes cast at such Referendum shall have been cast in favour of its enactment into law.*

47.2.1° *Every proposal, other than a proposal to amend the Constitution, which is submitted by Referendum to the decision of the people shall be held to have been vetoed by the people if a majority of votes cast at such Referendum shall have been cast against its enactment into law and if the votes so cast against its enactment into law shall have amounted to not less than thirty-three and one-third per cent of the voters on the register.*

47.2.2° *Every proposal, other than a proposal to amend the Constitution, which is submitted by Referendum to the decision of the people shall for the purposes of Article 27 hereof be held to have been approved by the people unless vetoed by them in accordance with the provisions of the foregoing sub-section of this section.*

47.3 *Every citizen who has the right to vote at an election for members of Dáil Éireann shall have the right to vote at a Referendum.*

47.4 *Subject as aforesaid, the Referendum shall be regulated by law.*

containing a proposal or proposals to amend the Constitution were also to contain a legislative proposal, the legislative proposal could not be referred to the Supreme Court for a decision on its constitutional validity under Article 26 because that Article excludes 'a Bill containing a proposal to amend the Constitution'.

A practical problem

The issue of whether every proposal must be put separately is of great practical concern to the Committee. The *Report of the Constitution Review Group* makes about a hundred recommendations for constitutional change; in addition it proposes that the text of the Constitution should be made gender-inclusive – a process that would involve additional changes in about eighty sections or subsections. If the Oireachtas were to propose all those changes, or a range of similar changes, and if it were to interpret Article 46 narrowly as requiring that each change should be put before the people as a separate proposal, it would need to arrange for about 180 referenda. Considering the time needed to conduct a single referendum, such a programme would stretch hopelessly far into the future.

It is critically important, therefore, to establish what flexibility the Oireachtas has in making proposals. Could it, for example, put a single proposal to the people to make the language of the Constitution gender-inclusive by carrying out multiple changes listed in a schedule to an Amendment Bill? Could it put an omnibus proposal to the people dealing with a series of technical and minor amendments listed in an Amendment Bill? Could it, in a single proposal, place the abolition of the Seanad, for instance, before the people, listing in an Amendment Bill all the changes in the wide range of Articles in which there are direct and indirect references to the Seanad and making provision for the redistribution of the powers and functions of the Seanad and its officers? A positive answer to these questions would greatly enhance the prospects of implementing a comprehensive programme of constitutional reform.

The role of the Oireachtas

Article 46 lays down that a referendum proposal must come in the form of a Bill initiated in Dáil Éireann and passed, or deemed to have been passed, by both Houses of the Oireachtas. The Constitution, therefore, lays down a process that ensures that the implications of a proposal are thoroughly teased out in the public national forum that the Oireachtas provides, with its regulated procedures and systems of recording, and is formulated in such a way that it will perform effectively as a constitutional provision. For a proposal needs to be clear and unambiguous, needs to be capable of implementation, needs to be consistent with the other provisions of the Constitution, or where it is not, needs to provide for consequential changes, and needs to ensure that if it relates to state institutions it does not violate the separation of powers which is an informing principle of the Constitution, and if it relates to individual rights that it does so in such a way that the public interest can be duly asserted. Moreover, Article 47.4 provides that, subject to the procedure laid down in the Constitution, the referendum shall be 'regulated by law'. The principal pieces of legislation governing the referendum are the Referendum Act 1942, the Electoral

51.1 *Notwithstanding anything contained in Article 46 hereof, any of the provisions of this Constitution, except the provisions of the said Article 46 and this Article, may, subject as hereinafter provided, be amended by the Oireachtas, whether by way of variation, addition or repeal, within a period of three years after the date on which the first President will have entered upon his office.*

51.2 *A proposal for the amendment of this Constitution under this Article shall not be enacted into law, if, prior to such enactment, the President, after consultation with the Council of State, shall have signified in a message under his hand and Seal addressed to the Chairman of each of the Houses of the Oireachtas that the proposal is in his opinion a proposal to effect an amendment of such a character and importance that the will of the people thereon ought to be ascertained by Referendum before its enactment into law.*

51.3 *The foregoing provisions of this Article shall cease to have the force of law immediately upon the expiration of the period of three years referred to in section 1 hereof.]*

Act 1963 and the Electoral (Amendment) Act 1972. It might be noted that when, in 1959, the Government was about to submit to the people a Bill running to several pages, it had hurriedly to introduce and get enacted the Referendum (Amendment) Act 1959, which provided that a proposal, which is the subject of a referendum, would be stated on the ballot paper by citing the Bill in which it is contained by its short title – under the Referendum Act 1942, the rules covering the form of the ballot paper prescribed that the proposal must 'be stated on the ballot paper in the same terms as nearly as may be as such proposal is stated in the Bill'.

The Constitution, then, leaves the responsibility for the process entirely to the Oireachtas, something we find underscored by the Supreme Court in *Slattery v An Taoiseach* [1993] 1 IR 286: '...with the exception of a Bill referred by the President to the Supreme Court under Article 26 of the Constitution, the courts have no jurisdiction to construe or review any Bill which has as its purpose the amendment of the Constitution, whatever its nature'. Furthermore, in *Finn v Minister for the Environment* [1983] IR 154, Barrington J stated that he was 'satisfied that by Article 46.1 the people intended to give themselves full power to amend any provision of the Constitution'. In using the referendum as the instrument of constitutional change the Oireachtas clearly has full freedom and wide powers within the provisions of Articles 46 and 47.

The experience of constitutional change

Since the enactment of the Constitution, the Oireachtas has proposed to amend it twenty times (see Appendices III, IV and V). The first two amendments were effected by the Oireachtas under the transitory provision of Article 51.1 which allowed the Oireachtas to propose constitutional changes for up to three years from the date of the inauguration of the first President, by having a Bill passed, or deemed to be passed, by both Houses of the Oireachtas and presented to the President for his or her signature. Under this procedure the President would sign the Bill unless, after consultation with the Council of State, he or she 'signified in a message under his hand and Seal addressed to the Chairman of each of the Houses of the Oireachtas that the proposal is in his opinion a proposal to effect an amendment of such a character and importance that the will of the people thereon ought to be ascertained by referendum before its enactment into law'.

The first amendment, enacted in 1939, provided for a state of emergency to secure 'the public safety and the preservation of the State in time of war or armed rebellion', by changing Article 28.3.3°. The second amendment of the Constitution, enacted in 1941, was an omnibus proposal, covering a range of disparate Articles, aimed at tidying up the Constitution in the light of experience since its enactment. It should be noted that since the President had powers to refer this Bill to the people if he was concerned about its constitutionality in terms of either its character or content but did not do so, a proposal of an omnibus character, which it was, is constitutionally valid. Of course, the Constitution itself had been presented to the people as a single proposal – an omnibus proposal *par excellence* – and it can hardly be doubted that the people could give themselves a totally new Constitution under the provisions of Article 46.

Of the eighteen proposals actually put to the people up to November 1996, none was *prima facie* an omnibus proposal, nor did any proposal affect more than one Article. However, the Oireachtas has used its power to amend a provision, by way of variation, addition or repeal, flexibly. Thus, the referendum on the voting system held in 1959 proposed to delete section 2 of Article 16 and insert in its place some twenty-two different elements of the proposed new electoral system, listed in a schedule to the Amendment Bill, including the introduction of single-member constituencies, a single non-transferable vote and a Constituency Commission. The electorate could be presumed to have different views on the merits of these different elements, but the Oireachtas chose to present the system as a single proposal. It might be argued that the proposal was an omnibus one. The referendum on European Union, held in 1992, was also a single proposal to delete one sentence in Article 29.4.3° and add three new subsections, each containing a separate provision. Here again the Oireachtas might have chosen to set forth those three provisions as separate proposals; and here again it might be argued that the proposal was an omnibus one. In the case of the referenda on the rights to life, travel and information held in 1993, the Oireachtas, on the contrary, placed three separate proposals before the people.

The people

Eamon de Valera once famously referred to *Bunreacht na hÉireann* in the following terms: '... if there is one thing more than another that is clear and shining through this whole Constitution, it is the fact that the people are the masters'. In making proposals for constitutional change to the people the Oireachtas brings to bear not only the deep legislative experience it itself has or can command through the civil service, but also its understanding of what the people want. Given this, the Oireachtas is bound to ensure that the form in which it presents its proposals is fair. In terms of decision making, fairness is most obviously achieved when a clear simple proposal is presented for a 'Yes' or 'No' answer. However, a reductive process can break any simple proposal down into a number of separate proposals. Thus the Fifteenth Amendment of the Constitution Act 1995, in a single proposal, replaced the constitutional prohibition on divorce with a provision which allowed divorce under a number of specified conditions. It could have been presented as a package of separate proposals such as:

i) a proposal to remove the absolute prohibition on divorce

ii) a proposal to permit divorce only where couples had separated for four out of the previous five years

iii) a proposal to permit divorce only where there was no reasonable prospect of reconciliation between the parties

iv) a proposal to permit divorce only where proper provision is made for children.

Thus, in theory, it might have been possible to arrive at the result which was achieved by a series of amendments in each of which a separate element of the package would have been put to the people for their decision. While the whole package would have fallen if i) fell, in principle any one or more of the others could have stood alone. Discretion as to what is the appropriate level of abstraction (and of detail) at which to make a particular proposal must be exercised by someone – in the case of referenda, by the Oireachtas. The Oireachtas judged, correctly in view of the result of the divorce referendum, that it was fair to the wishes of the people to link its proposals in a single proposal.

There are also good reasons why the Oireachtas might wish to put an omnibus proposal before the people: in circumstances where society was experiencing major changes in the political situation – in the case of contemporary Ireland the achievement of reconciliation in Northern Ireland would be such an event – the people might wish a completely new constitution; for the sake of convenience (and to avoid referendum fatigue) the Oireachtas might wish to cluster a large number of non-controversial amendments in a single proposal – thus the programme of constitutional renewal proposed by this Committee might conveniently feature a single proposal to put into effect a large number of technical and minor changes.

In its analysis of the referendum process the Committee has been impressed by the following points:

- the Oireachtas has sole responsibility for formulating the proposals that are to be put to the people

- the courts, in view of the constitutional principle of the separation of powers, are extremely reluctant to intervene in the legislative process, unless expressly empowered by the Constitution to do so, such as under Article 26

- the Oireachtas, in its experience of bringing about constitutional change, has found great flexibility in operating within the provisions of Articles 46 and 47.

The Committee is convinced, therefore, that the Oireachtas has the flexibility needed to carry out a comprehensive programme of constitutional reform over a reasonable period by a combination of single and omnibus proposals. However, if the Oireachtas has any doubt on the issue, it can propose to the people a facilitative amendment of Article 46.

Other mechanisms

In its analysis of Articles 46 and 47 the Constitution Review Group considered:

- the popular initiative, that is to say, the capacity of a certain specified minimum number of voters to concert to propose laws or amendments to the Constitution, and

- the preferendum, that is to say, the presentation to the electorate of a range of proposals which the voter would be invited to rank in order of his or her preference.

The popular initiative

There is no doubt that the popular initiative is a mechanism which would increase the capacity of the political system to express the democratic value. However, like other such mechanisms, it needs to be evaluated in terms of both its practicality and efficiency. The Constitution Review Group set forth arguments for and against its adoption and concluded that the practical problems associated with it outweigh its advantages (see Appendix VI). The fact that only a few states have adopted it supports this view. Modern Irish governments find the management of their legislative programmes through the Houses of the Oireachtas a stretching one. Provision for a popular initiative would, in the Committee's view, exacerbate a government's legislative difficulties and reduce its efficiency.

The preferendum

The Constitution Review Group agreed that a cogent theoretical argument could be made in favour of a preferendum system (see Appendix VI). Of the various preferenda systems, the de Borda preferendum is the one actively promoted in Ireland. The de Borda Institute, based in Belfast, sees the preferendum as promoting consensus politics. In a preferendum system the result arrived at depends on what options are placed before the voters and the sensitivity of the scoring system. The theoretical and technical aspects of the system are so complex as to arouse unease in the mind of the ordinary voter. The quality of the results produced by the preferendum would first need to be evaluated; and, if they were deemed to be superior to those produced by other systems, it would make sense to pilot the preferendum in relatively minor decision making areas before adopting it for such an important purpose as the amendment of the Constitution. The Committee concurs with the Constitution Review Group's view that the referendum has functioned well and that there is no pressing need to change it.

Funding

A referendum creates a situation in which every voter should inform himself or herself about what the Oireachtas proposes, weigh up the arguments for and against the proposal, and make a decision. Some proposals are relatively straightforward, for example the 1972 referendum to reduce the voting age at Dáil and Presidential elections from twenty-one years to eighteen years, but others – and this seems to be the usual case – are technical or complex, for example the referendum on the right to bail.

Governments have always undertaken the costs of an information campaign to place the issues before the voter. Of their nature such campaigns are low-key. But the mounting by political parties and interest groups of promotional campaigns, for and against, usually enlivens the debate.

Discussion is carried on mainly in the media and is resourced to a great extent by them in return for readers, listeners and viewers. The political parties and the interest groups also contribute promotional funds. However, each side needs to be able to reach the voter, above the welter of debate, with its salient, summative points. This involves publicity expenditure not readily available to voluntary organisations such as political parties and other interest groups.

Since the 1972 referendum on Ireland's accession to the European Communities, governments, through the ministers sponsoring proposals, have funded separate campaigns in favour of proposals. When in 1995 Dáil Éireann voted £500,000 to finance a government-sponsored promotional campaign in favour of a 'Yes' vote on the divorce referendum, Patricia McKenna, MEP, succeeded in having the proposed expenditure declared unconstitutional in the Supreme Court on the grounds that such expenditure had the effect of putting the voting rights of those citizens in favour of the amendment above the voting rights of those citizens opposed to it.

As a result, in the referendum on the right to bail the government funded a modest information programme conducted by an independent ad hoc commission, comprising the Ombudsman, the Clerk of the Dáil and the Clerk of the Seanad, but did not fund a promotional campaign in favour of the proposal. The low turnout and the widespread impression that voters had not been able to inform themselves sufficiently suggest a certain deficiency in the public debate. To evoke a vigorous democratic response it is necessary to work out how to underpin referendum campaigns with adequate informational and promotional resources.

Independent commission

In its report the Constitution Review Group said that there ought not to be a constitutional barrier to the public funding of a referendum campaign provided the equitable allotment of such funding is entrusted to an independent commission (see Appendix VII). The sum to be allotted would be subject to legislative regulation. According to the Constitution Review Group, Article 47.4 should be amended accordingly. Such a constitutional safeguard would meet the principal objection to the old funding arrangements identified in the *McKenna* case.

Functions

The commission would carry out two main functions:

i)   mount an adequate information campaign through radio, television, other electronic media, newspapers, periodicals, posters and leaflets

ii) allocate funds to political parties and interest groups to ensure a thorough, sustained debate on the proposal.

It might also monitor, and adjudicate on, the fairness of campaign activities.

In view of the *McKenna* case it would seem that the promotional funds must be divided equally between the groups for and against. It would be up to the commission to devise both the criteria for allocating the funds to political parties and interest groups and the systems to ensure they meet their own two critical values – fairness in the allocation, and efficiency in the use, of funds. So far as we can see there are no ready-made models in other countries for such a commission. We must rely on our own ingenuity.

Conclusion

The Committee agrees with the Constitution Review Group that an independent body should be established to regulate the funding and conduct of referenda. It feels, however, that it would be tidier to provide in the Constitution for a commission to carry out not just those functions but also those undertaken by the Constituency Boundary Commission, the Public Service Ethics Committee under the Ethics in Public Office Act 1995 and any commission which might be proposed to regulate election funding (see chapter 7).

3 Towards a Programme for Constitutional Renewal

Towards a Programme for Constitutional Renewal

The distinguished jurist Gerard Hogan has observed:

> ... recent Irish experience with referendums tends to prove a point which has also been noticed in other countries, namely that large-scale constitutional reform is often only possible at a defining moment in a country's history. This was true of Ireland in 1937 (when a new Constitution was clearly necessary to consolidate the gains of the 1920s and the 1930s) and, more recently, of Canada in 1982 and South Africa in 1994. However, once that moment has passed and society accustoms itself to existing constitutional arrangements, there is an in-built resistance to further and more radical changes, especially where controversial single-issue referendums are concerned.

However, government leaders who perform their functions in accordance with the provisions of a written constitution seem to become aware of numerous ways in which a constitution should be amended to adapt it to changing political needs. We have already adverted to Seán Lemass's sense that a constitution needs to be so adapted every generation or so; and in this context Thomas Jefferson (1743-1826) made a similar observation about the first written constitution, the constitution of the United States of America:

> Each generation is as independent of the preceding as that was of all which had gone before. It has, then, like them a right to choose for itself the form of government it believes most promotive of its own happiness; consequently, [it has the right] to accommodate to the circumstances in which it finds itself that [the constitution] received from its predecessors; and it is for the peace and good of mankind that a solemn opportunity of doing this every nineteen or twenty years, should be provided by the Constitution; so that it may be handed on, with periodical repairs, from generation to generation, to the end of time, if anything human can so long endure.

In the absence of a popular demand for change, the Committee's endeavour to draw up a programme of amendments aimed at renewing the Constitution in such a way that it will be contoured to meet the needs of the present generation and the next should therefore be seen in workaday rather than radical terms.

Description

- The Constitution consists of a Preamble and sixty-three Articles. Articles 51-63, referred to as the Transitory Provisions, do not appear in the official printed text of the

Constitution, as provided for in Article 52.1, but continue to have the force of law as provided for in Article 52.2

- Articles 1-11 deal with the Nation and the State

- Articles 12-37 deal with the strategic institutions of state (such as the President, Dáil Éireann, Seanad Éireann, the government, the courts)

- Articles 38-44 deal with the rights of the individual (the rights of those charged with a criminal offence and the fundamental rights of every individual)

- Article 45, called 'Directive Principles of Social Policy', sets forth principles intended for the general guidance of the Oireachtas in making laws, but a case brought before the courts cannot be decided on the basis of the Article, that is to say, the Article is not cognisable by the courts

- Article 46 deals with amendment of the Constitution

- Article 47 deals with the Referendum

- Articles 48-50 deal with the Repeal of the Constitution of Saorstát Éireann and the continuance of laws in force in Saorstát Éireann.

- Articles 51-63 called 'the Transitory Provisions' ensured continuity in the authority and effectiveness of the organs and institutions of the state in the course of transition from Saorstát Éireann to the state defined and described by *Bunreacht na hÉireann*.

Recommendations of the Constitution Review Group

The recommendations of the Constitution Review Group in relation to each of these elements of the Constitution were as follows:

i)   *Preamble*

A majority of the Review Group favoured the replacement of the present Preamble by the basic formula of enactment of the Constitution by the people of Ireland. They acknowledged that a more extensive Preamble may be preferred and provided guidelines for it.

ii)   *Articles 1-11*

The Constitution Review Group recommended changes to two Articles only.

The Name of the State In regard to Article 4 it recommended that it should be amended to read:

> Éire is ainm don Stát
> The name of the State is Ireland

26

Article 8

8.1 The Irish language as the national language is the first official language.

8.2 The English language is recognised as a second official language.

8.3 Provision may, however, be made by law for the exclusive use of either of the said languages for any one or more official purposes, either throughout the State or in any part thereof.

Article 12.4

12.4.1° Every citizen who has reached his thirty-fifth year of age is eligible for election to the office of President.

12.4.2° Every candidate for election, not a former or retiring President, must be nominated either by:

    i. not less than twenty persons, each of whom is at the time a member of one of the Houses of the Oireachtas, or

    ii. by the Councils of not less than four administrative Counties (including County Boroughs) as defined by law.

12.4.3° No person and no such Council shall be entitled to subscribe to the nomination of more than one candidate in respect of the same election.

12.4.4° Former or retiring Presidents may become candidates on their own nomination.

12.4.5° Where only one candidate is nominated for the office of President it shall not be necessary to proceed to a ballot for his election.

Article 12.8

12.8 The President shall enter upon his office by taking and subscribing publicly, in the presence of members of both Houses of the Oireachtas, of Judges of the Supreme Court and of the High Court, and other

Official languages In regard to Article 8 it recommended that the first and second sections should be replaced by English and Irish versions on the following lines:

1 The Irish language and the English language are the two official languages.

2 Because the Irish language is a unique expression of Irish tradition and culture, the State shall take special care to nurture the language and to increase its use.

1 Is iad an Ghaeilge agus an Béarla an dá theanga oifigiúla.

2 Ós í an Ghaeilge an chuid is dúchasaí de thraidisúin agus de chultúr na hÉireann, beidh sé de chúram ar an Stát an teanga a chaomhnadh agus a h-úsáid a leathnú.

References to God References to God in the Constitution came up for consideration in Article 6. Some members of the Constitution Review Group saw no need to change the text of Article 6, considering that the words 'under God' are widely acceptable. Other members preferred that religious references generally should be reviewed by the Oireachtas in the context of amendment of the Preamble and the other relevant parts of the Constitution.

iii) *Articles 12-37*

The President – Articles 12-14

The Constitution Review Group recommended substantive change in relation to two sections of Article 12. It recommended three minor or technical changes to the same Article.

Nomination of Presidential candidates The Constitution Review Group considered that the constitutional requirements for nominating a presidential candidate (Article 12.4) are too restrictive and in need of democratisation. The means of securing a popular element in the process should be explored. It suggested that another method that might loosen the nomination procedure would be to reduce the number of members of either House required for nomination.

Declaration or affirmation Article 12.8 provides that upon entering upon his or her office the President shall take and subscribe publicly a declaration beginning, 'In the presence of Almighty God I ...'. The Constitution Review Group recommended that provision should be made for the President to make either a declaration or an affirmation. It considered whether the presidential declaration should be amended to incorporate the values a President should uphold in discharging official functions, for example, human rights.

Minor or technical changes These are listed in Appendix VIII (1-3).

public personages, the following declaration:-

In the presence of Almighty God 'I   , do solemnly and sincerely promise and declare that I will maintain the Constitution of Ireland and uphold its laws, that I will fulfil my duties faithfully and conscientiously in accordance with the Constitution and the law, and that I will dedicate my abilities to the service and welfare of the people of Ireland. May God direct and sustain me.'

Article 15.2.1°

15.2.1° The sole and exclusive power of making laws for the State is hereby vested in the Oireachtas: no other legislative authority has power to make laws for the State.

Article 15.3.1°

15.3.1° The Oireachtas may provide for the establishment or recognition of functional or vocational councils representing branches of the social and economic life of the people.

The National Parliament – Articles 15-27

The Constitution Review Group did not recommend any change in the constitutional arrangements governing relations between the President, the Dáil and the Seanad or between the legislature and government. However, it recognised that such change may be necessary in the light of any comprehensive review of Seanad Éireann that might be carried out.

The Constitution Review Group recommended ten substantive changes in these Articles and eleven minor or technical changes (apart from those in relation to gender-inclusiveness).

Delegation of powers to legislate Article 15.2.1° vests the 'sole and exclusive' power of making laws in the Oireachtas and provides that no other legislative authority has power to make laws for the state. This provision has been interpreted to restrict severely the power of ministers and other authorities to make statutory instruments or subordinate legislation. In *Cityview Press Ltd v An Chomhairle Oiliúna* [1980] IR 381 the Supreme Court held that the test

> is whether that which is challenged as an unauthorised delegation of parliamentary power is more than a mere giving effect to principles and policies which are contained in the statute itself. If it be, then it is not authorised; for such would constitute a purported exercise of legislative power by an authority which is not permitted to do so under the Constitution. On the other hand, if it be within the permitted limits – if the law is laid down in the statute and details only are filled in or completed by the designated Minister or subordinate body – there is no unauthorised delegation of power.

The Constitution Review Group recommended that consideration should be given to an amendment to Article 15.2.1° whereby in addition to subordinate legislation which is already permissible within the limits of the *Cityview Press* test, the Oireachtas should have power to authorise by law the delegation of power to either the government or a minister (but no other body) to legislate, using the mechanism of a statutory instrument, in relation to the substance of the parent legislation (thereby exceeding the present limits of the *Cityview Press* test). However, if such a change were to be made, it should be accompanied by necessary safeguards to ensure that the legislative supremacy of the Oireachtas was not thereby undermined. These safeguards would have to include, at a minimum, a requirement that any legislation pursuant to this power could not enter into law until it had been the subject of a positive resolution of both Houses of the Oireachtas.

Democratic participation The Constitution Review Group suggested that Article 15.3.1° might be amended to incorporate a reference to community and voluntary groups as follows:

Article 15.4.2°

15.4.2° *Every law enacted by the Oireachtas which is in any respect repugnant to this Constitution or to any provision thereof, shall, but to the extent only of such repugnancy, be invalid.*

Article 16.2.4°

16.2.4° *The Oireachtas shall revise the constituencies at least once in every twelve years, with due regard to changes in distribution of the population, but any alterations in the constituencies shall not take effect during the life of Dáil Éireann sitting when such revision is made.*

The Oireachtas may provide for the establishment or recognition of advisory or consultative bodies representing branches of the social, community, voluntary and economic life of the people, with a view to improving participation in, and the efficiency of, the democratic process.

Date of invalidity of laws found unconstitutional The Constitution Review Group adverted to the fact that Article 15.4.2° may require amendment to clarify the time from which the invalidity of a law dates, in the light of its recommendations under Article 34 (see below).

Revision of constituencies In regard to the Article 16.2.4° requirement on the Oireachtas to revise the constituencies at least once in every twelve years, the Constitution Review Group considered that it may be appropriate to give constitutional status to a Constituency Commission as a permanent element in the electoral system.

Electoral systems The Constitution Review Group presented an analysis of the advantages and disadvantages of various electoral systems. It recommended that consideration of any proposal to change the electoral system should be guided by the following principles:

1 the present PR-STV system has had popular support and should not be changed without careful advance assessment of the possible effects

2 if there were to be change, the introduction of a PR-list or AMS system would satisfy more of the relevant criteria than a move to a non-PR system.

The Constitution Review Group considered that the objective of introducing a common voting method across Europe for elections to the European Parliament is proceeding towards realisation – and some form of PR-list system continues to be the likely common choice. Consideration might be given to using a PR-list system for such elections in Ireland as a way of testing some of the effects of a PR-list system in the Irish context.

Seanad Éireann (Articles 18 and 19) The Constitution Review Group recommended a separate, comprehensive, independent examination of all issues relating to Seanad Éireann. It considered that if such a review did not resolve the issue of representation and other substantive issues in a satisfactory manner, serious consideration would need to be given to the abolition of the Seanad and the transfer of its role and functions to other parts of the political system. It pointed out that Articles 23, 24 and 27 require attention in any review of the composition, powers and functions of the Seanad.

Constitutionality of Bills and laws The constitutionality of Bills arises under Article 26 which provides that the President may, after consultation with the Council of State, refer a Bill to the Supreme Court for a decision as to whether it is

Article 34.3.3°

34.3.3° No Court whatever shall have jurisdiction to question the validity of a law, or any provision of a law, the Bill for which shall have been referred to the Supreme Court by the President under Article 26 of this Constitution, or to question the validity of a provision of a law where the corresponding provision in the Bill for such law shall have been referred to the Supreme Court by the President under the said Article 26.

Article 26.2.2°

26.2.2° The decision of the majority of the judges of the Supreme Court shall, for the purposes of this Article, be the decision of the Court and shall be pronounced by such one of those judges as the Court shall direct, and no other opinion, whether assenting or dissenting, shall be pronounced nor shall the existence of any such other opinion be disclosed.

Article 34.4.5°

34.4.5° The decision of the Supreme Court on a question as to the validity of a law having regard to the provisions of this Constitution shall be pronounced by such one of the judges of that Court as that Court shall direct, and no other opinion on such question, whether assenting or dissenting, shall be pronounced, nor shall the existence of any such other opinion be disclosed.

Article 26.2.1°

26.2.1° The Supreme Court consisting of not less than five judges shall consider every question referred to it by the President under this Article for a decision, and, having heard arguments by or on behalf of the Attorney General and by counsel assigned by the Court, shall pronounce its decision on such question in open court as soon as may be, and in any case not later than sixty days after the date of such reference.

repugnant to the Constitution. The constitutionality of laws arises under Article 34.3.2°. It empowers the High Court and the Supreme Court to pronounce on the constitutional validity of any law (other than those tested as Bills under the Article 26 procedure).

- In relation to the validity of a law passed following the Article 26 procedure and the immutability given to such a law by Article 34.3.3°, the Constitution Review Group, on balance, considered that Article 34.3.3° should be deleted in its entirety. Such a deletion would leave Acts passed under the Article 26 procedure open to later challenge but would impact only marginally upon the legal certainty given by the procedure inasmuch as a decision of the Supreme Court upholding the constitutionality of the Bill would still be an authoritative ruling on the Bill which would bind all the lower courts and be difficult to dislodge. It is to be expected that the Supreme Court would not, save in exceptional circumstances, readily depart from its earlier decision to uphold the constitutionality of the Bill. Such exceptional circumstances might be found to exist where the Constitution had been later amended in a manner material to the law in question, or where the operation of the law in practice had produced an injustice which had not been apparent at the time of the Article 26 reference, or possibly where constitutional thinking had significantly changed.

- The one-judgment rule, that is to say, the constitutional provision that the Supreme Court, in pronouncing on the validity of a Bill or law, shall give one judgment only rather than indicating assenting or dissenting views, operates in relation to Article 26 reference cases (Article 26.6.2°) and challenges to legislation (Article 34.4.5°).

  In regard to Article 26 cases the Constitution Review Group did not reach a consensus. Some members considered that the special character of the reference procedure justified the retention of the rule while others felt it should be deleted. In regard to the Article 34.4.5° cases the Constitution Review Group considered, on the whole, that it should be deleted because the rule is unsatisfactory in its operation and is apt to create anomalies.

- The Constitution Review Group considered that the sixty-day time limit in Article 26.2.1°, within which the Supreme Court must deliver its judgment in reference cases, is too short and should be extended to ninety days, with the possibility of further extension to accommodate a reference to the European Court of Justice where this is necessary.

Minor or technical changes These are listed in Appendix VIII (4-14).

Article 28.3.1°

28.3.1° *War shall not be declared and the State shall not participate in any war save with the assent of Dáil Éireann.*

Article 28.3.3°

28.3.3° *Nothing in this Constitution shall be invoked to invalidate any law enacted by the Oireachtas which is expressed to be for the purpose of securing the public safety and the preservation of the State in time of war or armed rebellion, or to nullify any act done or purporting to be done in time of war or armed rebellion in pursuance of any such law. In this sub-section 'time of war' includes a time when there is taking place an armed conflict in which the State is not a participant but in respect of which each of the Houses of the Oireachtas shall have resolved that, arising out of such armed conflict, a national emergency exists affecting the vital interests of the State and 'time of war or armed rebellion' includes such time after the termination of any war, or of any such armed conflict as aforesaid, or of an armed rebellion, as may elapse until each of the Houses of the Oireachtas shall have resolved that the national emergency occasioned by such war, armed conflict, or armed rebellion has ceased to exist.*

Article 28.10

28.10 *The Taoiseach shall resign from office upon his ceasing to retain the support of a majority in Dáil Éireann unless on his advice the President dissolves Dáil Éireann and on the reassembly of Dáil Éireann after the dissolution the Taoiseach secures the support of a majority in Dáil Éireann.*

Article 29.5

29.5.1° *Every international agreement to which the State becomes a party shall be laid before Dáil Éireann.*

29.5 2° *The State shall not be bound by any international agreement involving a charge upon public funds unless the*

The Government – Article 28

The Constitution Review Group recommended substantive change in relation to three sections of Article 28 and one minor or technical change.

Declaration of war The Constitution Review Group considered that declaring war has become an outmoded formality. Because 'war' may still be understood in the restricted sense of a formally declared state, it recommended that the second and subsequent references to 'war' in Article 28.3 be extended to include 'or other armed conflict', so that the government would be prevented from participating in an external armed conflict without the authorisation of Dáil Éireann.

Limit on the period for which a law enacting a state of emergency continues to have effect The Constitution Review Group recommended that Article 28.3.3° should be amended to include a limit of not more than three years during which such legislation will have effect, with annual review thereafter. It also recommended that fundamental rights and liberties retained during a state of emergency should be specified in the Constitution because they are in the European Convention on Human Rights and the International Covenant on Civil and Political Rights.

Constructive vote of no confidence A vote of no confidence aims to bring down a government and lead to the dissolution of the Dáil. A constructive vote of no confidence combines a vote of no confidence in the government with the nomination to the House of a new Taoiseach. It replaces a government without first dissolving the Dáil and holding a general election. It aims to bring continuity and stability to government for the full term of the Dáil. A majority of the Constitution Review Group considered that the introduction of this procedure merits serious consideration. It could be achieved by amending Article 28.10 by deleting the text after 'Éireann' and replacing this with 'demonstrated by the loss of a motion of no confidence which at the same time nominates an alternative Taoiseach'. Article 13.2.2° would then become redundant.

Minor or technical changes The change is listed in Appendix VIII (15).

International Relations – Article 29

The Constitution Review Group recommended two substantive changes to this Article and two minor or technical ones.

Ireland's membership of the United Nations A majority of the Constitution Review Group favoured inserting a specific clause dealing with the state's membership of the United Nations. It envisaged that the clause might be modelled loosely on the corresponding provisions of Article 130(u)(3) of the Treaty of Rome in that such a clause would (a)

terms of the agreement shall have been approved by Dáil Éireann.

29.5.3° *This section shall not apply to agreements or conventions of a technical or administrative character.*

recognise our existing membership of the United Nations and (b) confirm the state's determination to comply with its obligations under the United Nations Charter. The following draft was suggested:

> Ireland, as a member of the United Nations, confirms its determination to comply with its obligations under the Charter of the United Nations.

A majority of the Constitution Review Group recommended the insertion of such a clause because it would have symbolic value and would remove any uncertainty concerning the validity of our membership of the United Nations.

Technical and administrative agreements The Constitution Review Group recommended an amendment to Article 29.5.3° so that Article 29.5.2° would also apply to technical and administrative agreements. As a consequence, where they involve a charge upon public funds they would require prior Dáil approval.

Minor or technical changes These are listed in Appendix VIII (16-17).

The Attorney General, the Council of State and the Comptroller and Auditor General – Articles 30-33

The Constitution Review Group recommended two substantive changes in these Articles and one technical one.

Delegation of Attorney General's functions The Constitution Review Group recommended that Article 30 should expressly permit delegation of the Attorney General's functions to another senior lawyer with the approval of the Taoiseach.

Article 31.4

31.4° *Every member of the Council of State shall at the first meeting thereof which he attends as a member take and subscribe a declaration in the following form:*

'In the presence of Almighty God,   , do solemnly and sincerely promise and declare that I will faithfully and conscientiously fulfil my duties as a member of the Council of State.'

Declaration or affirmation for Council of State members The Constitution Review Group recommended that Article 31.4 be amended to allow members of the Council of State to make a declaration or an affirmation at their first meeting.

Minor or technical changes The change is listed in Appendix VIII (18).

The Courts – Articles 34-37

The Constitution Review Group recommended ten substantive changes in these Articles and two minor or technical changes (apart from some in relation to gender-inclusiveness).

Article 34.2

34.2 *The Courts shall comprise Courts of First Instance and a Court of Final Appeal.*

Different court structures The Constitution Review Group recommended that Article 34.2 should be amended to give the Oireachtas greater flexibility to develop and experiment with different court structures. The following draft was suggested:

> The courts shall include the Courts of First Instance, a Court of Final Appeal and such other courts as may be prescribed by law.

Date of invalidity of a law The Constitution Review Group considered that the importance of the prohibition in Article 15.4 in ensuring that the Oireachtas operates within the limits set by the Constitution is recognised. A majority of the Constitution Review Group was, therefore, not disposed to recommend generally that the courts should have jurisdiction to declare invalid, otherwise than *ab initio*, a statutory provision which at the date of its passing was repugnant to the Constitution. However, a majority of the Constitution Review Group was in favour of amending the Constitution to provide the courts with an express discretion, where justice, equity or, exceptionally, the common good so requires, to afford such relief as they consider necessary and appropriate in respect of any detriment arising from acts done in reliance in good faith on an invalid law. The Constitution Review Group considered that such special consideration needs to be given to two exceptional categories (unanimously in regard to one and by a majority in regard to the other):

i)   the so-called 'creeping unconstitutionality' cases

ii)   cases where validity was originally confirmed on an Article 26 reference.

In relation to i), the Constitution Review Group recommended that given the uncertainties in this area, it favoured giving the courts express power, in cases where they declare an Act to be unconstitutional but determine that at the date of its enactment it was not repugnant to the Constitution, to determine the date upon which it became unconstitutional.

In relation to ii), a majority of the Constitution Review Group recommended that in the special case of declaration of invalidity of a law the Bill for which had been referred to the Supreme Court under Article 26, the Constitution should give the courts an express jurisdiction to declare the law to be unconstitutional as of a stated date other than the date of enactment.

A bar on the exclusion by law of a right of appeal from a decision to acquit an accused A majority of the Constitution Review Group recommended that consideration should be given to the question whether Article 34.4.4° should be amended so as to remove any doubt about the ability of the Oireachtas to exclude by law a right of appeal from a decision to acquit an accused.

Number of judges of the Supreme Court to determine the validity of laws As already noted, Article 26.2.1° requires the Supreme Court to consist of not less than five judges for a decision on a Bill referred by the President under Article 26. Article 34 does not specify any minimum number of judges for the determination by the Supreme Court of the constitutional validity of a law (though section 7 of the Courts (Supplemental Provisions) Act 1961 requires the Supreme Court to sit with five judges for such a decision). The Constitution Review Group recommended that constitutional

Article 34.4.4°

34.4.4° No law shall be enacted excepting from the appellate jurisdiction of the Supreme Court cases which involve questions as to the validity of any law having regard to the provisions of this Constitution.

Article 34.5.1°

34.5.1° Every person appointed a judge under this Constitution shall make and subscribe the following declaration:

'In the presence of Almighty God I,   do solemnly and sincerely promise and declare that I will duly and faithfully and to the best of my knowledge and power execute the office of Chief Justice (or as the case may be) without fear or favour, affection or ill-will towards any man, and that I will uphold the Constitution and the laws. May God direct and sustain me.'

Article 35.2

35.2 All judges shall be independent in the exercise of their judicial functions and subject only to this Constitution and the law.

Article 38.1

38.1 No person shall be tried on any criminal charge save in due course of law.

Article 38.3.1°

38.3.1° Special courts may be established by law for the trial of offences in cases where it may be determined in accordance with such law that the ordinary courts are inadequate to secure the effective administration of justice, and the preservation of public peace and order.

---

provision should be made for the Supreme Court to sit with not less than five judges for such cases.

Declarations taken by judges on appointment The Constitution Review Group recommended that the declaration in Article 34.5.1° should be amended by deleting the first and last phrases referring to God.

Judicial conduct While the Constitution Review Group was of the opinion that such 'disciplinary' provisions short of impeachment as at present apply to the District Court are probably not inconsistent with Article 35.2 or otherwise unconstitutional, lest there be any doubt in the matter, Article 35.2 should be amended to allow for regulation by the judges themselves of judicial conduct, in accordance with the doctrine of the separation of the powers.

Impeachment of judges The Constitution Review Group recommended that the Article 12.10 impeachment process (in relation to the President) should be provided for judges and other constitutional officers. However, a majority of the Constitution Review Group recommended that this process should not be extended to District and Circuit Court judges.

Minor or technical changes These are listed in Appendix VIII (19-20).

iv) *Articles 38-44*

Trial of Offences – Articles 38 and 39

The Constitution Review Group recommended four substantive changes in relation to these Articles. It recommended no minor or technical change.

Specific enumeration of an accused's rights The Constitution Review Group considered it desirable to amend Article 38.1 to give explicit constitutional recognition of, and protection for, the rights of the accused recognised in the European Convention on Human Rights, the International Covenant on Civil and Political Rights and Irish case law, provided:

- such explicit statement does not prevent the specification of further rights by the courts such as may be necessarily implied by the enumerated rights

- the power of the Oireachtas to qualify certain of these rights by law is also expressly acknowledged.

While the Constitution Review Group did not put forward any particular draft of such a qualifying clause, it suggested that useful models might be found in the European Convention on Human Rights (see Articles 5(1) and 10(2)) and the German Constitution (see Articles 18 and 19).

The position of special courts The Constitution Review Group, on balance, considered that Article 38.3 should be

Article 38.6

38.6 *The provisions of Articles 34 and 35 of this Constitution shall not apply to any court or tribunal set up under section 3 or section 4 of this Article.*

Article 38.3.2°

38.3.2° *The constitution, powers, jurisdiction and procedure of such special courts shall be prescribed by law.*

Article 38.4.1°

38.4.1° *Military tribunals may be established for the trial of offences against military law alleged to have been committed by persons while subject to military law and also to deal with a state of war or armed rebellion.*

amended so as to provide that special courts may be established only for a fixed period as prescribed by law.

The exemption of special courts from compliance with Articles 34 and 35 as provided for by Article 38.6 A majority of the Constitution Review Group considered that Article 38.6 should be amended so as to remove the exemption of special courts from compliance with Articles 34 and 35. This can be achieved by deleting 'section 3 or' from Article 38.6. If this recommendation is accepted, a majority of the Constitution Review Group recommended that Article 38.3.2° might also be amended so as to permit the trial of offences before special courts where the ordinary courts are inadequate to secure the effective administration of justice *or* the preservation of public peace and order. This would permit the enactment at a future date of appropriate legislation if it appeared that the ordinary courts with trial by jury were inadequate to secure the effective administration of justice.

Military tribunals The Constitution Review Group considered it desirable that there should be a constitutional requirement in relation to both categories of military tribunals: that they should be established by law for the trial of offences against military law, and that they should also have a clear legal basis for their operation during, and in dealing with, a state of war, armed conflict or armed rebellion. It considered that the section should be amended by the insertion of the words 'in accordance with law' after the word 'established' in the first line so that Article 38.4.1° would read:

> Military tribunals may be established in accordance with law for the trial of offences against military law alleged to have been committed by persons while subject to military law and also to deal with a state of war, armed conflict or armed rebellion.

Extra-territorial trial of offences The Constitution Review Group considered whether constitutional provision should be made to deal with extra-territorial trial of offences committed within the jurisdiction of the state and for the surrender of fugitive offenders either to other states or to international tribunals established to deal with any such offences. It considered that, in general, no constitutional amendment is required to permit the extra-territorial trial of offences committed within the jurisdiction of the state or the surrender of fugitive offenders to stand trial for such offences in another state or before an international tribunal. However, were it to be decided that priority should be afforded the assumption of jurisdiction over such an offence or offences by another state or international tribunal, constitutional provision should be made for this.

Fundamental rights – Articles 40-44

While the Constitution Review Group was struck by the general sophistication of Articles 40-44 and recognised that, by the standards of the day, they represented a far-sighted attempt to improve the method of protecting fundamental rights against legislative and executive attack, nevertheless there are three key features of these provisions which require attention, namely the incomplete nature of the rights protected; the development of the unenumerated rights doctrine and the varying language of the clauses which qualify both the enumerated and unenumerated rights protected by the Constitution. It was on these issues that the Constitution Review Group focused its attention.

The Constitution Review Group recommended twenty-four substantive changes in these Articles, counting the complete revision of Article 41 as one change, and the conflation of Articles 40.3.2° and 43, in respect of their application to property, as one also, and six minor or technical changes. (Please note that in the text immediately following some discussion of the Constitution Review Group that did not lead to majority recommendations is given because it has bearing on how important aspects of fundamental rights should be dealt with.)

Having regard to the provisions of Article 40, the Constitution Review Group did not favour the direct incorporation of the European Convention on Human Rights (ECHR) in the Constitution. It decided instead that it would be preferable to draw on the ECHR (and other international human rights conventions) where:

i) the right is not expressly protected by the Constitution

ii) the standard of protection of such rights is superior to those guaranteed by the Constitution; or

iii) the wording of a clause of the Constitution protecting such a right might be improved.

Equality before the law – Article 40.1

Equality – a core norm? The Constitution Review Group considered that equality before the law is a fundamental right whose position will be strengthened by constitutional amendments it recommended later in its report. However, a majority of the Constitution Review Group considered it unnecessary and inappropriate to designate a right to equality as taking precedence over others and preferred that reconciliation of rights, where they are in conflict, should remain a matter for the courts. A minority feared that the absence of such a provision would mean that equality would be subordinated to other constitutional values.

Guarantee for citizens only? The Constitution Review Group recommended that the words 'as human persons' should be deleted and that the guarantee of equality should not be confined to citizens but should be extended to all individuals.

Relevant differences A majority of the Constitution Review Group favoured replacement of the second sentence in Article 40.1 by:

Article 40.1

40.1 *All citizens shall, as human persons, be held equal before the law.*

This shall not be held to mean that the State shall not in its enactments have due regard to differences of capacity, physical and moral, and of social function

This shall not be taken to mean that the State may not have due regard to relevant differences.

Protection against unfair discrimination, direct or indirect A majority of the Constitution Review Group recommended that there should be added to Article 40.1 a section in the following terms:

> No persons shall be unfairly discriminated against, directly or indirectly, on any ground such as sex, race, age, disability, sexual orientation, colour, language, culture, religion, political or other opinion, national, social or ethnic origin, membership of the travelling community, property, birth or other status.

Men and women A majority of the Constitution Review Group did not regard it as necessary to have an express guarantee of equality between men and women having regard to the general guarantee of equality before the law and the prohibition on discrimination.

Equal access to justice Having regard to the generally liberal and flexible nature of our *locus standi* rules, the Constitution Review Group was not persuaded that there is any need for an express provision for equal access to justice along the lines of section 7(4) of the constitution of South Africa. However, if the Constitution Review Group's recommendations in respect of a Human Rights Commission were to be accepted, consideration should be given to permitting that body either to take constitutional actions on behalf of individual citizens or the public at large in appropriate circumstances. The commission might also be given the right to intervene as an *amicus curiae* in some constitutional actions involving fundamental rights.

Affirmative action The Constitution Review Group was divided on the basic issue whether it is necessary or desirable to include specific authorisation of 'affirmative action' in the Constitution. Because of the difficulty of defining 'affirmative action' and of appointing reasonable constitutional limits to the exercise of such authority and because of the primary responsibility of the government and the Oireachtas in determining the associated policies, some members preferred that pursuit of the objective of rectifying unfair disadvantage should continue to be legislatively authorised, at least until (if ever, given the amendments proposed) a constitutional barrier presents itself. Other members preferred that a specific provision should be included in the Constitution, loosely based on Article 9(2) of the South African constitution on the grounds that the realisation of any substantive degree of equality for marginalised social groups would be advanced by a constitutional provision and that it would give the government and the Oireachtas constitutional protection for any affirmative action policies they might wish to introduce.

Article 40.3

40.3.1° The State guarantees in its laws to respect, and, as far as practicable, by its laws to defend and vindicate the personal rights of the citizen.

40.3.2° The State shall, in particular, by its laws protect as best it may from unjust attack and, in the case of injustice done, vindicate the life, person, good name, and property rights of every citizen.

40.3.3° The State acknowledges the right to life of the unborn and, with due regard to the equal right to life of the mother, guarantees in its laws to respect, and, as far as practicable, by its laws to defend and vindicate that right.

This subsection shall not limit freedom to travel between the State and another state.

This subsection shall not limit freedom to obtain or make available, in the State, subject to such conditions as may be laid down by law, information relating to services lawfully available in another state.

Article 40.4

40.4.1° No citizen shall be deprived of his personal liberty save in accordance with law.

40.4.2° Upon complaint being made by or on behalf of any person to the High Court or any judge thereof alleging that such person is being unlawfully detained, the High Court and any and every judge thereof to whom such complaint is made shall forthwith enquire into the said complaint and may order the person in whose custody such person is detained to produce the body of such person before the High Court on a named day and to certify in writing the grounds of his detention, and the High Court shall, upon the body of such person being produced before that Court and after giving the person in whose custody he is detained an opportunity of justifying the detention, order the release of such person from such

Personal rights – Article 40.3.1° and 2°

On balance, the Constitution Review Group favoured an amendment of Article 40.3.1° which would provide a comprehensive list of fundamental rights which could specifically encompass the personal rights which have been identified by the Irish courts to date, and which might also include those set out in the European Convention on Human Rights and the International Covenant on Civil and Political Rights, so far as may be considered appropriate, and other personal rights which might be particularly appropriate in an Irish context, and which should confine further recognition of fundamental rights by the courts to those necessarily implicit in the rights expressly listed.

The Constitution Review Group recommended that, in general, personal rights should not be confined to citizens but should be extended to all human persons. There may be some rights which should be confined to citizens.

Death penalty The Constitution Review Group recommended that the right not to be sentenced to death or executed should be expressly provided for in the provision dealing with the right to life. If it were also provided that Article 28.3.3° (which refers to emergency legislation) could not be used to override such a provision, the other safeguards in the Constitution for persons sentenced to death (Article 40.4.5°) could be deleted. Otherwise they would have to remain.

Qualifying clause The Constitution Review Group recommended that the existing qualifying clauses contained in Article 40.3.1° and 2° should be replaced by a general and more comprehensive qualifying clause along the lines of Article 10(2) of the ECHR. Certain rights – such as the right to life and freedom from torture and slavery – may call for special treatment.

Right to life ('unborn' and mother) – Article 40.3.3°

The Constitution Review Group concluded that while in principle the major issues in regard to this subsection should be tackled by constitutional amendment, there is no consensus as to what that amendment should be and no certainty of success for any referendum proposed for substantive constitutional change in relation to this subsection.

The Constitution Review Group, therefore, favoured, as the only practical possibility at present, the introduction of legislation covering such matters as definitions, protection for appropriate medical intervention, certification of 'real and substantial risk to the life of the mother' and a time-limit on lawful termination of pregnancy.

Personal liberty – Article 40.4

The Constitution Review Group recommended a constitutional prohibition on the re-introduction of the death penalty. If this is not deemed desirable, Article 40.4.5° should

detention unless satisfied that he is being detained in accordance with the law.

40.4.3° *Where the body of a person alleged to be unlawfully detained is produced before the High Court in pursuance of an order in that behalf made under this section and that Court is satisfied that such person is being detained in accordance with a law but that such law is invalid having regard to the provisions of this Constitution, the High Court shall refer the question of the validity of such law to the Supreme Court by way of case stated and may, at the time of such reference or at any time thereafter, allow the said person to be at liberty on such bail and subject to such conditions as the High Court shall fix until the Supreme Court has determined the question so referred to it.*

40.4.4° *The High Court before which the body of a person alleged to be unlawfully detained is to be produced in pursuance of an order in that behalf made under this section shall, if the President of the High Court or, if he is not available, the senior judge of that Court who is available so directs in respect of any particular case, consist of three judges and shall, in every other case, consist of one judge only.*

40.4.5° *Where an order is made under this section by the High Court or a judge thereof for the production of the body of a person who is under sentence of death, the High Court or such judge thereof shall further order that the execution of the said sentence of death shall be deferred until after the body of such person has been produced before the High Court and the lawfulness of his detention has been determined and if, after such deferment, the detention of such person is determined to be lawful, the High Court shall appoint a day for the execution of the said sentence of death and that sentence shall have effect with the substitution of the day so appointed for the day originally fixed for the execution thereof.*

be retained. If it is prohibited, Article 28.3.3° will require amendment so that the death penalty cannot be imposed in any circumstances.

Freedom of expression – Article 40.6.1°i

Blasphemy The Constitution Review Group considered that the retention of the present constitutional offence of blasphemy is not appropriate.

Sedition The Constitution Review Group recommended that the word 'seditious' should be deleted from Article 40.6.1°i. If the Constitution Review Group's recommendation to the effect that any redrafted version of Article 40.6.1°i should be modelled on the provisions of Article 10 of the ECHR were accepted, the Oireachtas would retain the capacity to criminalise publications which posed a genuine and real threat to public order.

Indecent matter The Constitution Review Group recommended that the provisions of Article 40.6.1°i, which prescribe or require the creation or existence of the offence of publishing or uttering indecent matter, should be deleted. A replacement should provide for the regulation by law of obscene material so that the Oireachtas would be empowered to legislate in a manner which struck a fair balance in this sensitive area between the right of free speech and access to information on the one hand and pressing public interests on the other, such as the prevention of the portrayal of women in degrading fashion and the protection of children.

Public order and morality The Constitution Review Group recommended that the right to free expression should not be subject to 'the test of public order and morality and the authority of the State', since this test is too all-embracing. Instead, the Oireachtas should have the right to qualify by law the right of free expression for adequate reasons of public interest. This would be achieved if the recast version of Article 40.6.1°i was modelled on Article 10 of the ECHR as suggested by the Constitution Review Group.

Electronic media The Constitution Review Group recommended that any recast version of 40.6.1°i should follow the model of Article 10 of the ECHR and provide that the Oireachtas shall retain the capacity to insist on a licensing regime for electronic media.

Freedom of assembly – Article 40.6.1°ii

Control of meetings In regard to whether Article 40.6.1°ii gives the Oireachtas too great a latitude in preventing or controlling meetings the Constitution Review Group recommended that, because there is some risk that this aspect of Article 40.6.1°ii might be interpreted as enabling the authorities to curtail the right of free speech and assembly simply because the sensibilities of others might be offended, this aspect of the proviso to the Article be amended.

40.4.6° Nothing in this section, however, shall be invoked to prohibit, control, or interfere with any act of the Defence Forces during the existence of a state of war or armed rebellion.

Article 40.6.1°.i

40.6.1° The State guarantees liberty for the exercise of the following rights, subject to public order and morality:-

i. The right of the citizens to express freely their convictions and opinions.

The education of public opinion being, however, a matter of such grave import to the common good, the State shall endeavour to ensure that organs of public opinion, such as the radio, the press, the cinema, while preserving their rightful liberty of expression, including criticism of Government policy, shall not be used to undermine public order or morality or the authority of the State.

The publication or utterance of blasphemous, seditious, or indecent matter is an offence which shall be punishable in accordance with law.

Article 40.6.1°.ii

40.6.1° The State guarantees liberty for the exercise of the following rights, subject to public order and morality:-

ii. The right of the citizens to assemble peaceably and without arms.

Provision may be made by law to prevent or control meetings which are determined in accordance with law to be calculated to cause a breach of the peace or to be a danger or nuisance to the general public and to prevent or control meetings in the vicinity of either House of the Oireachtas.

The Constitution Review Group recommended that the existing qualifying clause should be replaced by a new re-modelled version based on Article 11(2) of the ECHR. They suggested the following draft:

1 All persons have the right to assemble peaceably and without arms.

2 No restrictions shall be placed on the exercise of this right other than such as are prescribed by law and are necessary in a democratic society in the interests of national security or public safety, for the protection of health or morals or for the protection of the rights and freedoms of others.

3 This Article shall not prevent the imposition of lawful restrictions on the exercise of these rights by members of the armed forces, of the police or of the administration of the State.

4 Without prejudice to subsection 2 of this section, provision may be made by law to prevent or control meetings in the vicinity of either House of the Oireachtas.

Freedom of association – Article 40.6.1°iii

Qualifying clause The Constitution Review Group recommended that the 'public order and morality' qualifying language of Article 40.6.1°iii should be replaced by a more carefully drafted qualifying clause modelled on Article 11(2) of the ECHR.

The family – Article 41

The Constitution Review Group recommended the following in relation to this Article:

1 All family rights, including those of unmarried mothers or fathers and children born of unmarried parents, should now be placed in Article 41.

2 Delete existing Articles 41.1.1°, 41.1.2°, 41.2.1°, 41.2.2° and 41.3.1°.

3 The description of any rights or duties specified in Articles 41 or 42 should not include adjectives such as 'inalienable' or 'imprescriptible'.

4 A revised Article 41 should include the following elements:

   i) recognition by the state of the family as the primary and fundamental unit of society

   ii) a right for all persons to marry in accordance with the requirements of law and to found a family

40.6.1° *The State guarantees liberty for the exercise of the following rights, subject to public order and morality:-*

iii. The right of the citizens to form associations and unions.

Laws, however, may be enacted for the regulation and control in the public interest of the exercise of the foregoing right.

Article 41 – The Family

41.1.1° *The State recognises the Family as the natural primary and fundamental unit group of Society, and as a moral institution possessing inalienable and imprescriptible rights, antecedent and superior to all positive law.*

41.1.2° *The State, therefore, guarantees to protect the Family in its constitution and authority, as the necessary basis of social order and as indispensable to the welfare of the Nation and the State.*

41.2.1° *In particular, the State recognises that by her life within the home, woman gives to the State a support without which the common good cannot be achieved.*

41.2.2° *The State shall, therefore, endeavour to ensure that mothers shall not be obliged by economic necessity to engage in labour to the neglect of their duties in the home.*

41.3.1° *The State pledges itself to guard with special care the institution of Marriage, on which the Family is founded, and to protect it against attack.*

41.3.2° *A Court designated by law may grant a dissolution of marriage where, but only where, it is satisfied that:*

i at the date of the institution of the proceedings, the spouses have lived apart from one another for a period of, or periods amounting to, at least four years during the previous five years,

iii) a pledge by the state to guard with special care the institution of marriage and protect it against attack subject to a proviso that this section should not prevent the Oireachtas from legislating for the benefit of families not based on marriage or for the individual members thereof

iv) a pledge by the state to protect the family based on marriage in its constitution and authority

v) a guarantee to all individuals of respect for their family life whether based on marriage or not

vi) an express guarantee of certain rights of the child, which fall to be interpreted by the courts from the concept of 'family life', which might include:

a) the right of every child to be registered immediately after birth and to have from birth a name

b) the right of every child, as far as practicable, to know his or her parents, subject to the proviso that such right should be subject to regulation by law in the interests of the child

c) the right of every child, as far as practicable, to be cared for by his or her parents

d) the right to be reared with due regard to his or her welfare

vii) an express requirement that in all actions concerning children, whether by legislative, judicial or administrative authorities, the best interests of the child shall be the paramount consideration

viii) a revised Article 41.2 in gender neutral form which might provide:

The State recognises that home and family life give society a support without which the common good cannot be achieved. The State shall endeavour to support persons caring for others within the home

ix) an amended form of Article 42.5 expressly permitting state intervention either where parents have failed in their duty or where the interests of the child require such intervention and a re-statement of the state's duty following such intervention

x) an express statement of the circumstances in which the state may interfere with or restrict the

ii there is no reasonable prospect of a reconciliation between the spouses,

iii such provision as the Court considers proper having regard to the circumstances, exists, or will be made for the spouses, any children of either or both of them and any other person prescribed by law, and

iv any further conditions prescribed by law are complied with.

41.3.3° No person whose marriage has been dissolved under the civil law of any other State but is a subsisting valid marriage under the law for the time being in force within the jurisdiction of the Government and Parliament established by this Constitution shall be capable of contracting a valid marriage within that jurisdiction during the lifetime of the other party to the marriage so dissolved.

Article 42 – Education

42.1 *The State acknowledges that the primary and natural educator of the child is the Family and guarantees to respect the inalienable right and duty of parents to provide, according to their means, for the religious and moral, intellectual, physical and social education of their children.*

42.2 *Parents shall be free to provide this education in their homes or in private schools or in schools recognised or established by the State.*

42.3.1° *The State shall not oblige parents in violation of their conscience and lawful preference to send their children to schools established by the State, or to any particular type of school designated by the State.*

42.3.2° *The State shall, however, as guardian of the common good, require in view of actual conditions that the children receive a certain minimum education, moral, intellectual and social.*

42.4 *The State shall provide for free primary education and shall endeavour to supplement and give*

exercise of family rights guaranteed by the Constitution loosely modelled on Article 8(2) of ECHR

xi) retention of the existing provisions in Article 41.3.3° relating to recognition for foreign divorces.

Education – Article 42

The Constitution Review Group recommended that the adjectives 'natural', 'inalienable' and 'imprescriptible' should be removed from the Article (as well as from Article 41).

Application to all parents The Constitution Review Group recommended that Article 42.1 should be amended to apply to all non-marital parents, provided they have appropriate family ties and connections with the child in question. They suggested the following wording:

> Article 42.1 The State acknowledges that the primary educator of the child is the family and guarantees to respect the right and duty of parents to provide, according to their means, for the education of their children.

Explicit statement of the right and its extension to second level The Constitution Review Group recommended that the right of every child to free primary education should be explicitly stated in the Constitution. The Oireachtas should also seriously consider extending this right to second level education as this may be defined by law. If the right is so extended, the new Article might read as follows:

> Every child has a right to free primary and secondary level education. The State shall provide for such education and shall endeavour to supplement and give reasonable aid to private and corporate educational initiative, and, where appropriate, provide other educational facilities or institutions with due regard, however, for the rights of the parents, especially in the matter of religious and moral formation.

Extension of right to all persons? Some members of the Constitution Review Group favoured the extension of the right to education to all persons and argued that the right could be qualified so that it would not entail unrealistic financial or other demands. A majority of the Constitution Review Group, however, was against such an amendment because of its indefinite nature and unassessable implications.

Definition of minimum education The Constitution Review Group considered that the Oireachtas should have the express power to define by law the meaning of the term 'certain minimum education'. The Constitution Review Group recommended that Article 42.1 and Article 42.3.2° might be amended as follows (see Article 42.1 above):

reasonable aid to private and corporate educational initiative, and, when the public good requires it, provide other educational facilities or institutions with due regard, however, for the rights of parents, especially in the matter of religious and moral formation.

42.5 *In exceptional cases, where the parents for physical or moral reasons fail in the duty towards their children, the State as guardian of the common good, by appropriate means shall endeavour to supply the place of the parents, but always with due regard for the natural and imprescriptible rights of the child.*

Article 40.3.2°

40.3.2° *The State shall, in particular, by its laws protect as best it may from unjust attack and, in the case of injustice done, vindicate the life, person, good name, and property rights of every citizen.*

Article 43 – Private Property

43.1.1° *The State acknowledges that man, in virtue of his rational being, has the natural right, antecedent to positive law, to the private ownership of external goods.*

43.1.2° *The State accordingly guarantees to pass no law attempting to abolish the right of private ownership or the general right to transfer, bequeath, and inherit property.*

43.2.1° *The State recognises, however, that the exercise of the rights mentioned in the foregoing provisions of this Article ought, in civil society, to be regulated by the principles of social justice.*

43.2.2° *The State, accordingly, may as occasion requires delimit by law the exercise of the said rights with a view to reconciling their exercise with the exigencies of the common good.*

Article 42.3.2° The State shall require that children receive a certain minimum education as may be determined from time to time by law, provided that the State shall at all times have due regard to the right of parents to make decisions concerning the religious and moral education of their children.

Specific provision for equality in education? A majority of the Constitution Review Group did not favour the inclusion of any absolute requirement in the Constitution which would remove the necessary discretion of government and Oireachtas in policy matters but would see no objection to a directive principle 'to promote equality of access to, and participation in, education' being included in Article 45, if retained.

Private Property – Articles 40.3.2° and 43

A majority of the Constitution Review Group favoured the following:

1   Article 40.3.2° (in so far as it concerns property rights) and Article 43 should be deleted and replaced by a single self-contained Article dealing with property rights.

2   Article 1 of the First Protocol to the European Convention on Human Rights should not be directly transposed into the Constitution. However, a slightly recast version of the opening sentence of Article 1 of the First Protocol might usefully replace the existing Article 43.1.1° as follows:

> Every natural person shall have the right to the peaceable possession of his or her own possessions or property.

3   A slightly altered version of Article 43.1.2° should be included. This might provide:

> The State guarantees to pass no law attempting to abolish the right of private ownership or the general right to transfer, bequeath and inherit property.

(Some members of the Constitution Review Group felt a general right to 'bequeath and inherit' property should not be consolidated in the Constitution because of its potential effect of increasing wealth differentials in society. The majority, however, considered that legislative fiscal freedom and the constitutional provision that property rights may be regulated by reference to the principles of social justice were adequate qualifications.)

4   A new qualifying clause which would provide that such property rights, since they carry with them

Article 44 – Religion

44.1 *The State acknowledges that the homage of public worship is due to Almighty God. It shall hold His Name in reverence, and shall respect and honour religion.*

44.2.1° *Freedom of conscience and the free profession and practice of religion are, subject to public order and morality, guaranteed to every citizen.*

44.2.2° *The State guarantees not to endow any religion.*

44.2.3° *The State shall not impose any disabilities or make any discrimination on the ground of religious profession, belief or status.*

44.2.4° *Legislation providing State aid for schools shall not discriminate between schools under the management of different religious denominations, nor be such as to affect prejudicially the right of any child to attend a school receiving public money without attending religious instruction at that school.*

44.2.5° *Every religious denomination shall have the right to manage its own affairs, own, acquire and administer property, movable and immovable, and maintain institutions for religious or charitable purposes.*

44.2.6° *The property of any religious denomination or any educational institution shall not be diverted save for necessary works of public utility and on payment of compensation.*

duties and responsibilities, may be subject to legal restrictions, conditions and formalities, provided these are duly required in the public interest and accord with the principles of social justice. Such restrictions, conditions and formalities may, in particular, but not exclusively, relate to the raising of taxation and revenue, proper land use and planning controls, protection of the environment, consumer protection and the conservation of objects of archaeological and historical importance.

A minority of the Review Group favoured the retention of Articles 43.2.1° and 43.2.2° in their present form.

Religion – Article 44

A majority of the Constitution Review Group favoured deletion of Article 44.1. If that were not deemed desirable or politic, they considered that the section might be re-formulated as follows:

The State guarantees to respect religion.

Worship in public In so far as it may be necessary to deal with the issue of worship in public and the open manifestation of religious beliefs, the Constitution Review Group recommended that this might be better achieved through an amendment of Article 44.2.1° by adding to it the following sentence (modelled on Article 9(1) of the European Convention on Human Rights):

These rights shall include the freedom, either alone or in community with others, and in public or in private, to manifest his or her religion or belief, in worship, teaching, practice and observance.

Qualifying clause A majority of the Constitution Review Group recommended that the qualifying language of Article 44.2.1° should be modelled on Article 9(2) of the European Convention on Human Rights:

The exercise of these rights and freedoms may be subject only to such limitations as may be imposed by law and are necessary in a democratic society in the interests of public safety, for the protection of public order, health and morals, or for the protection of the rights and freedoms of others.

Conscientious beliefs If the views of the Constitution Review Group as to the meaning of the words 'freedom of conscience' in Article 44.2.1° are correct and if the Constitution Review Group's earlier recommendation concerning the addition of an extra sentence to this subsection modelled on Article 9(1) of the European Convention on Human Rights is followed, no further change in Article 44.2.1 is necessary.

Religious ethos A majority of the Constitution Review Group considered that Article 44 should be amended to provide that

Article 45

The principles of social policy set forth in this Article are intended for the general guidance of the Oireachtas. The application of those principles in the making of laws shall be the care of the Oireachtas exclusively, and shall not be cognisable by any Court under any of the provisions of this Constitution.

45.1 *The State shall strive to promote the welfare of the whole people by securing and protecting as effectively as it may a social order in which justice and charity shall inform all the institutions of the national life.*

45.2 *The State shall, in particular, direct its policy towards securing:-*

i. That the citizens (all of whom, men and women equally, have the right to an adequate means of livelihood) may through their occupations find the means of making reasonable provision for their domestic needs.

ii. That the ownership and control of the material resources of the community may be so distributed amongst private individuals and the various classes as best to subserve the common good.

iii. That, especially, the operation of free competition shall not be allowed so to develop as to result in the concentration of the ownership or control of essential commoditles in a few individuals to the common detriment.

iv. That in what pertains to the control of credit the constant and predominant aim shall be the welfare of the people as a whole.

v. That there may be established on the land in economic security as many families as in the circumstances shall be practicable.

45.3.1° *The State shall favour and, where necessary, supplement private initiative in industry and commerce.*

institutions which retain a religious ethos should not be debarred from public funding, provided that they do not discriminate on grounds of religious practice or belief, save where this can be shown, in any given case, to be necessary in order to maintain their own religious ethos.

Minor or technical changes These are listed in Appendix VIII (21-26).

v) *Directive principles of social policy – Article 45*

The Constitution Review Group was divided as to whether Article 45 should be deleted or retained in an amended form. A majority considered if it is to be retained it should be amended so as to indicate that the principles are for the guidance of the government as well as the Oireachtas and relate to executive action as well as to the making of laws.

The Constitution Review Group recommended that the Article, if retained, should be amended by the addition of further principles to reflect modern concerns in regard to socioeconomic rights. In that process the language of the existing provisions could, as far as necessary, be revised.

vi) *Amendment of the Constitution – Article 46*

A majority of the Constitution Review Group did not favour the addition of a new provision which would permit by Act of the Oireachtas amendments of a purely stylistic and technical nature. It concluded that stylistic and technical amendments should be submitted collectively to the people by referendum at intervals, as convenient, and that the first such submission might comprise those stylistic and technical amendments identified as desirable in the course of the current review. The same view is taken of amendments involving minor or insignificant changes of substance.

viii) *The referendum – Article 47*

The Constitution Review Group recommended one substantial change to Article 47.

Public funding of referenda campaigns The Constitution Review Group considered that there ought not to be a constitutional barrier to public funding of a referendum campaign *provided* that the manner of equitable allotment of such funding is entrusted to an independent body such as the proposed Constituency Commission. The total sum to be allotted should be subject to legislative regulation. Article 47.4 should be amended accordingly. The Constitution Review Group considered that such a constitutional safeguard meets the principal objection to the old funding arrangements identified in the *McKenna* case by ensuring that the government does not spend public money in a self-interested and unregulated fashion in favour of one side only, thereby distorting the political process.

45.3.2° *The State shall endeavour to secure that private enterprise shall be so conducted as to ensure reasonable efficiency in the production and distribution of goods and as to protect the public against unjust exploitation.*

45.4.1° *The State pledges itself to safeguard with especial care the economic interests of the weaker sections of the community, and, where necessary, to contribute to the support of the infirm, the widow, the orphan, and the aged.*

45.4.2° *The State shall endeavour to ensure that the strength and health of workers, men and women, and the tender age of children shall not be abused and that citizens shall not be forced by economic necessity to enter avocations unsuited to their sex, age or strength.*

Article 47.4

47.4 *Subject as aforesaid, the Referendum shall be regulated by law.*

Since an extension of the logic of the *McKenna* judgment could possibly render unconstitutional proposals to fund political parties from the public purse, the constitutionality of public funding for political parties may also need to be similarly addressed.

Preferendum The Constitution Review Group considered that the referendum has worked well in practice and should be retained. While it agreed that a cogent theoretical argument could be made in favour of the preferendum system, it believes there is no pressing need for change. However, it is a mechanism which might usefully be kept under review, especially having regard to the potentially complex nature of future proposals to amend the Constitution.

ix) *Repeal of the Constitution of Saorstát Éireann and Continuance of Laws – Articles 48-50*

These Articles provide for the repeal of the Constitution of Saorstát Éireann and its supersession by *Bunreacht na hÉireann* (Article 48) and for the transfer of the powers, functions, rights and prerogatives in respect of Saorstát Éireann to the people provided such powers are exercisable only by or on the authority of the government. They also provide that the government shall be the successor of the government of Saorstát Éireann as regards 'all property, assets, rights and liabilities (Article 49), and they provide for the carrying over of the body of laws in force in Saorstát Éireann in so far as such laws were consistent with *Bunreacht na hÉireann* (Article 50).

The Constitution Review Group was divided on the question of whether these Articles should be deleted. Some felt that since they had performed their function they were spent and should be deleted. Others felt that they should be retained because they provided a 'root of title' in respect of pre-1937 property, assets etc, and legal continuity generally.

x) *The transitory provisions – Articles 51-63*

The Constitution Review Group was divided on the question of whether these Articles should be deleted or retained for the same reasons as obtain in relation to Articles 48-50.

xi) *New provisions*

The Constitution Review Group recommended three substantive changes in the form of new provisions.

The Ombudsman The Constitution Review Group recommended that a new Article should be inserted in the Constitution confirming the establishment of the office of the Ombudsman, providing for the independent exercise of such investigative and other functions of the office in relation to administrative actions as may be determined by law, and making other provisions similar to those applying to the Comptroller and Auditor General and consistent with the 1980 Act, as amended.

Local government The Constitution Review Group considered, by a majority, that a form of recognition in principle of local government should be inserted in the Constitution.

The environment A majority of the Constitution Review Group favoured the inclusion in the Constitution of a duty on the state and public authorities as far as practicable to protect the environment, to follow sustainable development policies, and to preserve special aspects of our heritage.

The Constitution Review Group recommended that such a provision could constitute a new Article or be incorporated in Article 10. Legislation would remain the chief source of specific provisions aimed at safeguarding the environment.

Human Rights Commission A majority of the Constitution Review Group considered that a Human Rights Commission should be established to maintain an overview of the extent to which human rights are protected at both the constitutional and legal levels, to assess the adequacy of this protection and to make recommendations to government for the better protection of these rights, as appropriate. The preferred view was that the commission should have legislative rather than constitutional status and that, if a legislatively-based commission were established and performed well over a number of years, the desirability of affording it constitutional status should be further considered.

xii) *General recommendations*

1   In the foreword to its report the Constitution Review Group made the general recommendation that 'the principle of gender-inclusiveness should be observed in the wording of the Constitution'.

2   In dealing with amendment of the Constitution (Article 46) the Constitution Review Group concluded that minor and technical amendments should be put to the people in an omnibus proposal.

Overview of recommendations

1) Preamble

2) Article 4   –   name of the State
3) Article 8   –   official languages

4) Article 12.4   –   nomination procedure for the President
5) Article 12.8   –   declaration/affirmation by the President

6) Article 15.2.1°   –   subordinate legislation
7) Article 15.3.1°   –   democratic participation
8) Articles 18, 19   –   Seanad Éireann

9)	Articles 26, 34	–	constitutionality of Bills and laws
10)	Article 28.3.1°	–	declaration of war 'or other armed conflict'
11)	Article 28.3.3°	–	emergency legislation – limit on time period
12)	Article 28.10	–	constructive vote of no confidence
13)	Article 29.3	–	public and private international law distinction
14)	Article 29.5.3°	–	technical and administrative agreements having a charge on public funds
15)	Article 29	–	United Nations provision
16)	Article 30	–	delegation of functions of the Attorney General
17)	Article 31.4	–	declaration/affirmation taken by Council of State members
18)	Article 34.2	–	different court structures
19)	Article 34.4.4°	–	exclusion by law of right of appeal from a decision to acquit an accused
20)	Article 34.5.1°	–	judge's declaration upon appointment
21)	Article 35.2 and 4	–	judicial conduct and the impeachment of judges
22)	Article 38.1	–	explicit enumeration of an accused's rights
23)	Article 38.3, 38.6 and 38.4.1°	–	special courts: their establishment for a fixed period, their exemption from compliance with Articles 34 and 35, and military tribunals
24)	Article 40.1	–	equality before the law
25)	Article 40.3.1° and 40.3.2°	–	personal rights
26)	Article 40.4	–	personal liberty
27)	Article 40.5	–	inviolability of the dwelling
28)	Article 40.6.1°i	–	freedom of expression
29)	Article 40.6.1°ii	–	freedom of assembly
30)	Article 40.6.1°iii	–	freedom of association
31)	Article 41	–	the family
32)	Article 42	–	education
33)	Articles 40.3.2° and 43	–	private property
34)	Article 44	–	religion
35)	Article 45	–	directive principles of social policy
36)	Articles 48 - 63	–	repeal of the Constitution of Saorstát Éireann, the continuance of laws and the Transitory Provisions
37)	new provision	–	Ombudsman
38)	new provision	–	environment
39)	new provision	–	local government

40)	general recommendation	–	gender-inclusiveness
41)	general recommendation	–	omnibus proposal containing minor and technical amendments

Feasibility of a programme

The recommendations of the Constitution Review Group, being the product of a thorough review, provide a broad measure of what a programme for constitutional renewal might contain. Even if one did not agree with many of the recommendations, it is likely that one would propose other recommendations that the Constitution Review Group itself did not come up with and thus end up with a programme of broadly similar dimensions.

Before proceeding to assess the Constitution Review Group's recommendations in terms of the arguments adduced by it and by the individuals who, and organisations which, have made submissions to the Committee, the Committee sought to assure itself that a programme of the necessary amplitude could be mounted and implemented within a reasonable period – and the Committee considered that to be five years.

When a referendum is being held the Oireachtas has the opportunity to place a number of different proposals to the people. On three occasions, in 1968, 1972 and 1979, two proposals were put to the people on the same day and in 1992 three proposals were put to the people on the same day. If one were to suppose that as many as five proposals could be put to the people on any one day and that referenda could be held twice a year over a five-year period, some fifty proposals could be accommodated in a programme. As we have seen from the overview, the Constitution Review Group's recommendations could be carried in forty-one proposals. One can therefore regard the programme approach proposed by the Committee as feasible.

Getting ahead

The Committee's *modus operandi* will be to work its way steadily through the recommendations of the Constitution Review Group and the submissions made to it both in writing and orally. It has decided to gather the fruits of the process together periodically and publish them in the form of progress reports. This will allow the people enough time to digest the recommendations.

In this first progress report the Committee presents, in addition to its strategy, some actual product of its deliberations. The Committee has dealt with seven elements of the programme upon which it could reach early consensus.

The Committee's recommendations in regard to the following substantive issues are dealt with in chapters 4–9:

- the power to dissolve Dáil Éireann (Articles 13 and 28)

- the constitutionality of Bills and laws (Articles 26 and 34)

- local government (new provision)

- the electoral and ethics commission (new provision)

- ombudsman (new provision)

- 'woman in the home' (Article 41.2) and gender-inclusive language in the Constitution.

The Committee's recommendations in regard to minor or technical amendments are dealt with in chapter 10:

- omnibus proposal: technical/minor amendments.

4 The Power to Dissolve Dáil Éireann

The Power to Dissolve Dáil Éireann

13.2.1° *Dáil Éireann shall be summoned and dissolved by the President on the advice of the Taoiseach.*

The Constitution provides (Article 13.2.1°) that the Dáil shall be summoned and dissolved by the President on the advice of the Taoiseach. This provision gives the Taoiseach the power to have the Dáil dissolved at whatever time he or she considers most suitable. It consequently gives Taoisigh a powerful means of exercising discipline over their cabinet colleagues (whether they are drawn from one party or a coalition of parties), the ordinary deputies of the government party or parties, and the body of deputies generally. It also offers a Taoiseach the opportunity to go to the people at a time he or she deems most favourable.

13.2.2° *The President may in his absolute discretion refuse to dissolve Dáil Éireann on the advice of a Taoiseach who has ceased to retain the support of a majority in Dáil Éireann.*

Article 13.2.2°, however, qualifies the provision by giving the President an absolute discretion to refuse to dissolve Dáil Éireann on the advice of a Taoiseach who has ceased to retain the support of a majority in Dáil Éireann. No President has used this discretion even though of the eighteen Dála convened under *Bunreacht na hÉireann* three followed upon dissolutions granted to Taoisigh who had lost formal votes of confidence and as many as eight others followed upon dissolutions granted to Taoisigh who could have been deemed to have lost the support of a majority in the Dáil. Constitutional tradition, then, has given Taoisigh the facility to have the Dáil dissolved on request to the President.

The Constitution Review Group's analysis

The Constitution Review Group considered whether the President should retain the discretion to refuse a dissolution of Dáil Éireann. Its discussion of the issue is given in Appendix IX. The Constitution Review Group concluded that:

> ... the involvement of the President in party political issues should, if possible, be avoided and, for that reason, has given consideration to other methods of dealing with the dissolution problem, principally the prescription of a fixed term for Dáil Éireann and provision for a constructive vote of no confidence.

Its discussion of those two mechanisms is also given in Appendix IX. It recommended as follows:

> There is no sufficient reason to advocate a fixed-term Dáil. A constructive vote of no confidence would reduce substantially the deadlock difficulty discussed above [following a general election or the fall of a government] and a majority of the Review Group considers that the introduction of this procedure merits serious consideration. It could be achieved by amending Article 28.10 by deleting the text after 'Éireann' and replacing this with 'demonstrated by the loss of a motion of no confidence which at the same time nominates an alternative Taoiseach.' Article 13.2.2° would then become redundant.

A different approach

To these issues the Committee takes a different approach. It does not share the Constitution Review Group's deep concern to remove the President from the risk of any political taint so completely that all discretion is removed from him or her. It considers, for instance, that there could be grave circumstances such as a time of violent civil unrest or invasion by foreign forces, when the preservation of the state might be best secured by a President's refusal to dissolve the Dáil – and therefore the source of the central authority within the state – simply at the request of a Taoiseach who had ceased to retain the support of a majority of Dáil Éireann.

The Constitution Review Group was also concerned with the Government formation process and in particular with the difficulties arising from deadlock either following a general election or the fall of a government. The Committee, however, feels that, since following an election, the Dáil has always embraced the paramount responsibility placed on it by the people of forming a government, it will continue to do so: it has shown itself capable of drawing upon the disparate elements of its membership to form stable coalitions; it has also succeeded in establishing stable minority governments.

The constructive vote of no confidence proposed by the Constitution Review Group is aimed at extending the life of a Dáil by giving it the power to elect a new Taoiseach when it has defeated the incumbent Taoiseach. The Committee considers that it is politically desirable to give the Dáil the formal power to elect a new Taoiseach to succeed a Taoiseach who has ceased to retain the support of a majority in Dáil Éireann without having the house dissolved and a general election held. Such a provision would give the Dáil another check on the power of a Taoiseach. It would also help to reduce the number of elections and increase the stability of government.

General elections inevitably create a period of uncertainty throughout the political system and in the economy. There may be weeks or even months of uncertainty as a Taoiseach shapes up to a decision to call for a dissolution of the Dáil; another period of uncertainty is the election campaign itself which usually lasts for three to four weeks. If a majority government is returned, there is immediate stability. However, if a new coalition government has to be formed, negotiations on a government programme may continue for many weeks after an election.

Political uncertainty impacts on the state's political endeavours generally, because it brings indecision to the direction of the organisational resources of the state, including those through which we pursue our interests in the EU. It impacts on our economic prospects, too, because it leads to the postponement of business decisions. It is, of course, one of the costs of democracy.

Although the maximum life of a Dáil has been fixed by law at five years, the average life of the Dáil, as the Constitution Review Group points out, has been two years and ten months. The political situation arising from this could not, generally speaking, be termed an unstable one because it has not made for difficulties on the financial markets or in the flow of inward investment, nor has it resulted in a faltering in our endeavours within the EU.

However, there have been some periods of frequent general elections in which governments have succeeded one another after short periods in office and following dissolutions of the Dáil. The trend towards coalition government may make for more frequent changes of government so that the issue of stability may become more acute.

The problem the Committee sees with the constructive vote of no confidence, which involves tabling a vote of no confidence in the Taoiseach and simultaneously agreeing on a replacement Taoiseach, is that it may facilitate stable but weak government over the period of a Dáil's term. A weak government formed following a general election may seek to avoid a constructive vote of no confidence by pandering to the interests of the opposition and a weak government which has come into power following the success of a vote of no confidence may seek to avoid all difficult issues in order not to provoke another constructive vote of no confidence. The mechanism might thus leave the people powerless to install a strong government.

The Committee believes that a sensible balance between the power of the people and of the Dáil would be struck if a Taoiseach who had lost the support of the Dáil were granted a dissolution by the President only if within ten days from the vote of no confidence the Dáil has not elected a new Taoiseach. There would of course be a need to define what would indicate the Taoiseach's loss of support of a majority in the Dáil. The Committee recommends the following indications: the loss of a vote of confidence or the loss of a vote of no confidence or the loss of a motion to approve or modify a charge upon the people or to appropriate revenue or other public monies (other than a charge or expenditure, as the case may be, which is subordinate and incidental to a legislative proposal).

Recommendation

Article 13.2.2° should be deleted and replaced by the following:

> If a Taoiseach formally ceases to retain the support of a majority of Dáil Éireann, as indicated by the loss of a vote of confidence or a vote of no confidence, or the loss of a motion to approve or modify a charge upon the people or to appropriate revenue or other public monies (other than a charge or expenditure, as the case may be, which is subordinate and incidental to a legislative proposal), the President shall accede to a request from the Taoiseach to dissolve the Dáil if within ten days from such a vote the Dáil has not elected a new Taoiseach.

A consequential amendment to Article 28.10 is to delete the words 'unless on his advice ... Dáil Éireann' (at the end of the section) and replace them with, 'as indicated by the loss of a vote of confidence or a vote of no confidence, or the loss of a motion to approve or modify a charge upon the people or to appropriate revenue or other public monies (other than a charge or expenditure, as the case may be, which is subordinate and incidental to a legislative proposal)'.

The revised Article 28.10 would read:

> The Taoiseach shall resign from office upon his or her ceasing to retain the support of a majority in Dáil Éireann, as indicated by the loss of a vote of confidence or a vote of no confidence, or the loss of a motion to approve or modify a charge upon the people or to

28.10 *The Taoiseach shall resign from office upon his ceasing to retain the support of a majority in Dáil Éireann unless on his advice the President dissolves Dáil Éireann and on the reassembly of Dáil Éireann after the dissolution the Taoiseach secures the support of a majority in Dáil Éireann.*

appropriate revenue or other public monies (other than a charge or expenditure, as the case may be, which is subordinate and incidental to a legislative proposal).

Effects

1   this scheme leaves it possible for a Taoiseach who has majority support in the Dáil to have the Dáil dissolved at will (Article 13.2.1°) and thus provides such a Taoiseach with a powerful means of disciplining the members of his or her own cabinet, the members of his or her supporting party or parties and the members of the Dáil generally

2   where a Taoiseach has ceased to retain the support of a majority in the house as indicated in specified ways, it provides an opportunity to the Dáil to replace the Taoiseach without resorting to a general election and thus reduces the risk of prolonged uncertainty in the political system.

The scheme does not deal with the historically more frequent situation where the Taoiseach informally ceases to retain the support of a majority in Dáil Éireann as, for example, in the case where a coalition partner has indicated publicly that it is withdrawing from the government but has not brought about a formal defeat of the government. The Committee considers that the President should still have an absolute discretion to refuse a request to dissolve Dáil Éireann from a Taoiseach who finds himself or herself in those circumstances.

The Committee proposes that where the President deems a Taoiseach, who requests a dissolution of the Dáil, to have ceased to retain the support of a majority in the Dáil, the President should have power to summon the Dáil within three days to vote on a motion of confidence in the Taoiseach. If the vote of confidence is carried, the President shall accede to the Taoiseach's request and dissolve the Dáil. If the motion of confidence is lost by the Taoiseach, the President shall dissolve the Dáil if within ten days the Dáil has not elected a new Taoiseach.

Recommendation

Insert a new subsection after Article 13.2.2° to read as follows:

If a Taoiseach who has not formally ceased to retain the support of a majority in Dáil Éireann but whom the President deems to have informally done so requests the President to dissolve Dáil Éireann, the President in his or her absolute discretion may, within three days, summon Dáil Éireann to vote on a motion of confidence in the Taoiseach. If the Taoiseach wins the vote, the President shall accede forthwith to his or her request for a dissolution. If the Taoiseach loses the vote, the President shall dissolve Dáil Éireann if within ten days the Dáil has not elected a new Taoiseach.

5 Constitutionality of Bills and Laws

Constitutionality of Bills and Laws

26.1.1° The President may, after consultation with the Council of State, refer any Bill to which this Article applies to the Supreme Court for a decision on the question as to whether such Bill or any specified provision or provisions of such Bill is or are repugnant to this Constitution or to any provision thereof.

26.1.2° Every such reference shall be made not later than the seventh day after the date on which such Bill shall have been presented by the Taoiseach to the President for his signature.

26.2.1° The Supreme Court consisting of not less than five judges shall consider every question referred to it by the President under this Article for a decision, and, having heard arguments by or on behalf of the Attorney General and by counsel assigned by the Court, shall pronounce its decision on such question in open court as soon as may be, and in any case not later than sixty days after the date of such reference.

34.4.5° The decision of the Supreme Court on a question as to the validity of a law having regard to the provisions of this Constitution shall be pronounced by such one of the judges of that Court as that Court shall direct, and no other opinion on such question, whether assenting or dissenting, shall be pronounced, nor shall the existence of any such other opinion be disclosed.

26.3.3° In every other case the President shall sign the Bill as soon as may be after the date on which the decision of the Supreme Court shall have been pronounced.

34.3.3° No Court whatever shall have jurisdiction to question the validity of a law, or any provision of a law, the Bill for which shall have been referred to the

When a Bill has been passed, or deemed to have been passed, by the Dáil and Seanad, it is sent to the President for signing into law and promulgation in *Iris Oifigiúil,* the official gazette. Article 26 of the Constitution provides that the President may, after consultation with the Council of State, refer a Bill to the Supreme Court for a decision on its constitutionality, that is to say, on whether the Bill, in whole or in part, is repugnant to the Constitution. If a Bill is found unconstitutional, the President declines to sign it and it has no legal effect.

The provision does not apply to all Bills. It excludes a Money Bill, or a Bill expressed to be a Bill containing a proposal to amend the Constitution, or a Bill the time for consideration of which has been abridged under Article 24.

The Article 26 reference procedure is as follows:

i) after consulting with the Council of State, the President refers the Bill to the Supreme Court within seven days after the Taoiseach has presented it to the President for signature (Article 26.1.1°-2°)

ii) the Supreme Court, consisting of not less than five judges, hears the arguments for the proposed Bill presented by the Attorney General, and the arguments against it presented by counsel appointed by the court (Article 26.2.1°)

iii) the Supreme Court gives its decision not later than sixty days after the date of reference by the President (Article 26.2.1°)

iv) the Supreme Court hands down a single judgment on constitutionality (as it does on the constitutionality of a law under Article 34.4.5°)

v) if the Supreme Court declares a Bill to be constitutional, the President signs the Bill into law as soon as may be (Article 26.3.3°)

vi) such an Act cannot thereafter be challenged in the courts (Article 34.3.3°).

As the Constitution Review Group observed, the procedure is used infrequently. In the past fifty-five years, during which over 1,900 Bills were enacted, it has been used ten times. Five of those referrals occurred in the past fourteen years. This indicates a trend of increasing, though still rare, use of the procedure.

Supreme Court by the President
under Article 26 of this
Constitution, or to question the
validity of a provision of a law
where the corresponding provision
in the Bill for such law shall have
been referred to the Supreme
Court by the President under the
said Article 26.

Recommendations

The Committee considered the recommendations made by the Constitution Review Group.

i) *Article 26 reference cases: number of judges*

Section 6 of the Courts and Court Officers Act 1995 increased the number of judges in the Supreme Court from the Chief Justice and four ordinary members to the Chief Justice and seven ordinary members. Under the 1961 Courts (Establishment and Constitution) Act 1961, the President of the High Court is *ex officio* an additional judge of the Supreme Court. Under the same Act, the Chief Justice has the power to request any ordinary judge or judges of the High Court to sit on the hearing of any appeal or other matter cognisable by the Supreme Court where, owing to the illness of a judge of the Supreme Court or for any other reason, a sufficient number of judges of the Supreme Court is not available for the transaction of the business of that court.

Article 26.2.1° provides that not less than five judges should sit to decide Article 26 reference cases. The Constitution Review Group considered that no change was necessary in the subsection:

> ... five represents more than half the total proposed Supreme Court membership and allows the court to deliver a judgment even if a number of judges cannot sit for such reasons as illness or absence abroad. If immunity from challenge is removed [as the Review Group recommended], the case for retaining the five-judge minimum would be all the stronger.

Owing to the importance of these cases, the Committee tends to favour the practice followed by the American Supreme Court which is to sit with its full membership when deciding constitutional cases. Since the Supreme Court now numbers nine (including the President of the High Court), the Committee takes the view that it should sit with seven members to decide Article 26 reference cases: that number allows for a depletion in the number of available judges through illness or absence and, since an uneven number is required for reaching decision by a majority, it is the highest such number available after allowing for depletion.

Amend Article 26.2.1° to begin 'The Supreme Court consisting of not less than seven judges ...'

In its discussion of the number of judges of the Supreme Court to determine the validity of laws (as distinct from Bills under the Article 26 procedure) the Constitution Review Group observed:

> Article 34 does not specify any minimum number of judges for the determination by the Supreme Court as to the constitutional validity of a law. Section 7 of the Courts (Supplemental Provisions) Act 1961 requires a Supreme Court of five judges for such decisions. The Review Group has already, in the section on the Constitutionality of Bills and Laws, expressed the view that it is desirable that a minimum of five judges for such decisions should be specified in Article 34. This would be particularly important if the Review Group

recommendation for the removal of immunity from challenge of Acts the Bills for which had been referred under Article 26 is accepted. The Constitution, having required five judges for the decision on the Bill referred under Article 26, should likewise require not less than five judges for the subsequent determination of the constitutional validity of the Act.

The Committee agrees with the view that the Supreme Court should sit with the same number of judges for Article 26 reference cases and cases to determine the validity of a law.

> Insert a subsection after Article 34.4.4° to read as follows:
>
> The decision of the Supreme Court on a question as to the validity of a law having regard to the provisions of this Constitution shall be made by not less than seven judges.

ii) *Article 26 reference cases: the time limit for pronouncing decisions*

Article 26.2.1° states that, in questions referred to it by the President under this Article the Supreme Court shall pronounce its decision on such questions in open court as soon as may be, and in any case not later then sixty days after the date of such reference.

The Constitution Review Group recommended that the period should be extended to ninety days. It argued as follows:

> It is accepted that Bills subject to reference require urgent attention. The rule may, however, result in a situation where counsel appointed by the Supreme Court to put the arguments against the Bill have too little time. The Government side is far better placed in this regard because it will have been dealing with the Bill before it has been referred. If the presentation of evidence were to be included in the process, the shortage of time would become grievous.

The Committee agrees with that recommendation.

The Constitution Review Group also considered that if a point of European law arises, and there is a need for reference to the European Court of Justice (ECJ), provision for an extension of the time limit in such cases should be made. The Committee, however, does not agree with this for the reason that since it may take years for the ECJ to arrive at a decision such a delay would remove the efficacy of the Article 26 procedure in providing almost immediate certitude on the constitutionality of a Bill. In any event, the Supreme Court is itself the interpreter of the operation of EU law within the state.

> Amend Article 26.2.1° to read '... and in any case not later than ninety days after the date of such reference'.

> The two changes should be incorporated in Article 26.2.1° as follows:
>
> The Supreme Court consisting of not less than seven judges shall consider every question referred to it by the President

under this Article for a decision, and, having heard arguments by or on behalf of the Attorney General and by counsel assigned by the Court, shall pronounce its decision on such question in open court as soon as may be, and in any case not later than ninety days after the date of such reference.

26.2.2° *The decision of the majority of the judges of the Supreme Court shall, for the purposes of this Article, be the decision of the Court and shall be pronounced by such one of those judges as the Court shall direct, and no other opinion, whether assenting or dissenting, shall be pronounced nor shall the existence of any such other opinion be disclosed.*

34.4.5° *The decision of the Supreme Court on a question as to the validity of a law having regard to the provisions of this Constitution shall be pronounced by such one of the judges of that Court as that Court shall direct, and no other opinion on such question, whether assenting or dissenting, shall be pronounced, nor shall the existence of any such other opinion be disclosed.*

iii) *Article 26 reference cases: one-judgment rule*

Article 26.2.2° provides that the Supreme Court shall pronounce a single judgment in these cases. The same rule applies (Article 34.4.5°) to cases where the Supreme Court decides on the validity of a law made under the Constitution, arising from cases on appeal from the High Court.

The Constitution Review Group was unable to reach a consensus on whether the rule should be abolished in regard to Article 26 reference cases. Some members were of the view that the special character of the Article 26 reference procedure justifies the retention of Article 26.2.2°. They set forth the arguments for and against deletion (see Appendix X).

The Committee believes that the arguments weigh overwhelmingly in favour of deletion of Article 26.2.2°. It feels that the two arguments against deletion do not carry great weight in modern conditions. The one-judgment rule seeks to give the decisions of the Supreme Court the character of an oracular utterance. However, it is not credible that people nowadays, who are habituated to the analysis of complex issues by the presentation of arguments for and against through the media, would presume that the members of the Supreme Court invariably reach an unanimous decision on the complex issues placed before them. The argument that the rule shields judges from improper influence or pressure does not take sufficient account of how easily such factors can be neutralised by the exposure of them in the media.

Delete Article 26.2.2°.

The Constitution Review Group reached unanimous agreement on the deletion of Article 34.4.5°: 'The rule is unsatisfactory in its operation and is apt to create anomalies'. The Constitution Review Group analysed the issue very closely in its report (see Appendix X) and the Committee endorses its conclusion.

Delete Article 34.4.5°.

iv) *Article 26 reference cases: immutability of the Supreme Court's decision*

Article 34.3.3° provides that, once the Supreme Court delivers its decision on the constitutionality of a Bill referred to it under Article 26, that decision stands immutable. The Article provides certainty about the validity of Bills referred under the procedure before their enactment. However, this certainty may be bought at too high a price. As the Constitution Review Group said:

Despite the care taken in preparing a Bill, doubt may arise as to its constitutionality. Some Bills concern fundamental issues on which doubt cannot be allowed, indeed where it is desirable that there should be certainty extending indefinitely, or at least over a long period. In relation to adoption, for instance, certainty for a period of over fifty years, that is to say, over about two generations, would seem desirable. On the constitutionality of elections to the Dáil an even longer period could be essential.

The certainty provided by the Article prevails indefinitely unless terminated by a referendum. However, with the efflux of time, changed circumstances and attitudes may bring about a situation where a referred Bill that has been enacted may operate harshly and unfairly, denying justifiable redress in a context not originally foreseen. The question to be addressed is whether the desirability of a measure of stability is reconcilable with an openness to challenge where reason and justice so demand.

The Constitution Review Group discussed the arguments for and against deletion of the Article in its report (see Appendix X). It recommended:

> On balance, Article 34.3.3° should be deleted in its entirety. Such a deletion would impact only marginally upon legal certainty, inasmuch as a decision of the Supreme Court upholding the constitutionality of the Bill would still be an authoritative ruling on the Bill which would bind all the lower courts and be difficult to dislodge. It is to be expected that the Supreme Court would not, save in exceptional circumstances, readily depart from its earlier decision to uphold the constitutionality of the Bill. Such exceptional circumstances might be found to exist where the Constitution had been later amended in a manner material to the law in question, or where the operation of the law in practice had produced an injustice which had not been apparent at the time of the Article 26 reference, or possibly where constitutional thinking had significantly changed.

The Committee agrees with the recommendations made by the Constitution Review Group.

Delete Article 34.3.3°.

v) *Constitutional cases: consequences of a declaration of invalidity*

The courts have interpreted Article 15.4 to mean that, if a court declares a provision of a post-1937 Act to be repugnant to the Constitution, it is void *ab initio* because Article 15.4 prevents it ever being valid law.

The Constitution Review Group discussed whether the courts should have express power to declare an Act to be unconstitutional not from the date of its enactment but from some later date (see Appendix X). It recommended:

> The importance of the prohibition in Article 15.4 in ensuring that the Oireachtas operates within the limits set by the Constitution is recognised. A majority of the Review Group

15.4.1° *The Oireachtas shall not enact any law which is in any respect repugnant to this Constitution or any provision thereof.*

15.4.2° *Every law enacted by the Oireachtas which is in any respect repugnant to this Constitution or to any provision thereof, shall, but to the extent only of such repugnancy, be invalid.*

is, therefore, not disposed (Article 26 cases and 'creeping unconstitutionality' cases apart) to recommend generally that the courts should have jurisdiction to declare invalid, otherwise than *ab initio,* a statutory provision which at the date of its passing was repugnant to the Constitution.

Note that in regard to Article 26 reference cases the Constitution Review Group recommended:

> In the special case of declaration of invalidity of a law the Bill for which had been referred to the Supreme Court under Article 26, a majority of the Review Group is in favour of amending the Constitution to give the courts an express jurisdiction to declare the law to be unconstitutional as of a stated date other than the date of enactment.

In the situation of 'creeping unconstitutionality' type cases, legislation which was constitutional at the date of its enactment has become unconstitutional by reason of changing circumstances (for example, the failure to revise monetary limits in line with inflation or the failure to revise constituency boundaries in line with population movements). In regard to such cases the Constitution Review Group recommended that:

> Given the uncertainties in this area, the Review Group favours giving the courts express power, in cases where they declare an Act to be unconstitutional but determine that at the date of its enactment it was not repugnant to the Constitution, to determine the date upon which it became unconstitutional.

To deal with the consequence of a declaration of invalidity a majority of the Constitution Review Group favoured amending the Constitution:

> to provide the courts with an express discretion, where justice, equity or, exceptionally, the common good so requires, to afford such relief as they consider necessary and appropriate in respect of any detriment arising from acts done in reliance in good faith on an invalid law.

The Committee endorses this majority view. However, it considers that such a general power would enable the courts to deal adequately with Article 26 reference cases and 'creeping unconstitutionality' type cases. They do not recommend therefore any special provision in relation to those two types of case.

Replace the deleted Article 34.3.3° with:

34.3.3° Where a law has been found to be invalid having regard to the provisions of this Constitution, the High Court or the Supreme Court (as the case may be) shall have jurisdiction to determine in the interests of justice the consequences of such a finding of invalidity.

Since the object of this suggested draft is to give the courts a general jurisdiction to determine the temporal and other effects of a finding of unconstitutionality, it may be expected that this

50.1 *Subject to this Constitution and to the extent to which they are not inconsistent therewith, the laws in force in Saorstát Éireann immediately prior to the date of the coming into operation of this Constitution shall continue to be of full force and effect until the same or any of them shall have been repealed or amended by enactment of the Oireachtas.*

jurisdiction would be exercised on a case by case basis and that the courts would balance the interests of good administration and the avoidance of legislative chaos against the *prima facie* right of the successful litigant to recover appropriate redress in the wake of a finding of unconstitutionality. The Committee recognises that it is difficult to come up with an *a priori* formula which would adequately deal with every contingency, but the present draft is suggested as a means of dealing with the very real difficulties identified in the *Report of the Constitution Review Group.*

An analogous provision is required for Article 50 to deal with findings of constitutional inconsistency in the case of pre-1937 laws.

Amend Article 50.1 by adding:

Where such a law has been found to be inconsistent having regard to the provisions of this Constitution, the High Court or the Supreme Court (as the case may be) shall have jurisdiction to determine in the interests of justice the consequences of such a finding of invalidity.

6 Local Government

Local Government

Local government is used here in the sense of local self-government, defined by the European Charter of Local Self-Government (Council of Europe) as: '...the right and the ability of local authorities, within the limits of the law, to regulate and manage a substantial share of public affairs under their own responsibility and in the interests of the local population'. It is thus distinguished from centrally controlled manifestations of the state in a particular locality such as a post office or Garda station.

Bunreacht na hÉireann is silent on the subject of local government apart from making a reference to administrative councils in relation to the nomination of Presidential candidates in Article 12.4.2° and a reference to local authorities in relation to money or loans raised by them for local purposes in Article 22.1.2°. Ireland in this regard is markedly different from the other thirteen member states of the European Union which have written constitutions.

The reason is mainly historical. The Local Government Act 1898 rationalised the system of local authorities and put them on a representative basis. But, as Dr Eunan O'Halpin says in *City and County Management 1929-1990 – A Retrospective,* 'Irish local government in the first decades of the twentieth century acquired a reputation for amateurishness, incompetence, venality and political favouritism'. A discredited system, it did not present as a likely candidate for constitutional protection.

Moreover, during the struggle for independence from 1916 to 1921, Irish politicians showed themselves anxious to depart from the inefficient system of government operated by the British in Ireland and wished to see a strong centralised state put in its place. Consequently the Constitution of the Irish Free State 1922 concentrated its attention on the organs of central government and omitted all references to local government. *Bunreacht na hÉireann* 1937, which followed the Constitution of the Irish Free State in many respects, did so in this respect too.

If the Constitution were being written today it is most likely that it would provide for local government: all our partners in the European Union except the UK do so, and the European Charter of Local Self-Government, which the Government is committed absolutely to ratify, urges that constitutional recognition be given to local government.

Constitutional recognition of local government would strengthen the democratic system. In doing so, it would counteract the dependency syndrome which, as many commentators have observed, strong centralised institutions create in their clients; it would concomitantly foster local creativity.

New Provision

Recognition could be provided for in either of two ways, one general, the other specific:

> by recognition in principle of local government, leaving almost entirely to legislation the definition of the structures and processes of local government

or

> by detailed provisions for the system of local government and for the relationship between it and central government.

In its report, the Constitution Review Group sets forth arguments for and against our having either general or specific provision for local government (see Appendix XI). A majority of the Constitution Review Group concluded that 'a form of recognition in principle of local government should be inserted in the Constitution', that is to say, a general recognition should be given. The All-Party Oireachtas Committee, having examined the arguments set forth against either form of constitutional recognition, concluded that those against providing for general recognition were nugatory. The submissions received by the Committee from the Department of the Environment, the General Council of County Councils, a number of local authorities, the Green Party and some interested individuals have all supported the constitutional recognition of local government. However, some individuals proposed specific recognition.

The arguments set forth by the Constitution Review Group against specific recognition are telling. It is clear from the number of official studies that have been or are being carried out on local government that there is widespread dissatisfaction with the structures that exist, their financing, their relationship with central government and their relationship to the community. One can discern steady attrition in the role of local authorities. Functions were removed and given to other institutions. The establishment of city and county management from 1929 onwards diminished the role of councillors and the abolition of rates on domestic property in the late 1970s reduced the autonomy of local authorities. However, in the 1990s there has been a marked movement to enlarge the role of local authorities, particularly in community and general development. In circumstances of such flux it would be ill-advised to set down specific provisions in the Constitution. The Committee therefore recommends that a new Article should be inserted in the Constitution providing general recognition of local government.

Because local authorities are at present the creature of legislation, it is possible to defer elections to local authorities for so prolonged a period that their representational character is discounted. In order to assert the democratic value further the Committee believes that there should be constitutional provision for periodic elections to local authorities.

Recommendation

The new Article should provide as follows:

1   Local authorities shall be empowered to carry out the functions which the Oireachtas may from time to time devolve upon them by law.

New Provision

2   Elections to local authorities shall be held at least once every five years.

7 The Electoral and Ethics Commission

The Electoral and Ethics Commission

In dealing with the issue of funding of referenda (chapter 2) the Committee concluded that the Constitution should provide for an independent commission to carry out the proposed functions. However, there are several cognate functions which, dealt with by two Bills and an Act, are at present designed to be carried out by three separate statutory commissions. (One embraces the informational but not the promotional function in regard to referenda.) The Committee feels that it would be more efficient and effective to entrust all those functions, as well as the functions in relation to the funding and promotion of referenda, to a single independent constitutional commission.

Commissions

The Public Offices Commission has been established under the Ethics in Public Office Act 1995. It is proposed that the ad hoc Dáil Constituency Commission be put on a statutory footing under the Electoral Bill 1994 and called the Constituency Commission. It is also proposed that the ad hoc Commission on Referendum Information should be placed on a statutory basis under the Independent Referendum Commission Bill 1996 (a Private Member's Bill).

Functions

The Public Offices Commission

The commission has two sets of functions:

a)   under the Ethics in Public Office Act 1995

The Act provides for the disclosure of interests by members of the Oireachtas, the holders of designated positions of employment in the public service and the directors of designated public bodies. To deal with complaints about members of the Dáil and Seanad it establishes a select committee on member's interests for each House. For office holders such as ministers and ministers of state and for the public service it establishes the Public Offices Commission.

The commission's main function under this Act is to deal with complaints that office holders specified in the Act have contravened the provisions of the Act. The commission may, where it considers it appropriate to do so, carry out an investigation to determine whether persons have contravened the Act when they were an office holder, or before they became an office holder.

New Provision

b)   under the Electoral Bill 1994

The Bill proposes to establish a Constituency Commission and to make provision for payments to political parties, disclosure of donations for political purposes, to regulate expenditure at elections by political parties and candidates, to provide voting arrangements for certain persons unable to vote at polling stations and to provide for other electoral matters.

The Bill proposes that the Public Offices Commission should carry out functions in relation to:

- recoupment of candidates' election expenses (for Presidential, Dáil, European Parliament elections)

- limitation of expenditure at elections

- funding of political parties

- donations to parties/individuals.

The commission has the following membership:

the Comptroller and Auditor General
the Ombudsman
the Ceann Comhairle
the Clerk of Dáil Éireann
the Clerk of Seanad Éireann.

Alternates are provided for in the Act where the above members are unable to act. The commission appoints one of its members to be chair.

Constituency Commission

The Electoral Bill 1994 provides for the establishment by the Minister for the Environment, following the publication of the Census Report on each census of population, of a Constituency Commission to report on the constituencies for Dáil and European Parliament elections in accordance with the terms set forth in the Bill (which include the provisions of Article 16.2.2°).

The commission will advise and report on the formation of constituencies for election of members in Dáil and European Parliament elections.   The proposed membership of the commission is:

a)   a Supreme or High Court judge (*chair*)
b)   the Ombudsman
c)   the Secretary, Department of the Environment
d)   the Clerk of Dáil Éireann
e)   the Clerk of Seanad Éireann.

New Provision

Independent Referendum Commission

The Independent Referendum Commission Bill 1996 proposes to provide for the establishment of an Independent Referendum Commission having the function of preparing and presenting to the public, information in an objective, impartial and informative manner thereby assisting the exercise of informed choice by the public in both constitutional and ordinary referenda.

The function of the Independent Referendum Commission is to supervise the production and communication to the electorate of objective information for and against proposed constitutional amendments.

The proposed membership of the commission, to be appointed by the President on the advice of the government, is:

    a)   the Clerk of the Dáil
    b)   the Clerk of the Seanad
    c)   the Ombudsman
    d)   the Comptroller and Auditor General
    e)   the President of The Law Reform Commission
    f)   two other suitably qualified persons.

The commission will appoint one of its members to be chair.

A single commission

Apart from the facts that a proliferation of commissions would readily lead to public confusion and that, in general, greater efficiency and effectiveness could be achieved by a single body, provision in the Constitution for a compendious commission would:

–   guarantee the independence and impartiality of the commission

–   generate greater confidence in public life

–   create greater transparency in public institutions

–   create consistency and continuity in developing the procedures for dealing with related functions

–   provide an independent source of advice and information in the areas of ethics in public life and electoral law reform.

This innovation would be in line with the trend in the economic sphere, such as in telecommunications and electricity production, to establish independent regulators. It would also provide a useful structure to which other appropriate functions or issues could be referred as the need arises. It would provide a powerful constitutional mechanism to guarantee the probity of public life. It would also provide protection to public representatives and public servants from gratuitous unsustained charges of corruption.

Membership

The qualities which the commission needs to carry out its functions in a manner that will command the trust of the people are:

- independence

- a deep knowledge and extensive experience of

  - the political system, including the system of public administration

  - the electoral system

  - financial affairs

  - the law.

Considering these criteria and prompted by the membership proposed for the commissions outlined above, the Committee recommends that the membership of the Electoral and Ethics Commission should be:

a) a serving or former Supreme or High Court judge nominated by the Chief Justice (*chair*)
b) the Comptroller and Auditor General
c) the Ombudsman
d) the Clerk of Dáil Éireann
e) the Clerk of Seanad Éireann.

The Committee considers that the Ceann Comhairle, who is a member of the Public Offices Commission, should not be a member of the commission because of its functions in relation to constituency boundaries. The Secretary of the Department of the Environment, who is proposed for membership of the Constituency Commission, should in principle also be excluded because of the possibility of a conflict of interest in regard to the same issue inasmuch as the Secretary is in charge of the public agency concerned with elections and answerable directly to a member of the government.

Recommendation

The Constitution should provide for an Electoral and Ethics Commission whose functions, in addition to those identified by the Committee in its examination of funding for referenda, would include those of the Public Offices Commission and the Constituency [Boundary] Commission. (The functions of the Independent Referendum Commission are included in the Committee's funding for referenda proposals.) The membership of the Commission would be:

a) a serving or former Supreme or High Court judge nominated by the Chief Justice (*chair*)
b) the Comptroller and Auditor General
c) the Ombudsman
d) the Clerk of Dáil Éireann
e) the Clerk of Seanad Éireann.

8 The Ombudsman

The Ombudsman

The office of the Ombudsman was established by the Ombudsman Act 1980. The Constitution Review Group considered whether the office should be strengthened by being put on a constitutional basis (see Appendix XII). The Constitution Review Group observed:

> The Constitution confirms various personal and other rights which are protected by the courts. Without prejudice to this basic and general protection, additional protection is available in defined areas through recourse to the Ombudsman and this can be of particular advantage to those who are poor and without social position. An effective democracy requires that public servants should be held accountable for their actions and that citizens be protected from maladministration by public officials.

It recommended that:

> A new Article should be inserted in the Constitution confirming the establishment of the office of the Ombudsman, providing for the independent exercise of such investigative and other functions of the office in relation to administrative actions as may be determined by law, and making other provisions similar to those applying to the Comptroller and Auditor General and consistent with the 1980 Act, as amended.

A majority of the Committee agrees with this recommendation. Apart from its objective merits, the recommmmendation congrues with the Committee's other recommendation for constitutional provision for an Electoral and Ethics Commission (see chapter 7), of which the Ombudsman would be a member.

Recommendation

Insert a new Article to read as follows:

The Ombudsman

1   There shall be an Ombudsman who shall independently perform such investigative and other functions in relation to administrative actions as may be determined by law.

2   The Ombudsman shall be appointed by the President on the nomination of Dáil Éireann.

3   The Ombudsman shall not be a member of either House of the Oireachtas and shall not hold any other office or position of emolument.

4   The Ombudsman shall report to Dáil Éireann at stated periods as determined by law.

New Provision

5   1°   The Ombudsman shall not be removed from office except for stated misbehaviour or incapacity, and then only upon resolutions passed by Dáil Éireann and by Seanad Éireann calling for his or her removal.

    2°   The Taoiseach shall duly notify the President of any such resolutions as aforesaid passed by Dáil Éireann and Seanad Éireann and shall send him or her a copy of each such resolution certified by the Chair of the House of the Oireachtas by which it shall have been passed.

    3°   Upon receipt of such notification and of copies of such resolutions, the President shall forthwith, by an order under his or her hand and Seal, remove the Ombudsman from office.

6   Subject to the foregoing, the terms and conditions of the office of Ombudsman shall be determined by law.

9 'Woman in the home' and gender-inclusive language in the Constitution

'Woman in the home' and gender-inclusive language in the Constitution

41.2.1° *In particular, the State recognises that by her life within the home, woman gives to the State a support without which the common good cannot be achieved.*

41.2.2° *The State shall, therefore, endeavour to ensure that mothers shall not be obliged by economic necessity to engage in labour to the neglect of their duties in the home.*

45.2 *The State shall, in particular, direct its policy towards securing:-*

i. That the citizens (all of whom, men and women equally, have the right to an adequate means of livelihood) may through their occupations find the means of making reasonable provision for their domestic needs.

'Woman in the home'

On one reading of Article 41.2 a domestic role as wives and mothers is envisaged for women. (Article 45.2.i, however, makes it clear that there was not an intention to limit women in such a way – it asserts that all citizens 'men and women equally have the right to an adequate means of livelihood'). It is a dated provision much criticised in recent years because it presumes that women, by reason of their gender, are predetermined to play a particular role in life, thus seeming to deny them the same freedom of choice as that enjoyed by men. Moreover, as the Constitution Review Group points out: 'Notwithstanding its terms, it has not been of any particular assistance even to women working exclusively within the home'.

The Constitution Review Group considered whether section 2 of Article 41 should be deleted or whether subsection 2° of section 2 should be retained in an amended form which might recognise the contribution of each or either spouse within the home. The Constitution Review Group was conscious of the importance of the caring function of the family. It considered it important that there be constitutional recognition for the significant contribution made to society by the large number of people who provide a caring function within their homes for children, elderly relatives and others. On balance it favoured the retention of Article 41.2 in a revised gender-neutral form. It also felt that the retention of Article 41.2.2° might not be appropriate to a gender-neutral form of the section (see Appendix XIII).

A majority of the Committee agrees with the position adopted by the Constitution Review Group on Article 41.2. However, it suggests a slight alteration in the form of the amendment offered by the Constitution Review Group so that it can decide the substantive issue in advance of its consideration of the constitutional definition of 'family'.

Recommendation

Delete Article 41.2 subsections 1° and 2° and replace it with the following:

Article 41.2: The State recognises that family life gives to society a support without which the common good cannot be achieved. The State shall endeavour to support persons caring for others within the home.

Gender-inclusive language

The text of the Constitution is a product of the patriarchal times in which it was written. Like most constitutions it is insensitive on the issue of gender and invariably, for instance, presumes that office-holders will be male. The Constitution Review Group suggested that:

> The principle of gender-inclusiveness should be observed in the wording of the Constitution. At various points the Review Group has drawn specific attention to this but there should be consistent adherence to the principle throughout the text of the Constitution.

The concern here is the same as that expressed in 'A General Outline for a Draft Revision of the Treaties' drawn up under the Irish presidency of the European Union, published in Brussels, 5 December 1996: 'The Presidency proposes that gender-neutral language should be incorporated into the Treaties wherever this is appropriate'.

The exclusive use of masculine pronouns in the Constitution does not create any constitutional disability for women because the Constitution has been interpreted by the courts in a sensible manner, taking the exclusive use of the male pronoun as merely reflecting the linguistic convention of the day whereby references to the masculine gender included the feminine save where the context excluded it.

However, a consistent rephrasing of the Constitution so as to ensure that it is gender-inclusive is a common courtesy the state should pay to more than half its citizens.

Recommendation

In order to make the Constitution gender-inclusive the amendments set forth in Appendix XIV should be made.

10 Omnibus Proposal: Technical/Minor Amendments

Omnibus Proposal: Technical/Minor Amendments

In its terms of reference the Committee was asked to consider 'whether there might be a single draft of non-controversial amendments to the Constitution to deal with technical matters'. Numerous minor and technical amendments to the Constitution have been identified in the course of the various constitutional reviews that have been carried out to date. Other such changes have been suggested in submissions to the Committee. The Committee will examine all of them in due course and make recommendations. It is clear to the Committee that it would be unmanageable for the people to consider and decide all the changes if they were presented in a single proposal. It recommends therefore that these changes should be effected through a series of omnibus proposals. The first such omnibus proposal should contain the recommendations that follow.

12.1 *There shall be a President of Ireland (Uachtarán na hÉireann), hereinafter called the President, who shall take precedence over all other persons in the State and who shall exercise and perform the powers and functions conferred on the President by this Constitution and by law.*

1   The Constitution does not describe the President as the Head of State. The need for this reticence disappeared with the coming into force of the Republic of Ireland Act 1948 and the removal from the British monarch of all functions in relation to external affairs and their assignment to the President.

Recommendation

Amend Article 12.1 by inserting after the first 'who' the words 'as the Head of State'.

12.2.3° *The voting shall be by secret ballot and on the system of proportional representation by means of the single transferable vote.*

2   Article 12.2.3° describes the method of election of the President as 'proportional representation by means of the single transferable vote'. The term 'proportional representation' denotes the filling of a number of seats by different parties in proportion to the votes they receive. It cannot refer to the filling of a single seat.

Recommendation

Delete the words 'and on the system of proportional representation' from Article 12.2.3°.

12.4.1° *Every citizen who has reached his thirty-fifth year of age is eligible for election to the office of President.*

12.4.1° *Gach saoránach ag a bhfuil cúig bliana tríochad slán, is intofa chun oifig an Uachtaráin é.*

3   There is an apparent discrepancy between the English and the Irish versions of Article 12.4.1°. The Irish version has 'ag a bhfuil cúig bliana tríochad slán' (that is, who has completed thirty-five years) whereas the English version is 'who has reached his thirty-fifth year of age', which could mean has entered rather than completed that year.

Recommendation

Substitute the word 'completed' for 'reached' in the English language version of Article 12.4.1°.

89

15.5 *The Oireachtas shall not declare acts to be infringements of the law which were not so at the date of their commission.*

4   Article 15.5 should be extended on the lines of Article 7 of the European Convention on Human Rights so as to provide that a heavier penalty shall not be imposed than was applicable at the time the offence was committed.

Recommendation

Amend Article 15.5 to read:

The Oireachtas shall not declare acts to be infringements of the law which did not constitute a criminal offence at the time of their commission. Nor shall a heavier penalty be imposed than the one that was applicable at the time the criminal offence was committed.

15.7 *The Oireachtas shall hold at least one session every year.*

15.7 *Ní foláir don Oireachtas suí uair sa bhliain ar a laghad.*

5   'The Oireachtas' consists of the President, Dáil Éireann and Seanad Éireann (Article 15.1.2°). Typically, the President does not sit with the Dáil and Seanad, nor do the Dáil and Seanad sit together. The clear object of Article 15.7 is to prevent government without parliament by ensuring that each House of the Oireachtas shall sit at least once every year.

Recommendation

Amend the English version of Article 15.7 to read:

Each House of the Oireachtas shall hold at least one meeting every year.

Amend the Irish version to read:

Ní foláir do gach Teach ar leith den Oireachtas cruinniú amháin ar a laghad sa bhliain a thionól.

15.15 *The Oireachtas may make provision by law for the payment of allowances to the members of each House thereof in respect of their duties as public representatives and for the grant to them of free travelling and such other facilities (if any) in connection with those duties as the Oireachtas may determine.*

6   It is not clear from the use of the term 'allowances' that Article 15.15 relates both to emoluments and expenses of deputies and senators. Accordingly, the word 'allowances' should be deleted and the word 'emoluments' inserted in its place.

Recommendation

Amend Article 15.15 to read:

The Oireachtas may make provision by law for the payment of emoluments to the members of each House thereof in respect of their duties as public representatives and for the grant to them of free travelling and such other facilities (if any) in connection with those duties as the Oireachtas may determine.

13.2.1° *Dáil Éireann shall be summoned and dissolved by the President on the advice of the Taoiseach.*

16.3.1° *Dáil Éireann shall be summoned and dissolved as provided by section 2 of Article 13 of this Constitution.*

7   Article 16.3.1° is the same as Article 13.2.1° and is therefore redundant.

Recommendation

Delete Article 16.3.1°.

17.1.2° Save in so far as may be provided by specific enactment in each case, the legislation required to give effect to the Financial Resolutions of each year shall be enacted within that year.

8   Article 17.1.2° has generally been understood as giving constitutional authority to the practice whereby the Dáil (but not the Oireachtas) anticipates the enactment of the Finance Act each year by the collecting of certain taxes on the authority of the resolutions passed by it in relation to the Budget. However, the matter should be put beyond doubt by explicit statement.

Recommendation

Amend Article 17.1.2° to read:

> Save in so far as may be provided by specific resolution in each case, the Financial Resolutions of each year passed by Dáil Éireann shall have immediate effect and full force of law provided that legislation confirming any such resolution is enacted within a year.

18.5 Every election of the elected members of Seanad Éireann shall be held on the system of proportional representation by means of the single transferable vote, and by secret postal ballot.

9   The word 'postal' in Article 18.5 makes the Seanad election process specifically – and unnecessarily – dependent on the postal services.

Recommendation

Delete the word 'postal' from Article 18.5.

18.8 A general election for Seanad Éireann shall take place not later than ninety days after a dissolution of Dáil Éireann, and the first meeting of Seanad Éireann after the general election shall take place on a day to be fixed by the President on the advice of the Taoiseach.

10   Article 18.8 does not envisage the possibility that a second general election might be called before the ninety days within which the Constitution provides that a Seanad election will take place. Such a possibility would create a situation where a second Seanad election would have to be called before the first one was completed.

Recommendation

Amend Article 18.8 to read:

> A general election for Seanad Éireann shall take place not later than ninety days after a dissolution of Dáil Éireann. If Dáil Éireann is dissolved before the general election for Seanad Éireann is completed, that Seanad election shall be cancelled and an election related to the more recent Dáil dissolution shall be held instead. The first meeting of Seanad Éircann after the general election shall take place on a day to be fixed by the President on the advice of the Taoiseach.

18.9 Every member of Seanad Éireann shall, unless he previously dies, resigns, or becomes disqualified, continue to hold office until the day before the polling day of the general election for Seanad Éireann next held after his election or nomination.

11   Article 18.9 does not define the polling day. The latest date upon which an elector can vote should be the polling day.

Recommendation

Amend Article 18.9 by adding:

> The latest date upon which an elector can vote shall be the polling day.

28.6.2° *The Tánaiste shall act for all purposes in the place of the Taoiseach if the Taoiseach should die, or become permanently incapacitated, until a new Taoiseach shall have been appointed.*

28.6.3° *The Tánaiste shall also act for or in the place of the Taoiseach during the temporary absence of the Taoiseach.*

29.4.2° *For the purpose of the exercise of any executive function of the State in or in connection with its external relations, the Government may to such extent and subject to such conditions, if any, as may be determined by law, avail of or adopt any organ, instrument, or method of procedure used or adopted for the like purpose by the members of any group or league of nations with which the State is or becomes associated for the purpose of international co-operation in matters of common concern.*

31.2 *The Council of State shall consist of the following members:*

ii. Every person able and willing to act as a member of the Council of State who shall have held the office of President, or the office of Taoiseach, or the office of Chief Justice, or the office of President of the Executive Council of Saorstát Éireann.

35.3 *No judge shall be eligible to be a member of either House of the Oireachtas or to hold any other office or position of emolument.*

35.3 *Ní cead aon bhreitheamh a bheith ina chomhalta de cheachtar de Thithe an Oireachtais, ná bheith in aon oifig ná post sochair eile.*

12 Article 28.6.2°–3° provides for the Tánaiste to act for the Taoiseach in certain circumstances but makes no disposition for what should happen if both the Taoiseach and the Tánaiste are unable to act in an emergency. There should be a provision for the nomination of a member of the government to act in such circumstances.

Since Article 28.7.1° requires the Taoiseach to be a member of Dáil Éireann and Article 28.7.2° permits two members of Seanad Éireann to be members of the government, the nominated member must be from Dáil Éireann.

Recommendation

Amend Article 28.6 by adding a subsection as follows:

If the Tánaiste is unable to act in the place of the Taoiseach in the circumstances defined in subsections 2° and 3° of this section, a designated member of the government who is also a member of Dáil Éireann shall so act.

13 Article 29.4.2° was designed to accommodate in the Constitution the arrangement whereby the British crown was authorised under legislation – Executive Authority (External Relations) Act 1936 – to carry out certain functions in relation to external affairs which included the accreditation of diplomatic representatives. The arrangement ceased with the coming into force of the Republic of Ireland Act 1948. The subsection is for all practical purposes spent.

Recommendation

Delete Article 29.4.2°.

14 Since all those who have held the office of President of the Executive Council of Dáil Éireann are dead, the words 'or the office of the President of the Executive Council of Saorstát Éireann' in Article 31.2.ii are obsolete.

Recommendation

Delete the words 'or the office of the President of the Executive Council of Saorstát Éireann' from Article 31.2.ii.

15 The Irish and English language versions of the text of Article 35.3 appear to be discordant. The English refers to 'eligible', whereas the Irish uses the words 'a bheith ina chomhalta'. The latter phrase suggests that, while a judge could stand for election to the Oireachtas, he or she could not take his or her seat if elected. It seems that the English phrase more accurately reflects the underlying purpose of this section, in that a serving judge would be simply debarred from standing for election. The Irish language text should be brought into conformity by substituting 'intofa mar chomhalta' for 'ina chomhalta'.

Recommendation

Amend the Irish language text of Article 35.3 by substituting 'intofa mar chomhalta' for 'ina chomhalta'.

16 The prohibition in Article 35.3 should extend to the Presidency and to membership of any elected assembly. In addition to being prohibited from taking up paid appointments, serving judges should, in order to uphold public confidence in the judiciary and public perception of their independence and impartiality, be prohibited from taking up any position which is inconsistent with the office of judge under the Constitution.

Recommendation

Amend Article 35.3 to read:

No serving judge shall be eligible to stand for election for the office of President or for membership of either House of the Oireachtas or for membership of any other elected assembly nor shall he or she hold any other office or position of emolument or any other position inconsistent with the office of judge.

11 Summary of Recommendations and Conclusions

Summary of recommendations and conclusions

Constitutional reviews (pages 1–11)

The Committee considers that:

- it should draw up a programme of constitutional reform to be implemented over a number of years

- it should engage the people from an early stage in discussion of the elements of the programme

- to get this process under way in an orderly and manageable fashion it should publish a series of reports dealing with the various elements of the programme

- it should draw up the programme in such a way that the people can most efficiently deal with it (so as to avoid referendum fatigue)

- the programme should be implemented in such a way that the economies of combining referenda with local, Dáil, Presidential and European Parliament elections are made.

The Referendum (pages 15–22)

The Committee agrees with the Constitution Review Group that an independent body should be established to regulate the funding and conduct of referenda. It feels, however, that it would be tidier to provide in the Constitution for a commission to carry out not just those functions but also those undertaken by the Constituency Boundary Commission, the Public Service Ethics Committee under the Ethics in Public Office Act 1995 and any commission which might be proposed to regulate election funding.

Towards a Programme for Constitutional Renewal (pages 25–50)

The Committee's *modus operandi* will be to work its way steadily through the recommendations of the Constitution Review Group and the submissions made to it both in writing and orally. It has decided to gather the fruits of the process together periodically and publish them in the form of progress reports. This will allow the people enough time to digest the recommendations.

The Power to Dissolve Dáil Éireann (pages 53–56)

Article 13.2.2° should be deleted and replaced by the following:

> If a Taoiseach formally ceases to retain the support of a majority of Dáil Éireann, as indicated by the loss of a vote of confidence or a vote of no confidence, or the loss of a motion to approve or modify a charge upon the people or to appropriate revenue or other public monies (other than a charge or expenditure, as the case may be, which is subordinate and incidental to a legislative proposal), the President shall accede to a request from the Taoiseach to dissolve the Dáil if within ten days from such a vote the Dáil has not elected a new Taoiseach.

A consequential amendment to Article 28.10 is to delete the words 'unless on his advice ... Dáil Éireann' (at the end of the section) and replace them with, 'as indicated by the loss of a vote of confidence or a vote of no confidence, or the loss of a motion to approve or modify a charge upon the people or to appropriate revenue or other public monies (other than a charge or expenditure, as the case may be, which is subordinate and incidental to a legislative proposal)'.

The revised Article 28.10 would read:

> The Taoiseach shall resign from office upon his or her ceasing to retain the support of a majority in Dáil Éireann, as indicated by the loss of a vote of confidence or a vote of no confidence, or the loss of a motion to approve or modify a charge upon the people or to appropriate revenue or other public monies (other than a charge or expenditure, as the case may be, which is subordinate and incidental to a legislative proposal).

Insert a new subsection after Article 13.2.2° to read as follows:

> If a Taoiseach who has not formally ceased to retain the support of a majority in Dáil Éireann but whom the President deems to have informally done so requests the President to dissolve Dáil Éireann, the President in his or her absolute discretion may, within three days, summon Dáil Éireann to vote on a motion of confidence in the Taoiseach. If the Taoiseach wins the vote, the President shall accede forthwith to his or her request for a dissolution. If the Taoiseach loses the vote, the President shall dissolve Dáil Éireann if within ten days the Dáil has not elected a new Taoiseach.

Constitutionality of Bills and Laws (pages 59–65)

Amend Article 26.2.1° to begin 'The Supreme Court consisting of not less than seven judges ...'

Insert a subsection after Article 34.4.4° to read as follows:

> The decision of the Supreme Court on a question as to the validity of a law having regard to the provisions of this Constitution shall be made by not less than seven judges.

Amend Article 26.2.1° to read '... and in any case not later than ninety days after the date of such reference'.

The two changes should be incorporated in Article 26.2.1° as follows:

> The Supreme Court consisting of not less than seven judges shall consider every question referred to it by the President under this Article for a decision, and, having heard arguments by or on behalf of the Attorney General and by counsel assigned by the Court, shall pronounce its decision on such question in open court as soon as may be, and in any case not later than ninety days after the date of such reference.

Delete Article 26.2.2°.

Delete Article 34.4.5°.

Delete Article 34.3.3°.

Replace the deleted Article 34.3.3° with:

> 34.3.3° Where a law has been found to be invalid having regard to the provisions of this Constitution, the High Court or the Supreme Court (as the case may be) shall have jurisdiction to determine in the interests of justice the consequences of such a finding of invalidity.

Amend Article 50.1 by adding:

> Where such a law has been found to be inconsistent having regard to the provisions of this Constitution, the High Court or the Supreme Court (as the case may be) shall have jurisdiction to determine in the interests of justice the consequences of such a finding of invalidity.

Local Government (pages 69–71)

The new Article should provide as follows:

1   Local authorities shall be empowered to carry out the functions which the Oireachtas may from time to time devolve upon them by law.

2   Elections to local authorities shall be held at least once every five years.

The Electoral and Ethics Commission (pages 75–78)

The Constitution should provide for an Electoral and Ethics Commission whose functions, in addition to those identified by the Committee in its examination of funding for referenda, would include those of the Public Offices Commission and the Constituency [Boundary] Commission. (The functions of the Independent Referendum Commission are included in the Committee's funding for referenda proposals.) The membership of the Commission would be:

a)   a serving or former Supreme or High Court judge nominated by the Chief Justice (*chair*)

b) the Comptroller and Auditor General
c) the Ombudsman
d) the Clerk of Dáil Éireann
e) the Clerk of Seanad Éireann.

The Ombudsman (pages 81–82)

Insert a new Article to read as follows:

The Ombudsman

1 There shall be an Ombudsman who shall independently perform such investigative and other functions in relation to administrative actions as may be determined by law.

2 The Ombudsman shall be appointed by the President on the nomination of Dáil Éireann.

3 The Ombudsman shall not be a member of either House of the Oireachtas and shall not hold any other office or position of emolument.

4 The Ombudsman shall report to Dáil Éireann at stated periods as determined by law.

5 1° The Ombudsman shall not be removed from office except for stated misbehaviour or incapacity, and then only upon resolutions passed by Dáil Éireann and by Seanad Éireann calling for his or her removal.

2° The Taoiseach shall duly notify the President of any such resolutions as aforesaid passed by Dáil Éireann and Seanad Éireann and shall send him or her a copy of each such resolution certified by the Chair of the House of the Oireachtas by which it shall have been passed.

3° Upon receipt of such notification and of copies of such resolutions, the President shall forthwith, by an order under his or her hand and Seal, remove the Ombudsman from office.

6 Subject to the foregoing, the terms and conditions of the office of Ombudsman shall be determined by law.

'Woman in the home' and gender-inclusive language in the Constitution (pages 85–86)

Delete Article 41.2 subsections 1° and 2° and replace it with the following:

Article 41.2: The State recognises that family life gives to society a support without which the common good cannot be achieved. The State shall endeavour to support persons caring for others within the home.

In order to make the Constitution gender-inclusive the amendments set forth in Appendix XIV should be made.

Omnibus Proposal: Technical/Minor Amendments (pages 89–93)

Amend Article 12.1 by inserting after the first 'who' the words 'as the Head of State'.

Delete the words 'and on the system of proportional representation' from Article 12.2.3°.

Substitute the word 'completed' for 'reached' in the English language version of Article 12.4.1°.

Amend Article 15.5 to read:

> The Oireachtas shall not declare acts to be infringements of the law which did not constitute a criminal offence at the time of their commission. Nor shall a heavier penalty be imposed than the one that was applicable at the time the criminal offence was committed.

Amend the English version of Article 15.7 to read:

> Each House of the Oireachtas shall hold at least one meeting every year.

Amend the Irish version to read:

> Ní foláir do gach Teach ar leith den Oireachtas cruinniú amháin ar a laghad sa bhliain a thionól.

Amend Article 15.15 to read:

> The Oireachtas may make provision by law for payment to the members of each House thereof in respect of their duties as public representatives and for the grant to them of free travelling and such other facilities (if any) in connection with those duties as the Oireachtas may determine.

Delete Article 16.3.1°.

Amend Article 17.1.2° to read:

> Save in so far as may be provided by specific resolution in each case, the Financial Resolutions of each year passed by Dáil Éireann shall have immediate effect and full force of law provided that legislation confirming any such resolution is enacted within a year.

Delete the word 'postal' from Article 18.5.

Amend Article 18.8 to read:

> A general election for Seanad Éireann shall take place not later than ninety days after a dissolution of Dáil Éireann. If Dáil Éireann is dissolved before the general election for Seanad Éireann is completed, that Seanad election shall be cancelled and an election related to the more recent Dáil dissolution shall be held instead. The first meeting of Seanad Éireann after the general

election shall take place on a day to be fixed by the President on the advice of the Taoiseach.

Amend Article 18.9 by adding:

The latest date upon which an elector can vote shall be the polling day.

Amend Article 28.6 by adding a subsection as follows:

If the Tánaiste is unable to act in the place of the Taoiseach in the circumstances defined in subsections 2° and 3° of this section, a designated member of the government who is also a member of Dáil Éireann shall so act.

Delete Article 29.4.2°.

Delete the words 'or the office of the President of the Executive Council of Saorstát Éireann' from Article 31.2.ii.

Amend the Irish language text of Article 35.3 by substituting 'intofa mar chomhalta' for 'ina chomhalta'.

Amend Article 35.3 to read:

No judge shall be eligible to be President or a member of either House of the Oireachtas or of any other elected assembly or to hold any other office or position of emolument or any other position inconsistent with the office of judge.

Appendices

Appendix I
Constitutional reviews 1966-1996

COMMITTEE ON THE CONSTITUTION 1967

In a speech in March 1966 Seán Lemass, then Taoiseach, suggested that:

> ... the time had come for a general review of *Bunreacht na hÉireann*. It is possible that some of the views regarding the procedures and institutional arrangements for applying the democratic principles on which the Constitution is framed, which prevailed thirty years ago, could now be modified in the light of our own experience or that of other countries in the intervening years.

He accepted that the principles of the Constitution continued to have a strong appeal, but he argued that 'the manner in which these principles were expressed and the procedures by which it was decided to apply them might not be as suitable to our present requirements as they were...' In any case, the Supreme Court had in some instances interpreted the Constitution 'in a way its drafters had not expected or intended'. He thought there was 'a case for carrying out a general review of the provisions of the Constitution'. In the Dáil, a week later, he made it clear that he was thinking of this as a routine operation: such a review ought to be undertaken 'every twenty-five years or so'.

In August 1966, the three political parties represented in the Dáil agreed to an informal committee of deputies and senators 'to review the constitutional, legislative and institutional bases of government'. The committee had twelve members with George Colley, TD, as chairman. The first meeting of the committee took place on 12 September 1966 and, in all, seventeen meetings were held. In its report, published in December 1967, the committee acknowledged that, in general, *Bunreacht na hÉireann* was still regarded as satisfactory: 'we are not aware of any public demand for a change in the basic structure of the Constitution'.

However, it reviewed the text and dealt with matters either by way of recommendation where the members were unanimous or, where they were not, by deploying the arguments for and against changes, 'leaving it to the government of the day to decide the items which should be selected for inclusion in any legislative proposals that may emerge'.

This report, which was intended by the committee to be an interim report, was the only report produced by the committee.

The committee, in addition, identified a number of legal ambiguities arising in the text of the Constitution and referred them to the Attorney General for examination by a legal committee under his chairmanship.

THE ATTORNEY GENERAL'S COMMITTEE ON THE CONSTITUTION 1966

This committee was established following a request by the Taoiseach to the Attorney General to set up a legal committee to consider constitutional review in conjunction with, but separately from, the informal Oireachtas Committee on the Constitution. There were seventeen members of this committee all of whom were members of the legal profession. The Attorney General's committee considered a number of matters including those which had been referred to it by the Oireachtas committee. The committee prepared a draft report dated August 1968. This draft was never finalised by the committee and therefore was not published. The draft report was made available to the Constitution Review Group by the present Attorney General, Dermot Gleeson, SC.

THE INTER-PARTY COMMITTEE ON THE IMPLICATIONS OF IRISH UNITY 1972

In November 1971, the Labour Party TD, Michael O'Leary, wrote to the Taoiseach, Jack Lynch, suggesting the establishment of an All-Party committee in response to an initiative by the leader of the British Labour Party, Harold Wilson, in relation to proposals on Northern Ireland. This led to discussions and consultations between the Taoiseach and ministers, on behalf of the Fianna Fáil Party, and representatives of the Fine Gael and Labour parties in December 1971 and early 1972. On 4 May 1972, the Taoiseach announced the establishment of the committee with the following terms of reference:

> With a view to contributing to a peaceful settlement of the Northern Ireland situation it has been agreed to set up an Inter-Party Committee to establish the common ground between the parties represented on the committee on the constitutional, legal, economic, cultural, social and other relevant implications of a united Ireland and to make recommendations as to the steps now required to create conditions conducive to a united Ireland.

The first meeting of the committee was held on 24 May 1972. Michael O'Kennedy, TD, was elected chairman.

The committee held eighteen meetings in all and had completed consideration of the constitutional aspects of the terms of reference. The points of agreement on this had been drawn up when the committee lapsed in February 1973 on the dissolution of the Dáil. A preliminary run-through of the legal matters covered by the terms of reference was also under way. This was to have been followed by a study of the economic, social and cultural aspects of the terms of reference.

THE ALL-PARTY COMMITTEE ON IRISH RELATIONS 1973

Following consultation with the leader of Fianna Fáil in June and July 1973, the Taoiseach, Liam Cosgrave, TD, on 12 July 1973, announced the establishment of this committee with the following terms of reference:

With a view to contributing to a peaceful settlement of the Northern Ireland situation, it has been agreed to set up an Inter-Party Committee to establish the common ground between the parties represented on the committee on the constitutional, legal, economic, cultural, social and other relevant steps required to bring about lasting reconciliation of all the people of Ireland so that conditions may be created conducive to a united Ireland; and, if thought appropriate, to make recommendations.

The committee held its first meeting on 27 July 1973. It elected Paddy Harte, TD, chairman.

The committee held fifteen meetings, the last one being in June 1975. It met various groups and individuals during the period 1973/74 for an exchange of views on matters coming within its terms of reference. The meetings included discussions with Northern political parties (SDLP, Alliance and NILP) as well as with church leaders and the Northern Ireland committee of ICTU.

The committee was unable to reach agreement on the amendment of any part of the Constitution. At a meeting on 4 December 1974, the committee decided that in view of the lack of agreement on constitutional reform, this aspect of its terms of reference should be left aside for the time being and attention given to other matters. Some preliminary consideration was then given by the committee to non-denominational education. The committee lapsed on the dissolution of the Dáil in May 1977.

In October 1977, the government gave some preliminary consideration to reconstituting the committee but it did not do so.

CONSTITUTION REVIEW BODY 1982

In a radio interview on 27 September 1981, three months after his election (and without consulting the Opposition), the Taoiseach Dr Garret FitzGerald, TD declared his intention of mounting a 'constitutional crusade' aimed at eliminating the sectarian and confessional nature of some parts of *Bunreacht na hÉireann* and replacing them with pluralist principles. His avowed purpose was to seek to allay the suspicions of Northerners and in this connection he referred particularly to Articles 2, 3 and 41 (the Article on the Family which contained the provision prohibiting divorce legislation). The subsequent Seanad motion, introduced at the earliest opportunity, at the first meeting of the new session in October, referred to 'the desirability of creating within this island conditions favourable to unity through a reconciliation of its people.' To this end it was proposed to undertake 'a constitutional and legislative review'.

A committee to review the Constitution was subsequently formed under the chairmanship of the then Attorney General, Peter Sutherland, SC. The body had nine members, all of whom were from the legal profession. The body met on a number of occasions but its work ceased with the collapse of the 1981-1982 FitzGerald administration. The body did not produce any report. However, a number of its working papers were made available to the Constitution Review Group by the Attorney General, Dermot Gleeson, SC.

THE NEW IRELAND FORUM 1983-1984

The New Ireland Forum was established in April 1983 for consultations on the manner in which lasting peace and stability could be achieved in a new Ireland through the democratic process and to report on possible new structures and processes through which the objective might be achieved. It reported in May 1984.

Participation in the Forum was open to all democratic parties who rejected violence and which had members elected or appointed to either House of the Oireachtas or the Northern Ireland Assembly. Four political parties took part in the Forum: Fianna Fáil, Fine Gael, the Labour Party and the Social Democratic and Labour Party (SDLP). The Forum sought the views of people of all traditions who agreed with its objectives and who rejected violence.

The establishment and work of the Forum had been of historic importance in bringing together, for the first time, since 1920, elected nationalist representatives from North and South to deliberate on the shape of a new Ireland. Its chairman was Colm Ó hEocha, President of University College Galway.

INITIATIVE OF THE PROGRESSIVE DEMOCRATS 1988

These Oireachtas and government reviews were followed by a review conducted by the Progressive Democrats the results of which were embodied in their publication *Constitution for a New Republic* (1988) and the accompanying explanatory memorandum. The party leader, Desmond O'Malley, TD, said they had put it out for public discussion.

The PDs were concerned to bring forward a truly republican and pluralist constitution which would be acceptable to all political and religious traditions. As a result they suggested the removal of the prohibition on divorce and the territorial claim to Northern Ireland. They suggested the jettisoning of the 'left luggage' of the 1930s – vocationalism, the Directive Principles of Social Policy, the limited role of women – and sought to balance the rights of parents and children. However, their redraft of the Constitution took care to preserve what was left of the large corpus of case-law relating to *Bunreacht na hÉireann*.

FORUM FOR PEACE AND RECONCILIATION – SUB-COMMITTEE ON OBSTACLES IN THE SOUTH TO RECONCILIATION 1994

The Downing Street Declaration of 15 December 1993 provided, on the undertaking of the then Taoiseach, for the establishment of the Forum for Peace and Reconciliation. It contained the following commitment which gave rise to the Forum's work on obstacles in the South to reconciliation:

> ... the Taoiseach will examine with his colleagues any elements in the democratic life and organisation of the Irish State that can be represented

to the Irish Government in the course of political dialogue as a real and substantial threat to their [Unionists'] way of life and ethos, or that can be represented as not being fully consistent with a modern democratic pluralist society, and undertakes to examine any possible ways of removing such obstacles.

The question of obstacles in the South to reconciliation was formally identified by the Forum as one of ten main sub-themes to be addressed by it.

The whole question of obstacles in the South to reconciliation had to be looked at from a number of perspectives, to which the various delegations gave differing degrees of emphasis. One perspective was that the Forum should take steps to promote pluralism for the greater benefit of society as a whole in the South. A second perspective was that of reconciliation. The Forum should examine what would make life in the South, and on the island of Ireland, more attractive and reassuring to the Northern Unionist outlook; this perspective did not necessarily coincide with the first. It had to be borne in mind that any change for the purpose of removing a real or perceived obstacle for the Unionist tradition could, unless handled with care and sensitivity, give rise to fears and anxieties for Irish nationalists. This latter consideration influenced the final view held by some delegations that any change contemplated must be considered in a wider context, including wider political negotiations, and therefore was best brought forward in the context of a political accommodation; others continued to hold to the view that change should come about now. All of these perspectives have been in play in the Forum's discussions, particularly those in relation to the more politically complex questions of the Constitution and symbols.

The Forum, which was chaired by Judge Catherine McGuinness, had not issued an agreed report on these matters when it adjourned *sine die* in March 1996.

THE CONSTITUTION REVIEW GROUP 1995–1996

A Government of Renewal, the policy agreement between Fine Gael, The Labour Party and Democratic Left, published when that administration came into power in December 1994, stated:

> To provide focus to the place and relevance of the Constitution, and to establish those areas where constitutional change may be desirable or necessary, the Government will propose the establishment of an all-Party Committee of the Oireachtas to review the Constitution. ... As a first step, the Government will appoint a group of experts to prepare a report on all aspects of the Constitution, and this report will be published and presented to the Oireachtas Committee ... .

The Constitution Review Group was established by the government, with Dr TK Whitaker as chairman, on 27 April 1995:

> to review the Constitution, and in the light of this review, to establish those areas where constitutional change may be desirable or necessary,

with a view to assisting the All-Party Committee on the Constitution, to be established by the Oireachtas, in its work. In their review, the Group should take into account that certain constitutional matters, that is, Articles 2 and 3, Divorce, the Right to Bail, Cabinet Confidentiality and Votes for Emigrants are the subject of separate consideration.

There were fifteen members of the Review Group selected from different backgrounds – administration, economics, education, law, political science and sociology – with lawyers being predominant. The Review Group presented its report to the Taoiseach on Friday 31 May 1996 – it was published on 3 July 1996. The Review Group's report, 350,000 words in extent and over 700 pages in length, is the most thorough analysis of the Constitution from the legal, political science, administrative, social and economic perspectives ever made.

Appendix II
Referenda arising from reviews

COMMITTEE ON THE CONSTITUTION 1967

Five proposals for amendment of the Constitution were put to the people in the twelve-year period 1967 to 1979 which were the subject of recommendation or discussion in the committee's report:

1   The Third Amendment of the Constitution Bill 1968 proposed that in forming Dáil constituencies the population per deputy in any case may not be greater or less than the national average by more than one-sixth and that regard must be had to the extent and accessibility of constituencies, the need for having convenient areas of representation and the desirability of avoiding the overlapping of county boundaries.

    This proposal was based on a recommendation in the report.

2   The Fourth Amendment of the Constitution Bill 1968 proposed:

    a) to substitute for the present system of voting at Dáil elections the 'straight vote' system in single-member constituencies

    b) to establish a Commission to determine constituencies, subject to the right of the Dáil to amend the constituencies as so determined

    c) to provide that whenever the Dáil is dissolved the outgoing Ceann Comhairle may be returned, without a contest, as a second deputy for a constituency chosen by him which consists of, or includes part of, the constituency he represented before the dissolution.

    a) and b) were issues discussed in the report but there was no consensus on them; c) was not discussed in the report.

    These two amendments (1 and 2) were rejected by the people on 16 October 1968.

3   The Fourth Amendment of the Constitution Bill 1972 proposed to reduce the minimum voting age at Dáil and Presidential elections and referenda from twenty-one years to eighteen years.

    This proposal was discussed in the report. Arguments for and against were given but no recommendation was made.

4   The Fifth Amendment of the Constitution Bill 1972 proposed to delete subsections 2° and 3° of Article 44.1 of the Constitution (the special position of the Roman Catholic Church).

This proposal was based on a recommendation in the report. Proposals 3 and 4 were accepted by the people on 7 December 1972.

5   The Seventh Amendment of the Constitution (Election of Members of Seanad Éireann by Institutions of Higher Education) Bill 1979 proposed the election by universities and other institutions of higher education specified by law of such members of Seanad Éireann, not exceeding six, as may be specified by law. Those so elected would be in substitution for an equal number of the members elected at present (three each) by the National University of Ireland and the University of Dublin. The Bill also proposed that nothing in Article 18 of the Constitution would prohibit the dissolution by law of those universities.

This proposal was based on discussion in the report. Arguments for and against were given but no recommendation was made.

This proposal was accepted by the people on 5 July 1979.

Appendix III

Referenda to amend the Constitution

There were two amendments of the Constitution made by Acts of the Oireachtas under the transitory provision Article 51.1. The first referendum was held in 1959. There have been eighteen referenda in all (to November 1996). Of these, five were rejected. The referendum procedure is as follows:

A Bill, for example the Third Amendment of the Constitution Bill 1971, is drawn up and debated by the Dáil. This specifies the proposed change or changes to be made in the Constitution. If the referendum is approved this Bill is signed by the President and thus formally enacted. In order to allow the referendum to take place a separate enabling Bill is passed by the Oireachtas and enacted by the President. This Act sets forth the arrangements for the referendum, for example the form of the proposal to appear on the polling card which is to be posted to every voter and the arrangements for publicising the Amendment of the Constitution Bill.

REFERENDUM	PROPOSAL(S)[1]	SPECIFIC AMENDMENT(S)[2]	OUTCOME
Referendum on the voting system: Third Amendment of the Constitution Bill 1958 Polling date: 17 June 1959	At present, members of Dáil Éireann are elected on a system of proportional representation for constituencies returning at least three members, each voter having a single transferable vote. It is proposed in this Bill to abolish the system of proportional representation and to adopt, instead, a system of single-member constituencies, each voter having a single non-transferable vote. It is also proposed in this Bill to set up a Commission for the determination and revision of the constituencies, instead of having this done by the Oireachtas, as at present.	Deletion of section 2 of Article 16 and the insertion in its place of the sections set out in Part II of the schedule to the Bill and the alteration of the numbers of sections 3, 4, 5, 6 and 7 from those numbers to '8', '9', '10', '11' and '12'.	Proposal rejected

[1] appearing on the polling card
[2] appearing in the Amendment of the Constitution Bill

REFERENDUM	PROPOSAL(S)	SPECIFIC AMENDMENT(S)	OUTCOME
Referenda on **a** the formation of Dáil constituencies: Third Amendment of the Constitution Bill 1968 (white ballot paper)	**a** proposes that in forming Dáil constituencies, the population per deputy in any case may not be greater or less than the national average by more than one-sixth and that regard must be had to the extent and accessibility of constituencies, the need for having convenient areas of representation and the desirability of avoiding the over-lapping of county boundaries.	**a** The subsection set out in Part II of the schedule to the Bill to be substituted for subsection 3° of section 2 of Article 16.	Both proposals rejected
b voting system: Fourth Amendment of the Constitution Bill 1968 (green ballot paper) Polling date: 16 October 1968	**b** proposes to (1) substitute for the present system of voting at Dáil elections the 'straight vote' system in single-member constituencies; (2) establish a Commission to determine constituencies, subject to the right of the Dáil to amend the constituencies as so determined; and (3) provide that whenever the Dáil is dissolved the outgoing Ceann Comhairle may be returned, without a contest, as a second deputy for a constituency chosen by him which consists of, or includes a part of, the constituency he represented before the dissolution.	**b** Article 16 to be amended as follows: delete sub-sections 1° and 2° of section 2 and replace them with the subsections set out in Part II of the schedule to the Bill. delete sub-sections 4°, 5° and 6° of section 2 and replace them with the subsection set out in Part IV of the schedule to the Bill. insert after section 2 the sections set out in Part VI of the schedule to the Bill. renumber the sections and subsections of this Article.	

REFERENDUM	PROPOSAL(S)	SPECIFIC AMENDMENT(S)	OUTCOME
Referendum on accession to the European Communities (1972): Third Amendment of the Constitution Bill 1971 Polling date: 10 May 1972	Proposes to add the subsection here following to Article 29.4 of the Constitution. 3° The State may become a member of the European Coal and Steel Community (established by Treaty signed at Paris on the 18th day of April, 1951), the European Economic Community (established by Treaty signed at Rome on the 25th day of March, 1957) and the European Atomic Energy Community (established by Treaty signed at Rome on 25th day of March, 1957). No provision of this Constitution invalidates laws enacted, acts done or measures adopted by the State necessitated by the obligations of membership of the Communities or prevents laws enacted, acts done or measures adopted by the Communities, or institutions thereof, from having the force of law in the State. The purpose of the proposal is to allow the State to become a member of the Communities commonly known as the European Communities.	Amend Article 29 by: adding to section 4 a subsection set out in Part II of the schedule to the Bill.	Proposal approved

REFERENDUM	PROPOSAL(S)	SPECIFIC AMENDMENT(S)	OUTCOME
Referenda on **a** the voting age: Fourth Amendment of the Constitution Bill 1972 (green ballot paper)	**a** proposes to reduce the minimum voting age at Dáil and Presidential elections and referendums from 21 years to 18 years.	**a** Amend Article 16 by: substituting 'eighteen years' for 'twenty-one years' in subsection 2° of section 1	Both proposals approved
b recognition of specified religions: Fifth Amendment of the Constitution Bill 1972 (white ballot paper) Polling date: 7 December 1972	**b** proposes to delete subsections 2° and 3° of Article 44.1 of the Constitution which provide as follows: 2° The State recognises the special position of the Holy Catholic Apostolic and Roman Church as the guardian of the Faith professed by the great majority of the citizens. 3° The State also recognises the Church of Ireland, the Presbyterian Church in Ireland, the Methodist Church in Ireland, the Religious Society of Friends in Ireland, as well as the Jewish Congregations and the other religious denominations existing in Ireland at the date of the coming into operation of this Constitution.	**b** Amend Article 44 by: deleting subsections 2° and 3° of section 1 renumbering subsection 1° of section 1 as section 1	

REFERENDUM	PROPOSAL(S)	SPECIFIC AMENDMENT(S)	OUTCOME
Referenda on **a** adoption: Sixth Amendment of the Constitution (Adoption) Bill 1978 (white ballot paper)	**a** proposes that an adoption which is in accordance with laws enacted by the Oireachtas shall not be invalid solely by reason of the fact that the relevant order or authorisation was not made or given by a judge or court but by a person or body designated for the purpose of those laws. The Bill relates to past as well as future adoptions. Its object is to ensure that adoption orders made by an Bord Uchtála (the Adoption Board) will not be in danger of being declared to be invalid because they were not made by a court.	**a** Amend Article 37 by: adding a section to the Article as set out in Part II of the schedule to the Bill. Article 37 shall be numbered as section 1 of that Article	Both proposals approved
b university representation in the Seanad: Seventh Amendment of the Constitution (Election of Members of Seanad Éireann by Institutions of Higher Education) Bill 1979 (green ballot paper) Polling date: 5 July 1979	**b** proposes the election by universities and other institutions of higher education specified by law of such number of members of Seanad Éireann, not exceeding 6, as may be specified by law. Those so elected would be in substitution for an equal number of the members elected at present (3 each) by the National University of Ireland and the University of Dublin. The Bill also proposes that nothing in Article 18 of the Constitution shall prohibit the dissolution by law of those universities.	**b** Amend Article 18 by: adding sub-sections to section 4 as set out in Part II of the schedule to the Bill. renumber section 4 as section 4.1°	

REFERENDUM	PROPOSAL(S)	SPECIFIC AMENDMENT(S)	OUTCOME
Referendum on the right to life of the unborn: Eighth Amendment of the Constitution Bill 1982 Polling date: 7 September 1983	Proposes to add the subsection here following to Article 40.3 of the Constitution. 3° The State acknowledges the right to life of the unborn and, with due regard to the equal right to life of the mother, guarantees in its laws to respect, and, as far as practicable, by its laws to defend and vindicate that right.	Amend Article 40 by adding to section 3 a subsection set out in Part II of the schedule to the Bill.	Proposal approved

REFERENDUM	PROPOSAL(S)	SPECIFIC AMENDMENT(S)	OUTCOME
Referendum on extension of voting right at Dáil elections: Ninth Amendment of the Constitution Bill 1984 Polling date: 14 June 1984	Proposes to extend the right conferred on citizens to vote at elections for members of Dáil Éireann to such other persons in the State who have reached the age of 18 years as may be specified by legislation enacted by the Oireachtas.	Amend Article 16 by: deleting subsection 2° of section 1 and replacing it with the subsection set out in Part II of the schedule to the Bill. inserting 'or other person' after 'disqualifying any citizen' in sub-section 3° of section 1.	Proposal approved

REFERENDUM	PROPOSAL(S)	SPECIFIC AMENDMENT(S)	OUTCOME
Referendum on dissolution of marriage: Tenth Amendment of the Constitution Bill 1986 Polling date: 26 June 1986	Proposes to delete subsection 2° of Article 41.3 of the Constitution, which states that no law shall be enacted providing for the grant of a dissolution of marriage, and to substitute the subsection here following: 2° Where, and only where, such court established under this Constitution as may be prescribed by law is satisfied that: i) a marriage has failed ii) the failure has continued for a period of, or periods amounting to, at least five years iii) there is no reasonable possibility of reconciliation between the parties to the marriage, and iv) any other condition prescribed by law has been complied with the court may in accordance with law grant a dissolution of marriage provided that the court is satisfied that adequate and proper provision having regard to the circumstances will be made for any dependent spouse and for any child of or any child who is dependent on either spouse.	Amend Article 41.3 by: deleting subsection 2° and replacing it with a subsection set out in the schedule to the Bill.	Proposal rejected

119

REFERENDUM	PROPOSAL(S)	SPECIFIC AMENDMENT(S)	OUTCOME
Referendum on ratification of the Single European Act 1987: Tenth Amendment of the Constitution Bill 1987 Polling date: 26 May 1987	Proposes to enable the State to ratify the Single European Act by inserting the sentence here following into subsection 3° of section 4 of Article 29 of the Constitution after the first sentence: The State may ratify the Single European Act (signed on behalf of the Member States of the Communities at Luxembourg on the 17th day of February, 1986, and at the Hague on the 28th day of February, 1986).	Amend Article 29 by: inserting in subsection 3° of section 4 a sentence, after the first sentence of that subsection, set out in Part II of the schedule to the Bill.	Proposal approved

REFERENDUM	PROPOSAL(S)	SPECIFIC AMENDMENT(S)	OUTCOME
Referendum on European Union (1992): Eleventh Amendment of the Constitution Bill 1992 Polling date: 18 June 1992	Relating to the amendment of Article 29 of the Constitution proposes to repeal the third sentence in subsection 3° of section 4 thereof and to insert the subsections here following into the said section 4: 4° The State may ratify the Treaty on European Union signed at Maastricht on the 7th day of February, 1992, and may become a member of that union. 5° No provision of this Constitution invalidates laws enacted, acts done or measures adopted by the State which are necessitated by the obligations of membership of the European Union or of the Communities, or prevents laws enacted, acts done or measures adopted by the European Union or by the Communities or by institutions thereof, or by bodies competent under the Treaties establishing the Communities, from having the force of law in the State. 6° The State may ratify the Agreement relating to community Patents drawn up between the Member States of the Communities and done at Luxembourg on the 15th day of December, 1989.	Amend Article 29 by: deleting the third sentence in sub-section 3° of section 4 and inserting in its place the text set out in Part II of the schedule to Bill.	Proposal approved

121

REFERENDUM	PROPOSAL(S)	SPECIFIC AMENDMENT(S)	OUTCOME
Referenda on **a** right to life: Twelfth Amendment of the Constitution Bill 1992 (white ballot paper)	**a** proposes to amend Article 40 of the Constitution by the addition of the text here following to subsection 3° of section 3 thereof: 'It shall be unlawful to terminate the life of an unborn unless such termination is necessary to save the life, as distinct from the health, of the mother where there is an illness or disorder of the mother giving rise to a real and substantial risk to her life, not being a risk of self-destruction.'	**a** Amend Article 40.3.3° by: adding to the text of subsection 3° of section 3 immediately after the words 'vindicate that right', the text set out in Part II of the schedule to the Bill.	Proposal **a** rejected
b right to travel: Thirteenth Amendment of the Constitution Bill 1992 (green ballot paper)	**b** proposes to amend Article 40 of the Constitution by the addition of the paragraph here following to subsection 3° of section 3 thereof: 'This subsection shall not limit freedom to travel between the State and another state.'	**b** Amend Article 40.3.3° by: inserting a second paragraph to the subsection as set out in Part II of the schedule to the Bill.	Proposal **b** approved
c right to information (1992): Fourteenth Amendment of the Constitution Bill 1992 (pink ballot paper) Polling date: 25 November 1992	**c** proposes to amend Article 40 of the Constitution by the addition of the paragraph here following to subsection 3° of section 3 thereof: 'This subsection shall not limit freedom to obtain or make available, in the State, subject to such conditions as may be laid down by law, information relating to services lawfully available in another state.'	**c** Amend Article 40.3.3° by: adding a paragraph the text of which is set out in Part II of the schedule to the Bill.	Proposal **c** approved

REFERENDUM	PROPOSAL(S)	SPECIFIC AMENDMENT(S)	OUTCOME
Referendum on dissolution of marriage: Fifteenth Amendment of the Constitution (No 2) Bill 1995 Polling date: November 1995	Proposes to substitute the subsection here following for subsection 2° of Article 41.3 of the Constitution: '2° A Court designated by law may grant a dissolution of marriage where, but only where, it is satisfied that – i at the date of the institution of the proceedings, the spouses have lived apart from one another for a period of, or periods amounting to, at least four years during the previous five years, ii there is no reasonable prospect of a reconciliation between the spouses, iii such provision as the Court considers proper having regard to the circumstances exists or will be made for the spouses, any children of either or both of them and any other person prescribed by law, and iv any further conditions prescribed by law are complied with.'	Amend Article 41 by: substituting the sub-section set out in Part II of the schedule to the Bill for subsection 2° of section 3	Proposal approved

REFERENDUM	PROPOSAL(S)	SPECIFIC AMENDMENT(S)	OUTCOME
Referendum on the right to bail: Sixteenth Amendment of the Constitution Bill 1996 Polling date: 28 November 1996	Proposes to add the following subsection to section 4 of Article 40 of the Constitution: '7° Provision may be made by law for the refusal of bail by a court to a person charged with a serious offence where it is reasonably considered necessary to prevent the commission of a serious offence by that person.'	Amend Article 40 by adding to section 4 the subsection set out in Part II of the schedule to the Bill.	Proposal approved

Appendix IV

Table of amendments to the Constitution

Title of Amendment	Date of coming into effect
First Amendment of the Constitution Act, 1939	2 September 1939
Second Amendment of the Constitution Act, 1941	30 May 1941
Third Amendment of the Constitution Act, 1972	8 June 1972
Fourth Amendment of the Constitution Act, 1972 Fifth Amendment of the Constitution Act, 1972	5 January 1973
Sixth Amendment of the Constitution (Adoption) Act, 1979	3 August 1979
Seventh Amendment of the Constitution (Election of Members of Seanad Éireann by Institutions of Higher Education) Act, 1979	3 August 1979
Eighth Amendment of the Constitution Act, 1983	7 October 1983
Ninth Amendment of the Constitution Act, 1984	2 August 1984
Tenth Amendment of the Constitution Act, 1987	22 June 1987
Eleventh Amendment of the Constitution Act, 1992	16 July 1992
*Thirteenth Amendment of the Constitution Act, 1992 Fourteenth Amendment of the Constitution Act, 1992	23 December 1992
Fifteenth Amendment of the Constitution Act, 1995	17 June 1996
Sixteenth Amendment of the Constitution Act, 1996	12 December 1996

* There is no Twelfth Amendment. On 25 November 1992, three proposals were put to the people:

> The Twelfth Amendment of the Constitution Bill, 1992
> The Thirteenth Amendment of the Constitution Bill, 1992
> The Fourteenth Amendment of the Constitution Bill, 1992

The people rejected the Twelfth Amendment Bill and approved the other two. These were enacted, therefore, as the Thirteenth Amendment of the Constitution Act, 1992 and the Fourteenth Amendment of the Constitution Act, 1992.

Appendix V
Referenda results

REFERENDUM	YEAR	% TURNOUT	VOTES		
			% Yes	% No	% Spoilt
Draft Constitution	1937	75.8%	51%	39%	
Voting system	1959	58.4%	46%	50%	4%
Dáil constituencies	1968	65.8%	38%	58%	4%
Voting system	1968	65.8%	38%	58%	4%
Accession to EEC	1972	70.9%	82%	17%	1%
Voting age	1972	50.7%	80%	15%	5%
Recognition of religions	1972	50.7%	80%	15%	5%
Adoption	1979	28.6%	97%	1%	2%
Universities/Seanad seats	1979	28.6%	89%	7%	4%
Right to life	1983	53.7%	66%	33%	1%
Voting rights at Dáil Elections	1984	47.5%	73%	24%	3%
Divorce	1986	60.8%	36%	63%	1%
Single European Act	1987	44.1%	70%	30%	---
European Union (Maastricht Treaty)	1992	57.3%	69%	31%	---
Right to life	1992	68.2%	33%	62%	5%
Right to travel	1992	68.2%	60%	36%	4%
Right to information	1992	68.1%	57%	39%	4%
Divorce	1995	62.1%	50.1%	49.6%	0.39%
Bail	1996	29.2%	75%	25%	---

Appendix VI

The popular initiative and the preferendum

Extract from the *Report of the Constitution Review Group*

whether provision should be made for a popular initiative to amend the Constitution otherwise than by the existing provisions of Articles 46 and 47

The Constitution may be amended only in accordance with Articles 46 and 47. These do not provide for a popular initiative. The Constitution of the Irish Free State (Article 48) provided for a popular initiative both for amendment of the Constitution and for enactment of non-constitutional legislation. For a history of this provision and commentary on it see Appendix 28.

The Review Group considered whether it is either desirable or necessary to recommend a change to provide for a popular initiative for amendment of the Constitution.

Arguments for

1   the initiative enables the people to propose constitutional amendments directly as well as through elected representatives, a facility that should be available in a democracy

2   the initiative has proved to be a practicable and popular method of effecting changes, particularly in some states of the United States

3   it enables a section of the people to submit to a referendum a proposal for amendment on a matter on which it feels the Houses of the Oireachtas are not responsive to its concerns; where a minority perceives that its concerns are not receiving adequate attention it may resort to undesirable action to secure that attention.

Arguments against

1   the by-passing of the Houses of the Oireachtas, comprising the elected representatives of all the people, in submitting a proposal for amendment is inappropriate to a representative democracy

2   there is no indication that people perceive the existing provisions for amendment to be inadequate

3   the initiative tends to favour the objectives of well-organised and well-funded pressure groups who have a disproportionate capacity to mobilise both proposers and voters for an amendment

4   the initiative carries the risk of enabling majoritarian concerns to be incorporated into the Constitution at the expense of minorities

5   as compared with a proposal for amendment emanating from the Houses of the Oireachtas one that arises from an initiative has several disadvantages, for example:

    i)   it lacks the quality of deliberation which the elected representatives could bring to bear upon it and is therefore less likely to command a majority

    ii) it lacks the benefit of the assistance provided by Government services in the analysis of issues and the refinement of proposals

    iii) the amendment proposal may lack the precise drafting required to ensure both that it is clear to the voter and that it achieves the objective of the initiative

6   a heavy administrative burden would be imposed by the need to check the authenticity of the proposers of the initiative because a substantial number would presumably be required.

The initiative therefore involves the dual risks of effecting inadequate or undesirable amendments to the Constitution and of leading to many fruitless and expensive referendums.

Conclusion

The consensus in the Review Group is that there should be no provision to allow constitutional change to be proposed either directly or indirectly by means of an initiative.

whether provision should be made for amendment of the Constitution by way of a preferendum instead of/as well as a referendum

A preferendum differs from a referendum in that the voter is given a choice between three or more proposals (including a 'no change' choice) rather than a choice between supporting or opposing a single proposal.

Preferendums have been used in some of the states of the United States of America. A preferendum was also used in Newfoundland in 1951 to determine whether or not that state should (among other options) join the Canadian federation.

In Ireland, there have been occasions when the complexity of the issue put to the people admitted of more than one appropriate response. This point might be illustrated by the 1992 referendum on the 12th Amendment of the Constitution Bill 1992 dealing with the 'substantive issue' of abortion in the wake of the Supreme Court's decision in *Attorney General v X* [1992] 1 IR 1. In that referendum the electorate were asked to amend Article 40.3.3° of the Constitution by inserting the following clause:

It shall be unlawful to terminate the life of the unborn unless such termination is necessary to save the life, as distinct from the health, of the mother where there is an illness or disorder of the mother giving rise to a real and substantial risk to her life, not being a risk of self-destruction.

It is plain that there was a substantial body of opinion which was unhappy with the proposal on the basis that it did not offer the electorate a 'real' choice in that it did not offer the possibility of voting to insert a complete and absolute ban on abortion in the Constitution. There were, then, at least four separate possibilities:

a) insert a complete and absolute ban on abortion into the Constitution

b) modify the decision in the X case by allowing abortion where the life of the mother was at risk in all cases other than suicide

c) accept the decision in the X case

d) admit of abortion in cases where the life or health of the mother was substantially put at risk by the continuation of the pregnancy.

An illustration of how voting in a preferendum might work is contained in a memorandum prepared by Gerard Hogan (see Appendix 27).

Argument for

It would give the voter a wide range of choices within which to express his or her preferences. At the moment the referendum system offers the voter a 'yes' or 'no' option on complex issues which may not admit of a simple yes or no. The voter should therefore be offered the option of voting on a reasonable range of the possible responses such complex issues evoke.

Arguments against

1 the referendum system offers the voter the right to say 'Yes' or 'No' to an option formulated by the Oireachtas. It is the task of the Oireachtas to draft the precise wording of the Bill to amend the Constitution which is put before the people and the Oireachtas may be relied upon to define the precise issue for the referendum

2 at a referendum there is a majority one way or the other on the issue before the people. A preferendum might result in an option, which had never obtained the support of a majority of the electorate, being nonetheless adopted following the vote

3 with referendums on complex issues, it is often necessary to formulate the proposal in a particular way so that the electorate can vote 'Yes' or 'No'. Preferendums introduce more complexity and the possibility of confusion

4 the referendum system has worked well in practice and does not require change

5   it is not clear who would formulate the range of proposals to be put to
     the electorate and how they would be so formulated

6   because there are three or more proposals, the terms in which each is
     formulated could be used to manipulate or distort the choices to be made,
     by, for instance, splitting a proposal supported by a majority into a
     number of proposals and leaving a proposal supported by a minority
     intact and therefore predominant.

Conclusion

The referendum system has worked well in practice and should not be
changed. While the Review Group agrees that a cogent theoretical argument
could be made in favour of the preferendum system, it believes there is no
pressing need for change. However, it is an issue which might usefully be
kept under review, especially having regard to the potentially complex nature
of future proposals to amend the Constitution.

Appendix VII

Funding of referenda

Extract from the *Report of the Constitution Review Group*

whether there should be an amendment to permit State funding of support for a proposal for an amendment

Exchequer funding to promote, and to seek to secure the passage of, proposed amendments to the Constitution occurred in relation to a number of amendments which were accepted by the people. These included the 1972 amendment to authorise entry into the EEC and subsequent amendments approving ratification of the Single European Act and the Maastricht Treaty. Public funding was also used in 1992 to support the series of referendums concerning Article 40.3.3°, relating to the rights to life, travel and information. Recently, the question of public funding in relation to a referendum became a matter of controversy resulting in litigation. The use of public funding was initially upheld by a decision of the High Court in *McKenna v An Taoiseach (No 1)* [1995] 2 IR 1 and (it seems) also by the Supreme Court in the case of *Slattery v An Taoiseach* [1993] 1 IR 286. However, in *McKenna v An Taoiseach (No 2)* [1995] 2 IR 10 it was ruled that the provision and use of such funding in order to seek to secure the passage of the divorce amendment was unconstitutional. This decision was handed down a week prior to the referendum taking place and gave rise to a petition to the court seeking to overturn the result of the referendum.

The Review Group has considered whether the Constitution should authorise the use of such public funding and, if so, in what circumstances.

A possible approach would be to extend Article 47.4 (which reads, 'Subject as aforesaid, the Referendum shall be regulated by law') on the following lines:

> Such law may provide for limited public funding in relation to any proposed amendment and shall entrust the equitable distribution of such funding to an independent body.

Arguments for

1   it appears unreasonable that a Government with a programme of constitutional reform approved by the Oireachtas may not spend public money in order to promote that reform

2   a political party may campaign and be elected on the basis of advocating constitutional change either generally or specifically and may form a Government on this basis. The position following the *McKenna* case

appears to be an unreasonable hindrance to the fulfilment of democratic objectives already sanctioned by the people

3   apart from any constitutional reform resulting from the current review, circumstances now unforeseen or some interpretation of existing provisions of the Constitution may create a popular demand for constitutional amendment and it would be unreasonable that the Government could not expend public monies, voted by Dáil Éireann, in seeking to secure such changes

4   on one view of the logic of the *McKenna* case, namely, that the public should not have their money spent in an effort to persuade them against their will in relation to the merits of any particular proposal, the result might be to impede any meaningful discussion of a constitutional amendment in so far as it was publicly funded, either directly or indirectly.

Arguments against

the arguments against the proposal were fully canvassed in the *McKenna* case and are set out in the majority judgments of the Supreme Court. They need not be reproduced in full here. They include respect for the equality of the voting power of the citizens, the right not to be forced to finance the enactment of views contrary to one's own wishes, fairness of procedure, equality of treatment, respect for the democratic rights of citizens, the alleged lack of any Government role in ensuring the passage of the amendment proposed.

Recommendation

There ought not to be a constitutional barrier to the public funding of a referendum campaign *provided* that the manner of equitable allotment of such funding is entrusted to an independent body such as the proposed Constituency Commission. The total sum to be allotted should be subject to legislative regulation. Article 47.4 should be amended accordingly. Such a constitutional safeguard meets the principal objection to the old funding arrangements identified in the *McKenna* case by ensuring that the Government does not spend public money in a self-interested and unregulated fashion in favour of one side only, thereby distorting the political process.

Since an extension of the logic of the *McKenna* judgment could possibly render unconstitutional proposals to fund political parties from the public purse, the constitutionality of public funding for political parties may also need to be similarly addressed.

Appendix VIII

Minor/technical amendments recommended by the Constitution Review Group

1	Article 12.1	amend this section to describe the President as Head of State.
2	Article 12.2.3°	delete the words 'and on the system of proportional representation' from this subsection.
3	Article 12.4.1°	substitute the word 'completed' for 'reached' in the English language version of this subsection.
4	Article 15.5	this section should be extended on the lines of Article 7 of the European Convention on Human Rights so as to provide that a heavier penalty shall not be imposed than was applicable at the time the offence was committed.
5	Article 15.7	if a consecutive series of individual sittings is intended by the use of the word 'session', the Irish version should be amended as follows:

> Ní foláir do Thithe an Oireachtais suí tréimhse amháin sa bhlian ar a laghad.

6	Article 15.13	a suitable amendment should be made to reflect that the distinction between 'felony' and 'misdemeanour' is anachronistic and does not serve any useful purpose. An appropriate reference, for example, to 'serious criminal offence', should be inserted.
7	Article 15.15	in order to clarify that this section relates not simply to expenses but to the total emolument of deputies and senators, the second word 'the' in line 1 and the words 'of allowances' in line 2 in the official printed text should be deleted.
8	Article 16.3.1°	delete this subsection because it is the same as Article 13.2.1°.
9	Article 16.7	provide for a limit on the time within which a bye-election should be held. The Constitution Review Group proposed ninety days.

10	Article 17.1.2°	amend this subsection to qualify 'effect' by 'permanent' or 'continuing'.
11	Article 18.5	delete the word 'postal' from this section because it makes the process specifically dependent on the postal services.
12	Article 18.8	if the current sequence of Dáil and Seanad elections is retained, this section should be amended to provide that the originally occasioned Seanad election should be aborted, and that an election related to the second Dáil dissolution should be held instead.
13	Article 18.9	this section does not define the polling day. The latest date upon which an elector can vote should be regarded as the polling date.
14	Article 23.2.1°	a technical amendment of this subsection is necessary in regard to Bills deemed to have been passed.
15	Article 28.6	an express constitutional provision should be made in this section for the nomination of a senior minister in the event of a situation arising in which neither the Taoiseach nor the Tánaiste was available to act.
16	Article 29.3	amend this section to make it clear that it covers public international law only and not private international law.
17	Article 29.4.2°	delete this subsection as it is, for all practical purposes, spent.
18	Article 31.2.ii	delete the words 'or the office of President of the Executive Council of Saorstát Éireann' because they are obsolete.
19	Article 35.3	amend the Irish language text of this section by substituting 'intofa mar chomhalta' for 'ina chomhalta'.
20	Article 35.3	amend this section to make serving judges ineligible to be President or a member of any elected assembly and to prohibit judges, in addition to the existing prohibitions, from holding 'any other position inconsistent with the office of judge'.
21	Article 40.1	the words 'as human persons' should be deleted.
22	Article 40.4.1°	the word 'person' should be substituted for 'citizen'
23	Article 40.5	the word 'person' should be substituted for 'citizen'.
24	Article 40.6.1°iii	the word 'persons' should be substituted for 'citizens'.
25	Article 44.2.1°	the word 'person' should be substituted for 'citizen'.

26 Article 44.2.6°   delete the word 'diverted' in Article 44.2.6° and
                       replace it by the words 'compulsorily acquired'.

*In general, personal rights should not be confined to citizens but should be
extended to all human persons. There may be some rights which should be
confined to citizens.*

Appendix IX

The power to dissolve Dáil Éireann

Extracts from the *Report of the Constitution Review Group*

whether the President should have discretion to refuse a dissolution of Dáil Éireann

Article 13.2.2° states that the President may in his absolute discretion refuse to dissolve Dáil Éireann on the advice of a Taoiseach who has ceased to retain the support of a majority in Dáil Éireann. Ambiguity arises over how a President may determine whether or not the Taoiseach has lost the support of the Dáil. Is a Dáil vote necessary? Or is a public announcement of withdrawal of support by a crucial number of deputies sufficient? If a Taoiseach sought to pre-empt the President's exercise of discretion by advice to dissolve the Dáil in advance of a Dáil vote, might not the President be able somehow to satisfy himself or herself that the Taoiseach had lost the support of the Dáil and therefore refuse a dissolution? No President has exercised this important power.

To remove the constitutional ambiguity there are the following possibilities:

i)   delete the latter half of Article 13.2.2° so that it reads, 'The President may in the President's absolute discretion refuse to dissolve Dáil Éireann.'

This would remove the Taoiseach's power to dissolve the Dáil at will when he or she has a majority and seeks an opportunity to enhance the Government's Dáil support. It would politicise the presidency by making the President a factor in the strategy of political parties. It might be argued that the President as Head of State should not be put in a politically divisive position, especially if the President's actions are to be exempt from debate in the Dáil.

ii) delete Article 13.2.2° in its entirety and in effect allow the Taoiseach to have power under Article 13.2.1° to dissolve Dáil Éireann whenever he or she so wishes.

It is arguably undemocratic for a Taoiseach to be able to call an election whenever he or she wishes. It might be argued that the checks the Dáil has on the Government are limited and would be strengthened by denying to the Taoiseach the initiative to dissolve the Dáil.

On the other hand, the power of dissolution is an invaluable aid to a Taoiseach in maintaining party and ministerial discipline and so sustaining government, the executive power of the State (as defined by the Constitution), while leaving the final decision, democratically, with the electorate. It can exercise a stabilising influence conducive to economic and social well-being.

   iii) let the Constitution define the circumstances in which the President might exercise absolute discretion, namely,

      a) following the loss of a vote of confidence

      b) following the rejection of a budget.

This would leave the initiative with the Taoiseach to seek a dissolution before either condition obtains. It would also politicise the President if he or she does exercise absolute discretion and refuses a dissolution.

Conclusion

The Review Group would prefer that the involvement of the President in party political issues should, if possible, be avoided and, for that reason, has given consideration to other methods of dealing with the dissolution problem, principally the prescription of a fixed term for Dáil Éireann and provision for a constructive vote of no confidence. These are discussed in the context of Article 28; to give them effect, amendments would be required in Article 13.2.

whether the President should have a role in the formation of a new Government

Articles 13.1.1° and 13.1.2° give the President no discretion in the selection and appointment of a new Taoiseach and Government. This is quite unusual in parliamentary government systems, and underscores a desire to maintain a position for the President impeccably remote from party politics. However, two problems may present themselves:

   i) where a new Dáil assembles and no party or group of parties has an overall majority

Recent Irish experience suggests that the parties in such circumstances feel obliged by the electorate to construct a stable Government based on an agreed programme. It is not clear that the intervention of the President in these circumstances would secure such a Government more quickly.

The Review Group considers that the President should not be given any role in this circumstance.

   ii) where a Government resigns voluntarily or on foot of a vote of no confidence, or the threat of one

A problem can arise where the Dáil cannot agree quickly on a nominee for Taoiseach and a defeated Government may be faced with a protracted term in office on an acting basis. In many other parliamentary government systems this problem is addressed in one of two ways:

i)   the Head of State is given a role in the process of identifying a new Prime Minister. The Head of State's intervention provides an alternative in what otherwise might be a chaotic, protracted process, but does not in all cases avoid the problem

ii) a constructive vote of no confidence is used to force the legislature to nominate a new Prime Minister when voting no confidence in the old one.

Conclusion

On balance, the Review Group feels once more that the proposal to introduce a constructive vote of no confidence is preferable to increasing the powers of the President in the government formation process.

dissolution of the Government

Article 28.9.1° provides that the Taoiseach may resign from office at any time by placing his or her resignation in the hands of the President.

Article 28.11.1° provides that if the Taoiseach resigns from office, the other members of the Government shall be deemed to have resigned from office also.

Article 28.10 provides that the Taoiseach shall resign from office upon his or her ceasing to retain the support of a majority in Dáil Éireann, unless on his or her advice the President dissolves Dáil Éireann, and on the re-assembly of Dáil Éireann, after the dissolution, the Taoiseach secures the support of a majority in Dáil Éireann.

Article 13.2.2° provides that the President may in his or her absolute discretion refuse to dissolve Dáil Éireann on the advice of a Taoiseach who has ceased to retain the support of a majority in Dáil Éireann.

While these constitutional procedures have worked, they are open to the risks (a) of Government formation being deadlocked or (b) of an early election being called simply to capitalise on favourable opinion poll ratings. Whether Article 13.2.2° can properly or effectively be invoked to lessen these risks is discussed in chapter 3 – 'The President'. Two other approaches are discussed below. Risk (b) need not be regarded as serious; the 'snap' election has been a rarity and seems destined to be rarer still as coalitions rather than single-party governments become the norm. While the average life of a Dáil has been relatively short – two years and ten months – this is attributable much more to the voting system producing a precarious balance of political representation than to resort to 'snap' elections. In any case, the result achieved by such elections could scarcely be described as undemocratic. Risk (a) is the more serious, and the possibility of its being lessened by introducing the procedure of a constructive vote of no confidence deserves prior examination. A fixed-term Dáil, the second possibility to be discussed, is concerned with the stability of parliament and government rather than avoidance of deadlock in the formation of government.

No country has both a fixed-term parliament and a provision for a constructive vote of no confidence.

a) constructive vote of no confidence

Difficulty in forming a government (without going back to the people by way of a general election) can arise *either* when a Dáil reassembles after a general election and no candidate for Taoiseach can obtain a majority *or* if the Government loses its control of the Dáil during a Dáil term. That can arise as the result of the break-up of a coalition or through deaths, resignations, bye-election defeats, or defections. In any of these events the replacement of a defeated Government may pose difficulty.

A constructive vote of no confidence, first introduced in Germany, and subsequently elsewhere, forces the legislature to agree upon a viable alternative before it can defeat the Government. This can be achieved by amending Article 28.10 by deleting the text after 'Éireann' and replacing this by 'demonstrated by the loss of a motion of no confidence which at the same time nominates an alternative Taoiseach.' Only if an alternative Taoiseach were simultaneously agreed could the incumbent Government be defeated.

A constructive vote of no confidence is an efficient response to the potential for deadlock that can arise if a Government is defeated in a critical vote which establishes that it has ceased to retain majority support yet the legislature cannot agree upon a replacement. It provides a means of determining whether an alternative Taoiseach is acceptable to a majority of the Dáil without the need for a general election to follow every government defeat.

Another advantage of this procedure is that it excludes the possibility of the President being drawn into party politics.

However, consideration also needs to be given to the situation in which a Taoiseach resigns *in anticipation* of losing a constructive vote of no confidence. This eventuality could be dealt with in the Constitution (Dáil standing orders might not be enough) by precluding a Government resignation once a constructive motion of no confidence had been tabled. While this might encourage the opposition to table such motions at the first whiff of a resignation, it may address adequately what is likely to be a rare contingency.

b) a fixed-term Dáil

To give effect to a fixed-term Dáil, Articles 13.2.1°, 13.2.2°, 16.3.1°, and the text after 'unless' in Article 28.10 would all need to be deleted. The timetable for elections could then be set by law, as provided for in Article 16.5. With all provisions for dissolving the Dáil deleted from the

Constitution, it would effectively have a fixed term. It might be felt to be more secure to provide over and above this for a fixed term in the Constitution, with an Article replacing Article 16.5 that would take the form: 'Elections to Dáil Éireann will take place every four years, according to a schedule regulated by law'.

A fixed-term Dáil need not involve any departure from the present procedure for filling vacancies by bye-elections. Its introduction would remove the possibility of a Government calling a general election while still undefeated in the hope of strengthening its position. A fixed-term Dáil would also eliminate the uncertainty which tends to prevail in the final twelve to eighteen months of a Dáil term because the incumbent Government is under strong inducement to choose the most propitious occasion to dissolve the legislature and 'go to the country'.

As against its contribution to stability, the main disadvantage of a fixed-term Dáil is that it is less democratic as it involves less consultation with the electorate. Moreover, a political deadlock might arise which would make it impossible to form a new Government from the existing legislature. This could arise if an incumbent Government were defeated but no alternative government was acceptable to a legislative majority. It would be necessary to install a way of breaking such a deadlock by providing for a dissolution of the Dáil, after a Government resignation or defeat, if no Taoiseach had been elected after, say, sixty days. Provision would also need to be made for early dissolution in the event of an emergency or crisis. One possibility would be to allow this on passage of a resolution by a qualified majority (for example sixty-six or seventy-five per cent) of the Dáil.

Fixed-term parliaments are a rarity. The nearest geographical example is Norway where parliament sits for four years and can be dissolved before this term has expired only in extraordinary circumstances. A government that falls during this term must be replaced by the sitting legislature. Norwegian experience is not persuasive as to the superior merits of a fixed-term system.

Recommendation

There is no sufficient reason to advocate a fixed-term Dáil. A constructive vote of no confidence would reduce substantially the deadlock difficulty discussed above and a majority of the Review Group considers that the introduction of this procedure merits serious consideration. It could be achieved by amending Article 28.10 by deleting the text after 'Éireann' and replacing this with 'demonstrated by the loss of a motion of no confidence which at the same time nominates an alternative Taoiseach.' Article 13.2.2° would then become redundant.

whether the President should have a role in the formation of a new Government

Conclusion

This was discussed in the chapter on the President [see page 137 of this text]. Having considered the question in the light of the foregoing discussion, the Review Group is, on balance, of the opinion that the introduction of a constructive vote of no confidence would be preferable to the involvement of the President in the Government-formation process.

Appendix X

Constitutionality of Bills and laws

Extracts from the *Report of the Constitution Review Group*

whether the one-judgment rule should be retained where the validity of laws is in question

This rule applies to constitutional decisions of the Supreme Court on the validity of post-1937 laws, not just to those arising from Article 26 references.

Article 34.4.5° was inserted into the Constitution by the Second Amendment of the Constitution Act 1941 during the transitional period when the Constitution could be amended by ordinary legislation. It parallels Article 26.2.2° (the italicised portions of which were also inserted by the Second Amendment) which provides:

> The decision of the majority of the judges of the Supreme Court shall, for the purposes of this Article, be the decision of the Court *and shall be pronounced by such one of the judges of that Court as that Court shall direct, and no other opinion, whether assenting or dissenting, shall be pronounced, nor shall the existence of any such other opinion be disclosed.*

Both provisions seem to have been inserted as a direct result of the decision of the Supreme Court in *In re Article 26 and the Offences Against the State (Amendment) Bill 1940* [1940] IR 470. In this very sensitive case, the Supreme Court upheld the constitutionality of the Offences Against the State (Amendment) Act 1940 (which provided for internment) a few months after the High Court had pronounced that similar legislation was unconstitutional. Chief Justice Sullivan commenced the judgment of the court by announcing that it was the 'decision of the majority of the judges' and as Chief Justice Finlay was later to state in *Attorney General v Hamilton (No 1)* [1993] 2 IR 250:

> This was apparently seen to indicate a dissenting opinion which, it was felt, could greatly reduce the authority of the decision of the court and, we are informed, and it is commonly believed, led directly to the additional clauses by the Act of 1941 in both Article 26 and Article 34.

This is borne out by Mr de Valera's comments in the Dáil during the debate on the Second Amendment of the Constitution Bill (82 *Dáil Debates* 1857-9):

From an educational point of view, the proposal [for separate judgments] would, no doubt, be valuable, but, after all, what do we want? We want to get a decision ... The more definite the position is the better, and, from the point of view of definitiveness, it is desirable that only one judgment be pronounced ... [and] that it should not be bandied about from mouth to mouth that, in fact, the decision was only come to by a majority of the Supreme Court. Then you have added on, perhaps, the number of judges who dealt with the matter in the High Court before it came to the Supreme Court, as might happen in some cases. You would then have an adding up of judges, and people saying: 'They were five on this side and three on the other, and therefore the law is the other way.'

What is important is legal certainty as to the judgment, which may affect fundamental issues. It was also suggested that the one-judgment rule allows the Supreme Court to provide the legislature with certainty without any of its members becoming the subject of political criticism and, possibly, pressure. Moreover, certainty would not be provided by a three-to-two judgment where at any time in the future a judge might change his mind on a fundamental issue.

It was argued, on the contrary, that a diversity of judgments would reflect society's diversity on issues, would provide the losing side with the comfort that its views had been taken into consideration, and, as a result, society's satisfaction with the court would be increased. A variety of judgments would enrich the development of jurisprudence. Moreover, the judgments of the individual judges would be formulated in a manner designed to convince reasonable people.

The 'one-judgment rule' operates in the case of the Court of Criminal Appeal (see s 28 of the Courts of Justice Act 1924) and the Special Criminal Court (see s 40 of the Offences Against the State Act 1939). It may be noted that in *The State (Littlejohn) v Governor of Mountjoy Prison* (1976) the Supreme Court appeared to accept that this statutory 'one-judgment' rule was designed to protect individual members of the three-member Special Criminal Court from untoward pressures. A similar rule applies in the case of the European Court of Justice (although not in the European Court of Human Rights). Here again the 'one-judgment' rule is thought to protect individual members of that court, as otherwise in sensitive cases affecting the vital interests of one state the judges of that particular nationality might be expected to pronounce in favour of that state.

Proposals for change

The Review Group considered the following:

   i)   delete Article 34.4.5°

   ii) delete Article 26.2.2°

   iii) retain Article 26.2.2° but delete Article 34.4.5°.

1   a) the rule does not apply to pre-1937 legislation and multiple
        judgments have been delivered in important cases such as the *Norris*
        case which examined the constitutionality of such pre-1937 laws.
        The courts also have had difficulty in determining whether the rule
        applies to 'mixed' cases where pre-1937 laws have been
        subsequently amended by post-1937 laws

    b) the rule does not apply where a Divisional High Court (that is, where
        the High Court sits as a court of three) pronounces on the validity of
        a post-1937 law. Such a court may deliver several judgments. In *In
        re Haughey* [1971] IR 217 several judgments were delivered by the
        High Court, yet the Supreme Court was bound by the one-judgment
        rule as far as the constitutionality of the law was concerned

    c) the rule obliges the Supreme Court to engage in an often artificial
        division between the constitutionality of the law and the other related
        constitutional issues raised by a case. This point was adverted to by
        Blayney J in *Meagher v Minister for Agriculture and Food* [1994] 1
        IR 239, a case where one judgment was delivered on the validity of
        the law, yet several judgments were delivered on the validity of
        statutory instruments promulgated pursuant to that law, even though
        the court plainly found it difficult to separate the issues in that case.
        In this respect, *Meagher* is not an isolated case, as 'split' Supreme
        Court judgments (that is, where one judgment is given on the issue
        of the validity of the law, with several judgments given on the
        subsidiary issues arising) have been delivered in upwards of twenty
        cases

    d) as *Meagher* confirms, the one-judgment rule does not apply to
        statutory instruments made pursuant to a post-1937 law

    e) the rule does not apply to constitutional cases (for example the *X*
        case) which do not concern the validity of a law

2   the rule may give rise – and possibly it already has done so – to serious
    practical difficulties in its application. Suppose that two judges are in
    favour of invalidating the law on ground A, but reject ground B, whereas
    another two are in favour of invalidating the law on ground B, but reject
    ground A. The fifth member of the court is in favour of invalidating the
    law on ground C, while rejecting grounds A and B. How is the judgment
    of the court to be delivered? Or is the court merely to state that the law
    is invalid?

3   the rule is itself completely out of harmony with the common law
    tradition which has always permitted individual judgments. Moreover,
    even in some civil law jurisdictions where the 'one-judgment' rule is the
    norm, it has been considered desirable to abandon the rule in the
    Constitutional Court. This has already happened in Germany and Spain

4   empirical evidence – admittedly impressionistic – suggests that the one-
    judgment rule affects the quality of the judgment, since dissent is

artificially suppressed and the court strives for the lowest common denominator so that a majority of the court can endorse the judgment. It certainly inhibits the development and clarification of the law in the manner envisaged in the common law case by case system which is of the essence of our legal system. As the Attorney General's Committee on the Constitution (1968) noted:

> A single majority judgment may be a compromise and so less precise in its reasoning than an individual judgment .... Concurring and dissenting judgments will help to clarify the law for the authorities in implementing a Bill held valid under Article 26 and in drafting similar legislation, and may express a view which later on may obtain public support. Where the majority decision declares an Act or Bill invalid, separate judgments might be useful in indicating what alternative legislation would be permissible ... If the majority judges disagreed on their reasons for the decision, the majority judgment might give quite a misleading impression of the weight of authority for a particular view. The possibility of separate judgments should help to ensure clarification of the thinking of the majority who will be compelled to answer criticisms of their views more explicitly than they otherwise would. There might be a chance that a judge who knew he was in a minority might fail to write a judgment which, if fully reasoned and written, would have changed his colleagues' minds

5   the rationale for the rule was that the authority of the court's judgment might be undermined if dissents were to be published.

This contention remains to be established. Several judgments have been delivered in many of the key constitutional cases: see, for example, *The People (Director of Public Prosecutions) v O'Shea* [1982] IR 384, *Norris v Attorney General* [1984] IR 36, *Crotty v An Taoiseach* [1987] IR 713, *Attorney General v X* [1992] 1 IR 1, *Attorney General v Hamilton (No 1)* [1993] 2 IR 250 (the *Cabinet Confidentiality* case) and *In the matter of a Ward of Court* [1995] 2 ILRM 401. The authority of these decisions has not been shaken by the presence of minority judgments. As the Attorney General's Committee on the Constitution (1968) added:

> The 'uncertainty' resulting from public knowledge of the existence of dissenting or concurring judgments, which will be primarily of interest to lawyers, is probably unlikely to be a serious problem.

The presence of dissents in each of the above cases has added to the richness of our constitutional law

6   as the former US Supreme Court judge, Holmes J put it, a dissent in a constitutional case is essentially an appeal to a later generation of judges and lawyers. His dissents in a series of free speech cases in the 1920s are perhaps the most famous judgments in the entirety of US constitutional law and led the US Supreme Court later to accept them as good law and to the over-turning of the majority judgments. In this jurisdiction, dissents have sometimes later proved the basis for the over-

ruling of the first decision: see, for example, the Supreme Court's acceptance in *The State (Browne) v Feran* [1967] IR 147 of the correctness of Johnston J's dissent in *The State (Burke) v Lennon* [1940] IR 136

7　even if the presence of minority judgments tended to encourage political dissent, such a consequence is not, as the Attorney General's Committee (1968) observed, 'necessarily undesirable' in a democratic society. Indeed, it supported the principle of freedom of expression. The one-judgment rule requires the judges to form a consensus. A consensus is usually based on either the lowest common level of agreement, or neutral grounds. In neither instance would one expect to find the soil most suitable for the development of jurisprudence. If each judge could make a judgment, the quality of judgments would tend to rise as each judge would articulate a position which must necessarily engage reasonable people. Moreover, the public would see the expert weighing of arguments for and against; they would appreciate that their views, even if they were on the losing side, were properly taken into account; the public's appreciation of the whole process would be enhanced because it would fairly reflect the diverse opinions within society. Furthermore, the procedure would sharpen people's perception of the independence of each judge.

Arguments for retaining Article 34.4.5°

1　it is the decision of the majority of the Supreme Court which really counts and only uncertainty is created by allowing the publication of dissenting opinions

2　the publication of dissenting opinions serves only to weaken the authority of the court's pronouncement and impair its persuasiveness.

Arguments for deleting Article 26.2.2°

1　the arguments already set out above apply with equal force to Article 26.2.2°

2　while it is admitted that an Article 26 reference is a special, unique procedure, in essence it is simply another mechanism by which the Supreme Court adjudicates on the validity of a parliamentary measure. On this view, there is no reason why the one-judgment rule should apply to Article 26 references

3　even if one rationale of the one-judgment rule was to emphasise the collective nature of the Supreme Court's pronouncement and thereby to protect individual judges from untoward pressure in sensitive cases, this still does not justify retaining the rule for Article 26 references. While it is admitted that the majority of Article 26 references have involved matters of fundamental constitutional importance (although some have not), there have been many cases of fundamental importance (for example the *X* case and the *Cabinet Confidentiality* case) where the one-judgment rule did not apply and multiple judgments were delivered. The fact that multiple judgments were delivered does not appear to have compromised the stance of any individual judge.

Arguments for retaining Article 26.2.2° while deleting Article 34.4.5°

1   the special character of the Article 26 procedure justifies the retention of the 'one-judgment' rule. Here it is not a case of private litigants seeking a reasoned judgment but rather of one organ of the State requiring a straight, unqualified answer from another organ of the State on the constitutionality of proposed legislation. The certainty needed on such an important matter justifies the retention for Article 26 references of the one-judgment rule. Article 26 involves the Supreme Court in giving a decision of a binding nature and it may be contended that the President, Government, Oireachtas and the wider public are entitled to have that advice tendered with one voice. In this regard, it may be noted that on the one occasion when the Supreme Court dealt with an Article 26 reference prior to the adoption of the one-judgment rule – namely, the Offences Against the State (Amendment) Bill 1940 – the Chief Justice merely announced that the decision was that of the majority, even though no dissenting opinions were delivered. It was evidently felt that, even in the absence of a formal one-judgment rule, it would have been inappropriate to permit the delivery of dissenting opinions in an Article 26 reference

2   many of the Bills referred to the Supreme Court under the Article 26 procedure involve sensitive and fundamental issues. In such circumstances, it is appropriate that the court should speak collectively and with one voice. This shields individual judges from improper influence or pressure.

Recommendation

On the whole, Article 34.4.5° should be deleted. The rule is unsatisfactory in its operation and is apt to create anomalies. There is not, however, a consensus that Article 26.2.2° should be deleted, some members of the Review Group being of the view that the special character of the Article 26 reference procedure justifies the retention of Article 26.2.2°.

whether a decision in an Article 26 reference by the Supreme Court should be immutable

Article 34.3.3°, which confers immunity from legal challenge, was inserted into the Constitution by the Second Amendment of the Constitution Act 1941 during the transitional period when that Constitution could be amended by ordinary legislation. At that stage, only one Article 26 reference had taken place and a majority of the Supreme Court had upheld the validity of the internment provisions of the Offences Against the State (Amendment) Act 1940. Similar legislation had previously been invalidated by the High Court in December 1939. The language of Article 34.3.3° 'shall have been referred ...' suggests the drafters wished to ensure that the internment provisions of the 1940 Act should enjoy a permanent immunity from constitutional attack.

Despite the care taken in preparing a Bill, doubt may arise as to its constitutionality. Some Bills concern fundamental issues on which doubt cannot be allowed, indeed where it is desirable that there should be certainty extending indefinitely, or at least over a long period. In relation to adoption, for instance, certainty for a period of over fifty years, that is to say, over about two generations, would seem desirable. On the constitutionality of elections to the Dáil an even longer period could be essential.

The certainty provided by the Article prevails indefinitely unless terminated by a referendum. However, with the efflux of time, changed circumstances and attitudes may bring about a situation where a referred Bill that has been enacted may operate harshly and unfairly, denying justifiable redress in a context not originally foreseen.

The question to be addressed is whether the desirability of a measure of stability is reconcilable with an openness to challenge where reason and justice so demand.

The arguments for retaining and for relaxing the present unchallengeability rule may be summarised as follows:

Arguments for the retention of Article 34.3.3° in its present form

1   the object of the Article 26 procedure might be undermined if a Bill which had been upheld by the Supreme Court could be open to later challenge. In this regard, certainty and finality might be said to be a seamless web: once the possibility of later challenge was admitted, the entire fabric unravels and the object of the procedure is defeated

2   even if the rule were to be relaxed and a limited period of immunity (of, say, seven years) were to be put in its stead, such a period would be essentially arbitrary. It might also have undesirable consequences in that as the end of the seven-year period approached a degree of uncertainty might be engendered, with the threat of fresh litigation.

Arguments for relaxing the present unchallengeability rule

1   while the need for some stability is recognised, the absolute nature of the present Article 34.3.3° is open to objection. As the number of Article 26 references increases and with on-going constitutional development, there is a real risk that this rule will operate to protect the validity of law in circumstances where, if the Supreme Court could later consider the matter afresh in the light of new circumstances, it would probably take a different view. The law should never be frozen. It should be free to flow with the needs of the people

2   a substantial degree of certainty is accorded by an affirmative decision on a reference to the Supreme Court. Such a decision would not be easy to dislodge, though it would not, of course, be immutable

3   at the time Article 34.3.3° was enacted (1941), it was assumed that the
     Supreme Court was strictly bound by its own previous decisions and
     could not overrule them (by reason of the doctrine of *stare decisis*).
     Now that this doctrine has been itself relaxed (in that the Supreme Court
     will over-rule previous decisions which have been shown to be clearly
     wrong), the retention of Article 34.3.3° is anomalous.

Arguments in favour of deleting Article 34.3.3°

1   the rule is inflexible and risks denying justifiable redress in
     circumstances not envisaged in the arguments on the Article 26 reference

2   if it appears likely that the reasoning underlying a judgment upholding
     the constitutionality of a law is defective and would not now be
     supported or endorsed by the Supreme Court, would it not be
     unsatisfactory if litigants or other persons affected by the law were to be
     required to wait for the expiration of some essentially arbitrary period
     (for example seven years) before being allowed to challenge the law in
     question?

3   the rule is apt to create anomalies such as the situation which would arise
     where, after the decision of the Supreme Court upholding the validity of
     the Bill, the Article or Articles upon which it based the decision is or are
     amended by referendum

4   furthermore, any immunity conferred by Article 34.3.3° could, of
     necessity, apply only to a challenge based on domestic constitutional
     law. It does not – and could not – immunise such a law against a
     challenge based on supposed incompatibility with European Union law

5   the unchallengeability feature of Article 34.3.3° may tend to inhibit the
     President from invoking his or her powers under Article 26. If the
     immunity were removed, the potentially useful reference procedure
     might be invoked more often

6   a further consequence of Article 34.3.3° is that the Supreme Court may
     be more prepared (especially, perhaps, where the arguments for and
     against the constitutionality of the Bill are finely balanced or where the
     practical consequences of the measure might be difficult to foresee) to
     strike down a Bill as unconstitutional, rather than to risk upholding the
     Bill in such circumstances.

Possible compromises

The Committee on the Constitution (1967) suggested that the immunity from
legal challenge in Article 34.3.3° should be retained but limited to seven
years. The Review Group reconsidered this solution as it has the benefit of
appearing to give certainty, albeit for a limited period, whilst not calcifying
the law for all time. However, the Review Group rejects this solution
primarily for the following reasons:

a)   the Supreme Court in *Murphy v Attorney General* [1982] IR 241 decided
     that a declaration that a post-1937 law is repugnant to the Constitution
     means that it is invalid from the date of its enactment. Without

amendment of the present wording of Article 15.4, the same invalidity *ab initio* would probably apply to an Act for which the Bill had been referred to the Supreme Court if that Act were declared unconstitutional on a challenge after the seven-year period. The certainty contemplated by the seven-year stay could thus prove to be illusory, with undesired consequences, for example an obligation to compensate numerous claimants for loss or damage during the seven years. The desirability of amended provisions as to the date from which the invalidity of an Act declared unconstitutional takes effect, particularly where there has been an Article 26 reference, is discussed later

b) where the Supreme Court has given a favourable decision on an Article 26 reference it can be assumed that a subsequent successful challenge to the Act could only be brought by a person prejudicially affected in a manner not envisaged at the time of the reference or because of some other significant change of circumstances. It appears undesirable that anyone so affected should be delayed from challenging the constitutionality of the Act for a seven-year period

c) any period specified would of necessity be arbitrary and different time limits might be appropriate to different types of legislation. Such detailed selective provision would not be appropriate to the Constitution.

Two further suggestions were considered by the Review Group but did not receive general approbation:

a) that, on an Article 26 reference, the Supreme Court be asked to give an opinion rather than a decision on the constitutionality of the Bill. The majority of the Review Group are of the view that the role of the Supreme Court and separation of powers provided for in the Constitution make it preferable that the Supreme Court should give a decision rather than an opinion

b) that Article 34.3.3° be replaced by a provision which would require a person seeking to challenge the constitutionality of an Act, the Bill for which had been the subject of an Article 26 reference, to obtain leave from the court upon showing that a *prima facie* case existed. The majority of the Review Group considered that such a provision was not appropriate to the Constitution and would not be preferable to the simple deletion of Article 34.3.3°.

Some current difficulties

Attention should be drawn to some potentially anomalous features of Article 34.3.3°:

i) where an Act of the Oireachtas (the constitutionality of which while in Bill form has been upheld by the Supreme Court under an Article 26 reference) is subsequently amended by later legislation, perhaps in a radical fashion, may it be presumed that Article 34.3.3° does not also apply to the amendments? Would there come a point when the cachet of Article 34.3.3° could cease to apply, not only to the amendments, but perhaps also to the original Act following these radical amendments?

ii) where the Constitution was amended following the Supreme Court's decision upholding the constitutionality of a particular Bill, would Article 34.3.3° continue to apply? Although this question has not been authoritatively determined by the courts, the answer would appear to be that it would not.

Recommendations

On balance, Article 34.3.3° should be deleted in its entirety. Such a deletion would impact only marginally upon legal certainty, inasmuch as a decision of the Supreme Court upholding the constitutionality of the Bill would still be an authoritative ruling on the Bill which would bind all the lower courts and be difficult to dislodge. It is to be expected that the Supreme Court would not, save in exceptional circumstances, readily depart from its earlier decision to uphold the constitutionality of the Bill. Such exceptional circumstances might be found to exist where the Constitution had been later amended in a manner material to the law in question, or where the operation of the law in practice had produced an injustice which had not been apparent at the time of the Article 26 reference, or possibly where constitutional thinking had significantly changed.

date of operation of judicial declaration of invalidity of an Act of the Oireachtas

The Review Group considered whether the courts should have power to place temporal limits on the effect of a finding of unconstitutionality. It recognised that a court decision which finds that a particular item of legislation is unconstitutional can have potentially far-reaching effects, particularly where the legislation has been in place for some time and has been widely acted upon. Accordingly, it considered the question whether the Constitution should be amended to ensure that the courts have power to place some form of temporal limitation on the scope of a finding of unconstitutionality. It seems appropriate first to consider briefly some of the case law in this area.

The nature of the problem is illustrated by examining the consequences which might have followed the Supreme Court's decision in *de Búrca v Attorney General* [1976] IR 38. In this case, the court held that key provisions of the Juries Act 1927 were unconstitutional because they excluded women and non rate-payers. The question immediately arose as to whether prisoners convicted by juries whose composition had been found to be unconstitutional would not have to be released. In the event, only one such prisoner sought to challenge the validity of his conviction. While a majority of the Supreme Court acknowledged the invalidity of that conviction, the prisoner was adjudged in the very special facts of that case to have forfeited his right to challenge it, as he had deliberately elected to proceed with a trial in full knowledge of the *de Búrca* case decision which had been handed down in the course of his trial: see *The State (Byrne) v*

Frawley [1978] IR 326. It remains an open question what the position might have been had these special factors not been present.

In the seminal decision of *Murphy v Attorney General* [1982] IR 241, a majority of the Supreme Court ruled that a law enacted by the Oireachtas which was later ruled to be unconstitutional was void *ab initio*. Speaking for a majority of the court, Henchy J articulated what he termed the 'primary rule' of redress:

> Once it has been judicially established that a statutory provision is invalid, the condemned provision will normally provide no legal justification for any acts done or left undone or for transactions undertaken in pursuance of it; and the persons damnified by the operation of the invalid provision will normally be accorded by the courts all permitted and necessary redress.

However, Henchy J recognised that this rule was subject to important exceptions, especially having regard to the need to avoid injustice to third parties who had changed their position in good faith in reliance on the validity of the (now condemned) statutory provisions. Moreover, Henchy J also drew attention to the possibility of 'transcendent considerations which make such a course [of redress] undesirable, impractical or impossible'.

In the *Murphy* tax case, the invalidation of a key provision of the Income Tax Act 1967 raised the possibility of enormous claims for arrears of tax which – in the light of the Supreme Court decision – it was clear had been unconstitutionally collected. This did not happen because the Supreme Court held that the State was entitled to defeat the vast majority of such past claims for repayment of taxes by reason of its change of position and expenditure of public funds in reliance in good faith on the validity of the provisions in question. Even where such public policy considerations do not directly come into play, the potentially disruptive consequences of a finding of unconstitutionality may be mitigated by analogous pleas such as laches (that is, undue delay coupled with prejudice) or the Statute of Limitations. Thus, in *Murphy v Ireland* (1996), Carroll J held that a teacher who had been dismissed in 1973 by operation of section 34 of the Offences Against the State Act 1939 was now debarred by both laches and the Statute of Limitations from pursuing a claim for damages against the State, despite the fact that the section in question had been declared to be unconstitutional by the Supreme Court in 1991: see *Cox v Ireland* [1992] 2 IR 503.

While it is true that the Supreme Court ruled in the *Murphy* tax case that a statute of the Oireachtas which is later found to be unconstitutional must be deemed to be void *ab initio*, the Review Group considers that there may be a category of instances of so-called 'creeping unconstitutionality' which the court might not have had directly in mind. Thus, there may be instances where a statute was perfectly valid and constitutional at the date it was enacted, but *became* unconstitutional by reason of changing circumstances such as inflation or population movements. It is possible, for example, for an item of legislation fixing the maximum rent a landlord can recover for his or her property which was perfectly valid at the date of its enactment to have become unconstitutional with the passage of time because of the failure of the Oireachtas to revise the monetary limit upwards in line with inflation.

Experience in other jurisdictions

The question when constitutional invalidity becomes operative has also caused considerable difficulties in other jurisdictions possessing similar powers of judicial review. The United States Supreme Court has held that it has the inherent power to place temporal limits on the effect of its judgments and that it may decline to give a particular ruling or finding of invalidity retrospective effect: see *Linkletter v Walker* 381 US 618 (1965). In that case the court ruled that the US constitution 'neither prohibits nor requires retrospective effect', so that it was the judicial task 'to weigh the merits and demerits' of retroactivity of the rule in question by looking 'to the prior history', to the 'purpose and effect of the new constitutional rule' and to whether 'retrospective operation will further or retard its operation'. This approach has the merit of pragmatism in that it leans against retrospectivity, but it is intellectually difficult to defend. It also leads to arbitrary results, in that, in practice, the benefit of judicial rulings is confined to the litigants in the case before the US Supreme Court or where similar cases are definitively pending at the date of the pronouncement of the judgment. It may be noted that such an approach did not commend itself to our Supreme Court in the *Murphy* case with Henchy J speaking of the arbitrariness and inequality, in breach of Article 40.1, that would result in a citizen's constitutional right depending on the fortuity of when a court's decision would be pronounced.

However, despite these criticisms, it must be noted that pragmatism is also the approach of the European Court of Justice (ECJ) which has frequently asserted the right to place temporal limitations on the scope of its own decisions: see, for example, Case 43/75 *Defrenne v Sabena* [1976] ECR 455 and Case 24/86 *Blaizot v Université de Liege* [1988] ECR 379. Moreover, the ECJ has asserted that it alone has the power to impose such a temporal limitation on the effect of its own judgments: see Case 309/85 *Barra v Belgium* [1988] ECR 355. A further refinement of this point is that a judgment must be deemed to have retroactive effect, *unless* the ECJ itself places 'a limitation of the effects in time of an interpretative preliminary ruling ... in the actual judgment ruling upon the interpretation sought': Case C-57/93 *Vroege* [1994] ECR 1-4541. A recent indication of the criteria governing the decision to place a temporal limitation is supplied by the decision in Joined Cases C-38/90 and C-151/90, *Lomas v United Kingdom* [1992] ECR 1-1781, where the ECJ said that such a limitation might be imposed on the basis of 'overriding considerations of legal certainty involving all the interests in the case concerned'.

The ECJ's case law in this area is highly complex, a point illustrated by the aftermath of its decision in Case 262/88 *Barber v Guardian Royal Exchange* [1990] ECR 1-1889, a case where it was held for the first time that the requirements of Article 119 of the EEC Treaty governing equal pay for men and women applied also to redundancy payments and 'contracted out' pension schemes. The ECJ did purport to place a temporal limitation on the scope of this judgment, but the ambiguities in that portion of the judgment led directly to a special Protocol in the Maastricht Treaty. Protocol No 2 was designed to clarify these ambiguities by restricting further the temporal effect of the *Barber* decision, while containing a saving clause 'in the case of workers or those claiming under them who have before [17 May 1990 – *Barber* judgment] initiated legal proceedings or introduced an equivalent claim under the applicable national law'. The *Barber* decision has given rise to no less that nine separate judgments of the ECJ, each of which seeks to clarify aspects of the ruling as a temporal limitation: see Hyland 'Temporal Limitation of the Effects of the Judgments of the Court of Justice' (1995) 4 *Irish Journal of European Law* 208.

The practice of continental constitutional courts is to lean against retroactivity. Thus, in practice, all rulings of the German constitutional court are prospective in nature, save that a specific legislative provision (section 79(2) of the Federal Constitutional Court Act) permits new trials in criminal cases where a court convicts a defendant under a subsequently voided statute. The German constitutional court has also devised new strategies designed to deal with the impact of rulings of unconstitutionality. A law may be declared null and void (*nichtig*), in which case the law will cease to be operative as and from the date of the decision. In addition, the law may be declared to be incompatible (*unvereinbar*) with the Basic Law, in which case the law remains unconstitutional, but not void. In such instances, the law in question is allowed a temporary transitional period in order to allow for the enactment of fresh legislation. This is an example of a so-called 'admonitory' decision of the constitutional court, a strategy which is designed to permit the legislature 'time to adjust to changing conditions or to avoid the political and economic chaos that might result from a declaration of unconstitutionality: see Kommers, *The Constitutional Jurisprudence of the Federal Republic of Germany*, Duke University Press, 1989, p 61.

The Irish courts have to date declined to accept any 'admonitory' jurisdiction of this character. As Keane J said in *Somjee v the Minister for Justice* [1981] ILRM 324:

> The jurisdiction of the court in a case where the validity of an Act of the Oireachtas is questioned because of its alleged invalidity ... is limited to declaring the Act in question to be invalid, if that indeed is the case. The court has no jurisdiction to substitute for the impugned enactment a form of enactment which it considers desirable or to indicate to the Oireachtas the appropriate form of enactment which should be substituted for the impugned enactment.

This passage was expressly approved by the Supreme Court in *Mhic Mhathúna v Ireland* [1995] 1 ILRM 69. Perhaps the only example of where our courts have adopted something approaching the 'unconstitutional but not void' admonitory practice of the German courts may be found in *Blake v Attorney General* [1981] IR 117. In this case, having declared that key elements of the Rent Restrictions Acts 1946-1967 were unconstitutional, the Supreme Court expressly indicated that the Oireachtas should take steps to fill the immediate 'statutory void' and indicated that any new legislation 'may be expected to provide for the determination of fair rents, for a degree of security of tenure and for other relevant social and economic factors'.

The court also strongly hinted that in this transitional period the applications brought by landlords for possession of rented property should normally either be adjourned or decrees of possession granted with 'such stay as appears proper in the circumstances'.

whether the courts should be expressly given discretion to determine the date of operation of a judicial declaration of invalidity of an Act of the Oireachtas and/or afford relief from the consequences of such a declaration

In the light of the foregoing discussion, two aspects of the invalidity issue need to be considered:

1   the date from which the unconstitutional provision is declared invalid

2   the consequences of such a decision.

1   date of invalidity

At present Article 15.4 expressly prohibits the Oireachtas from enacting any law repugnant to the Constitution. The Review Group has not recommended any change in this Article. The courts have interpreted Article 15.4 to mean that, if a court declares a provision of a post-1937 Act to be repugnant to the Constitution, it is void *ab initio* because Article 15.4 prevents its ever being a valid law. This principle may not apply to a law declared unconstitutional which was not at the date of the passing of the Act repugnant to the Constitution but became so thereafter ('creeping unconstitutionality').

If the courts were now to be given power to declare an Act invalid from, say, a prospective date only, notwithstanding that it was repugnant to the Constitution when passed, this would mean that an Act which was enacted in contravention of Article 15.4 was to be treated as a valid law for the period prior to the effective date of the declaration of invalidity. The arguments for and against doing so may be summarised as follows:

Arguments for

1   at present the potentially chaotic aftermath of a finding of unconstitutionality is avoided only by the somewhat dubious invocation of doctrines such as laches (*Murphy v Attorney General* [1982] IR 241) and estoppel (*The State (Byrne) v Frawley* [1978] IR 326). To give the courts a general power of fixing the date of validity of a finding of unconstitutionality would be to do no more than recognise the reality that the courts will in practice find it necessary to limit the retroactive effect of their rulings

2   if the courts were given such a general power to be exercised on a 'just and equitable' basis, it is to be expected that the power would be exercised in a flexible manner so as to mitigate the unfairness of the

arbitrary 'cut-off' dates which is a feature of US and European Court of Justice (ECJ) jurisprudence in this area

3   at present, the fear of the retroactive consequences of a finding of invalidity may deter the courts from ruling that a statute is unconstitutional.

Arguments against

1   the doctrine of voidance *ab initio* is the normal sanction attaching to both unconstitutional statutes and invalid administrative acts

2   if the courts were given the power to limit the temporal effect of a finding of invalidity, this could lead – as demonstrated by the US and ECJ jurisprudence – to arbitrary results and indefensible distinctions

3   it is not clear how the courts would exercise this power if it were conferred. What criteria could be employed to determine the date on which the law became unconstitutional? What parties would be heard by the courts before this power was exercised? In this regard, it may be noted that the successful plaintiff will often be indifferent as to the extent to which a finding of invalidity is given general retroactive effect.

Recommendation

The importance of the prohibition in Article 15.4 in ensuring that the Oireachtas operates within the limits set by the Constitution is recognised. A majority of the Review Group is, therefore, not disposed (Article 26 cases and 'creeping unconstitutionality' apart) to recommend generally that the courts should have jurisdiction to declare invalid, otherwise than *ab initio,* a statutory provision which at the date of its passing was repugnant to the Constitution.

2   consequences of a declaration of invalidity

Although a provision in an Act may be void *ab initio,* it is a separate issue as to whether the courts have adequate jurisdiction to deal with claims arising in relation to acts done prior to the declaration of invalidity in good faith and in reliance on the invalid law. To date, the courts have shown a willingness to exercise such a jurisdiction based upon doctrines such as laches (*Murphy v Attorney General*), and estoppel (*The State (Byrne) v Frawley* [1978] IR 326) or on the Statute of Limitations (*Murphy v Ireland* (1996)).

The courts appear to recognise that, notwithstanding the invalidity *ab initio,* the clock either cannot or should not be turned back. As Henchy J stated in *Murphy v Attorney General.*

> For a variety of reasons, the law recognises that, in certain circumstances, no matter how unfounded in law certain conduct may have been, no matter how unwarranted its operations in a particular case, what has happened has happened and cannot and should not be undone.

A majority of the Review Group is, however, concerned that, while to date the courts have taken a pragmatic approach to claims resulting from declarations of unconstitutionality of laws and relied upon estoppel etc to prevent claims being pursued in relation to matters done pursuant to the invalid statute, circumstances might arise that would prevent the courts from relying on such expedients. Unacceptable situations could thus arise where relief could not be granted to persons who had acted in good faith, albeit on an invalid law, or where damaging consequences for society could not be averted.

Consideration was, therefore, given to providing the courts with an express constitutional jurisdiction to deal with such situations. The majority of the Review Group saw a special need for such an express provision where the courts were not authorised to fix a date from which invalidity of a law took effect other than the date of the original enactment. Some grounds for a cautious approach were first noted:

1   such a provision should not be drawn so widely as to provide a temptation for enacting legislation of uncertain constitutionality and relieving the State of the consequences, to the prejudice of those unable to obtain relief for damage suffered. This would greatly reduce the protection Article 15.4 is intended to give to individuals

2   if criteria are to be set for the exercise of discretion by the courts, they should include the need to balance the different rights involved: the rights of individuals who had suffered detriment by reason of the invalid law or acts done thereunder; the rights of individuals to be protected where in good faith they had acted in reliance on the invalid law; and, in exceptional circumstances, the interests of the common good where a declaration of invalidity would have adverse consequences for society.

Other members of the Review Group, while recognising that the courts should have jurisdiction to deal with the consequences of a declaration of invalidity, consider that the courts have shown a willingness to date to exercise such a jurisdiction and that the development of this jurisdiction should be left to the courts on a case by case basis. The members who take this view consider that the risks attached to giving an express jurisdiction to the courts in the Constitution (which might lead to a weakening of the protection intended by Article 15.4) are greater than the risk of the courts not developing their jurisdiction to prevent any damaging consequences for society of a declaration of invalidity.

Recommendation

A majority of the Review Group is in favour of amending the Constitution to provide the courts with an express discretion, where justice, equity or, exceptionally, the common good so requires, to afford such relief as they consider necessary and appropriate in respect of any detriment arising from acts done in reliance in good faith on an invalid law.

157

While the foregoing comments are of general application to findings of constitutional invalidity, special consideration needs to be given to two exceptional categories:

1   the so-called 'creeping unconstitutionality' cases

2   cases where validity was originally confirmed on an Article 26 reference.

1   'creeping unconstitutionality' type cases

In this situation, legislation which was constitutional at the date of its enactment has become unconstitutional by reason of changing circumstances (for example, the failure to revise monetary limits in line with inflation or the failure to revise constituency boundaries in line with population movements). It would seem that it would not be correct, even when judged from a purely theoretical standpoint, to describe a law rendered unconstitutional on this ground as void *ab initio* and that to give the courts express power to determine the date on which such a law became unconstitutional would be simply to acknowledge the realities of this special type of case. Indeed, it is likely that the courts will assert such an inherent power to determine the date the law became unconstitutional in the special instance of 'creeping unconstitutionality', despite some judicial dicta to the contrary: see, for example, the comments of Murphy J in *Browne v Attorney General* [1991] 2 IR 58.

Recommendation

Given the uncertainties in this area, the Review Group favours giving the courts express power, in cases where they declare an Act to be unconstitutional but determine that at the date of its enactment it was not repugnant to the Constitution, to determine the date upon which it became unconstitutional.

2   Article 26 reference cases

These are cases where the Acts in their Bill form were referred to the Supreme Court under Article 26 of the Constitution and whose validity was originally upheld but in respect of which the Supreme Court has subsequently taken a different view and ruled the legislation in question to be unconstitutional. This situation could, of course, arise only if the Review Group's recommendation to amend Article 34.3.3° (which at present confers a permanent immunity on a Bill upheld under the Article 26 procedure) were accepted.

Argument for

1   the special features attending a declaration of invalidity in these circumstances means that the courts should have discretion in such cases

to fix a date of invalidity other than the date of enactment. These special features are:

a) one of the principal purposes of Article 26 is to create legal certainty, particularly where the Bill is of a type which, if it were not referred and were subsequently declared unconstitutional, there would be serious consequences for society or for those who had acted in reliance upon it

b) the Bill will have been signed into law by the President only after receiving a decision of the Supreme Court to the effect that the Bill is not unconstitutional

c) having been signed into law pursuant to the express provisions of Article 26.3.3° the Act should never be considered to be protected by Article 15.4 at the time of its enactment and it is thus distinguished from the position of an Act where there has been no Article 26 reference

d) those administering the legislation and those affected by it must of necessity be entitled to rely on the Supreme Court decision upholding the validity of the law, especially as in the course of an Article 26 reference the court is obliged to consider every possible set of circumstances and arguments which might render the Bill unconstitutional. (In the course of ordinary litigation the *locus standi* rules generally prevent the court from doing this, because it is confined to dealing with such arguments as are relevant to the plaintiff's personal circumstances.)

e) many persons may have acted to their detriment, or altered their position in good faith, in reliance on the Supreme Court's decision upholding the constitutionality of the Bill.

Argument against

1   the power to impose a temporal limitation results – as is evidenced by the jurisprudence of the European Court of Justice and the US Supreme Court – in arbitrary cut-off dates and indefensible distinctions. This is true of the Article 26-type case as much as of the ordinary case where the court has declared a law to be invalid.

Recommendation

In the special case of declaration of invalidity of a law the Bill for which had been referred to the Supreme Court under Article 26, a majority of the Review Group is in favour of amending the Constitution to give the courts an express jurisdiction to declare the law to be unconstitutional as of a stated date other than the date of enactment.

Appendix XI

Local Government

Extract from the *Report of the Constitution Review Group*

INTRODUCTION

The Review Group received a number of representations in favour of constitutional recognition being given to local government.

Article 2 of the Council of Europe European Charter of Local Self-Government states:

> The principle of local self-government shall be recognised in domestic legislation and where practicable in the constitution.

Article 4 states:

> The basic powers and responsibilities of local authorities shall be prescribed by the constitution or by statute.

Ireland is not yet a signatory of the Charter.

Rights to local self-government are constitutionally recognised in most western European countries, including Belgium, Denmark, Finland, France, Germany, Italy, Luxembourg, The Netherlands, Spain, Portugal, Sweden and Switzerland. Most of these countries are unitary as opposed to federal states, and some of them are considerably smaller than Ireland. With the exception of the United Kingdom, Ireland currently has the largest local authorities in western Europe, measuring these in terms of average population per local authority area.

A 1988 Council of Europe survey found that a range of functions and services, which are probably better performed at local rather than national level, were the responsibility of most European local government systems. Core functions of local government in at least fourteen of the fifteen European countries surveyed include: construction and upkeep of primary and post-primary schools; roads; local planning; building and demolition permits; refuse collection; social assistance; homes for the elderly; library services; tourism promotion; sports facilities; fire service; water supply; sewage disposal; waste disposal; cemeteries; cultural and artistic heritage conservation; subsidised housing; museum services; parks and recreation facilities. Local authorities in Ireland perform all of these functions (except those related to primary and most post-primary schools) but can raise only limited local taxes.

Views in favour of constitutional recognition

1   while the Constitution is not, of course, a textbook on all aspects of the running of the country, it does set out the fundamental rules governing the key political institutions of the State. In virtually every modern constitution, one of these basic rules concerns the relationship between central and local government. The omission of any mention of this relationship from the Irish Constitution is unusual and may reflect a preoccupation at the time with the central organs of government and a taking-for-granted of the inherited local government system. More recently, the trend in many countries has been towards decentralising decision-making with the consequence that local government, outside Britain and Ireland, has increased rather than decreased in importance

2   there is thus a more general appreciation of the special importance of local government as a basis for a fully participative democracy and as a practical expression in the sphere of government of the principle of subsidiarity – the devolution of functions to the lowest levels of organisation at which their fair and efficient exercise is practicable

3   local government in Ireland has suffered as a result of its lack of constitutional protection. Obvious examples include the postponement by the central government, on occasion, of local government elections – something that would be almost unthinkable in most democratic systems – and the promised abolition during a Dáil election campaign of one of the main sources of local government revenue, domestic rates

4   the downgrading of the importance of local government in Ireland, only possible as a result of its lack of constitutional protection, has meant that local people often have no effective local redress for their grievances. This in turn forces them to put pressure on their national representatives to put right what are essentially local problems more appropriately dealt with by an effective local government system. Many analysts have identified this as at least one of the causes of excessive constituency pressure on local TDs (see Appendix 4: 'Electoral systems')

5   local government could, therefore, appropriately receive the cachet and protection of express constitutional recognition. This is the norm almost everywhere else in Europe, where it clearly presents few problems. The main country where it is not the norm is Britain where, despite protestations that local government was protected by the 'unwritten' constitution, local government has recently come under persistent attack from central government, leading, for example, to the jailing of local councillors and the unilateral abolition of the entire Greater London Council. As a result, local government has become the subject of political controversy in Britain.

Views against constitutional recognition

1   local government in Ireland is already recognised in a substantial volume of statute law. In this way the requirements of the Council of Europe Charter are met. Local authorities are already responsible for all the functions mentioned in the Council of Europe survey, except primary

and most post-primary schools. This has occurred without specific constitutional 'recognition'. There is no constitutional bar on the development of smaller – or larger – local authorities, or more or less local authorities, with greater or lesser powers. Local government in Ireland exhibits a high degree of professionalism and in the statutory management system has developed a uniquely Irish contribution to administrative development, again without constitutional backing

2 the Constitution should not be lumbered with unnecessary provisions. Ireland is smaller than many European countries – and even than regions in Europe. Regional autonomy may be a basic requirement of good government in those countries. Countries with more 'local government' than Ireland generally have fewer representatives in Parliament per head of population. With 166 members in the Dáil elected from constituencies all over the country, sixty members in the Seanad and up to 1,500 local authority members in about 150 authorities, there is already, without constitutional recognition, a very large degree of representative democracy in the State. Constitutional 'recognition' would not affect the position of local government in this context one way or another

3 the statutory basis for local government allows Parliament to decide the forms and procedures for local government. The administrative system in Ireland is subject to change and with developments in technology and in Europe this is likely to continue. Thus justice, once the concern of Grand Juries, which were local authorities, is now centrally administered. The old system of public assistance, once administered by local authorities, has become the modern centralised welfare system. Health, which used to be a local government function, is now administered regionally by health boards. National roads administration is developing similarly. Thus, over time, the organisation of government *by area* has *not* been found to be the best way of delivering a service. The tendency in Ireland, as elsewhere, has been to develop by reference to *functions*: and this tendency is reinforced, in fact often made imperative, by EU requirements. Further developments, at present unforeseeable, could be necessary, for example, in the event of an 'agreed Ireland'. The 'recognition' of local government in the Constitution could impose an unnecessary rigidity on the system – subjecting any change to the possibility of judicial review

Indeed, any constitutional clause with teeth could give rise to new separation of powers issues between government and regions (a fruitful source of litigation in countries such as the USA and Germany). It could also lead to the invalidation of a whole range of central government controls (examples might include controls to secure the soundness of local finances, control of bye-laws etc) and might require the insertion of a specific equalisation clause similar to Article 107 of the German constitution allowing the redistribution of local government income (rates, service charges etc) to poorer local authority regions

4 Parliament has always had the authority to abolish and vary taxes. Rates were abolished, partly because they were assessed on a proportion of the

population – the 'occupiers' of property – without, in effect, reference to ability to pay, and on an inequitable system of valuations. They were in most areas increasing more rapidly than incomes or inflation

5   whether or not a constitutional provision should determine the timing of local elections is arguable

6   the government of the day will, in practice, under the Irish political system and culture, be held accountable in the Dáil for the operation of the local government system and for the application of more or less agreed standards of service throughout the country. The 'recognition' of local government in the Constitution is unlikely to change this or to affect the degree of clientelism in the Irish political system.

FORM OF RECOGNITION

Basic issues concerning the future of local government are at present under examination by two commissions: one, set up under the Local Government Act 1994, is due to report shortly to the Minister for the Environment on the reorganisation of *town* local government; the second, set up by the Taoiseach in July 1995, is to make recommendations on the phased devolution of significant additional functions to local authorities, and these recommendations are to be considered by a Cabinet committee chaired by the Taoiseach. The question of Ireland becoming a signatory of the Council of Europe European Charter of Local Self-Government is also expected to be decided in this context.

Recommendation

The Review Group considered, by a majority, that a form of recognition in principle of local government should be inserted in the Constitution. Whether or not this should be accompanied by extensive provisions might be decided when the reports of two commissions have been received and considered but with due advertence to the arguments above.

Appendix XII

The Ombudsman

Extract from the *Report of the Constitution Review Group*

INTRODUCTION

The word 'Ombudsman' is Swedish in origin and originally meant representative of the people. The concept has evolved over two centuries, from being a reaction to State absolutism and an assertion of the rights and dignity of the individual, to becoming a unique method of strengthening democratic control in society. Because of its special meaning, the title Ombudsman has been imported without translation into some languages but has been rendered as Parliamentary Commissioner or some similar vernacular title in others. The word 'Ombudsman' is not intended to have a gender connotation and was the title used in the Ombudsman Act 1980 which established the office here. Some members of the Review Group take the view that there could be misunderstanding on this point and would prefer a gender-neutral term.

The majority of Western European democracies provide for an Ombudsman in their constitutions. In addition, Article 138 of the Treaty of Rome (as inserted by the Maastricht Treaty) provides for the establishment of the office of Ombudsman in relation to the European Union. In the new democracies emerging in Eastern Europe, Africa and Latin America, the institution of Ombudsman is being included in their new constitutions, often with a role in relation to fundamental human rights. The concept came to attention in Ireland with the publication in 1969 of the report of the Public Services Organisation Review Group, which recognised the need for the development of new means of redress for an aggrieved citizen in the light of that Group's central recommendation relating to a restructured public service. The subsequent establishment of an all-party committee provided the impetus which led to the 1980 Act. It is clear that in recent years a consensus has emerged in the two Houses of the Oireachtas about the desirability of not only maintaining the institution of Ombudsman but strengthening and developing it.

The Constitution confirms various personal and other rights which are protected by the courts. Without prejudice to this basic and general protection, additional protection is available in defined areas through recourse to the Ombudsman and this can be of particular advantage to those who are poor and without social position. An effective democracy requires that public servants should be held accountable for their actions and that citizens be protected from maladministration by public officials.

The Constitution already provides for the office of Comptroller and Auditor General. That office monitors financial accountability by ensuring that moneys raised by, or given to, public authorities are used not only properly, but also in an efficient and effective manner. Similarly, the office of the Ombudsman monitors administrative accountability by ensuring that public service activities and, in particular, the exercise of discretionary decision-making powers are carried out in a manner consistent with fairness and good administrative practice. The role of the office will become all the more necessary if devolution and delegation within the public service develops as envisaged.

FUNCTIONS

The Ombudsman Act 1980 entitles the Ombudsman to investigate any administrative action taken by or on behalf of a Department of State or other specified persons or bodies which appears to have had an adverse effect and may have been faulty on one or other of seven grounds. The Ombudsman may follow up the investigation by seeking reasons for the action, by requiring the matter to be further considered or by recommending measures to remedy, mitigate or alter the adverse effect of the action.

The office of the Ombudsman operates in the area of administrative accountability – the process of ensuring that public service activities and, in particular, the exercise of decision-making powers, whether discretionary or otherwise, are carried out not only in a proper legal manner but fairly and consistently with good administrative practice. The Ombudsman gives the citizen the capacity to question the administration and may, in many instances, be an avenue of last resort for a citizen aggrieved by actions of the public service. The office has also developed a role in contributing to the elimination of the root causes of many of the complaints encountered, and to raising standards of public administration by identifying the underlying causes of maladministration and suggesting improvement.

As is the case in most countries, the legislation provides for areas where the writ of the Ombudsman does not run. These can be summarised as follows:

- the presidency, the courts and Seanad Éireann

- prisons

- Garda Síochána

- matters relating to national security or intergovernmental activity

- matters on which an appeal can be made to independent tribunals

- public service recruitment

- public service personnel matters.

Section 5(3) of the Ombudsman Act 1980 provides that a Minister may direct the Ombudsman to cease any investigation into matters within his or her departmental remit. This discretion has never been exercised. Should it be exercised, the Ombudsman may make a special report on the matter to the Oireachtas.

Independence is the foundation stone upon which the office of the Ombudsman is based. The Ombudsman must be able to operate without being influenced by Government action. It is not enough for him or her to be independent in fact – he or she must also be seen as such by those who use the office. A constitutional guarantee for this independence would reinforce freedom from conflict of interest, from deference to the executive, from influence by special interest groups, and it would support the freedom to assemble facts and reach independent and impartial conclusions.

Recommendation

A new Article should be inserted in the Constitution confirming the establishment of the office of the Ombudsman, providing for the independent exercise of such investigative and other functions of the office in relation to administrative actions as may be determined by law, and making other provisions similar to those applying to the Comptroller and Auditor General and consistent with the 1980 Act, as amended.

Appendix XIII

'Woman in the home'

Extract from the *Report of the Constitution Review Group*

the reference to the role of women and mothers or other persons within the home

Article 41.2 assigns to women a domestic role as wives and mothers. It is a dated provision much criticised in recent years. Notwithstanding its terms, it has not been of any particular assistance even to women working exclusively within the home. In the *L v L* case the Supreme Court rejected a claim by a married woman who was a mother and had worked exclusively within her home to be entitled to a 50% interest in the family home. At common law, it has been held that a married woman who makes a financial contribution directly or indirectly to the acquisition of a family home is entitled to a proportionate interest in it. However, this principle is of no help to the significant number of women who do not have a separate income from which they can make financial contributions to a family home but who contribute by their work within the home and in many instances relieve their husbands of domestic duties thereby permitting them to earn money. The Supreme Court considered that, while Article 41.2.2° imposed an obligation on the judiciary as well as on the legislature and the executive to endeavour to ensure that 'mothers should not be obliged by economic necessity to engage in labour outside the home to the neglect of their duties within the home', this Article did not confer jurisdiction on the courts to transfer any particular property right within a family.

These provisions have also been cited by the State in support of legislation which appeared to discriminate on grounds of sex. In *Dennehy v The Minister for Social Welfare* (1984) Barron J used Article 41.2 to support his conclusion that the failure of the State to treat deserted husbands in the same way as deserted wives for the purposes of Social Welfare was justified by the proviso in Article 40.1 (the recognition of a difference in capacity and social function).

The Review Group considered whether this Article should simply be deleted or whether section 2.1° should be retained in an amended form which might recognise the contribution of each or either spouse within the home.

The Review Group is conscious of the importance of the caring function of the family. It considers it important that there is constitutional recognition for the significant contribution made to society by the large number of people who provide a caring function within their homes for children, elderly relatives and others. On balance, therefore, the Review Group favours the retention of Article 41.2 in a revised gender-neutral form. The retention of

Article 41.2.2° may not be appropriate to a gender-neutral form of the Article. The revised form of Article 41.2 might read:

> The State recognises that home and family life gives to society a support without which the common good cannot be achieved. The State shall endeavour to support persons caring for others within the home.

Recommendation

A revised Article 41.2 in gender-neutral form which might provide:

> The State recognises that home and family life give society a support without which the common good cannot be achieved. The State shall endeavour to support persons caring for others within the home.

Appendix XIV
Making the Constitution gender-inclusive

PRINCIPLES

The following approach has been taken in drawing up the list of amendments designed to make the Constitution gender-inclusive:

1 The use of *'he or she'*, *'him or her'*, *'his or her'* asserts gender-inclusiveness but where used frequently leads to inelegance.

2 'He or she' is used whenever a constitutional officer, for example the President, is first mentioned in order to assert gender-inclusiveness.

3 Thereafter, inelegance is avoided as much as possible by repeating the name of an office (though not to the point that the repetition itself becomes inelegant), by rephrasing to avoid singular pronouns, for example, *'Every citizen who has reached thirty-five years of age'* instead of *'Every citizen who has reached his thirty-fifth year of age'*, or by contriving plural references instead of singular ones – *'they, them, their'* are gender neutral.

4 Certain functionaries, for example, *'chairman'*, are gender-exclusive. Use of such a term as *'the chair'* is gender-inclusive and, because it is less consciously so than the use of *'chairperson'*, is preferred.

5 Certain forms in Irish, for example, *'Ceann Comhairle'*, *'Cathaoirleach'*, are gender-inclusive, unlike their English counterparts. Where they are now acceptable in English usage they are used in the English text.

AMENDMENTS

The line through a word indicates deletion of the text; words in bold indicate insertions.

GENDER-PROOFING

THE PREAMBLE

*In the name of the Most Holy Trinity, from Whom is all authority and to Whom, as our final end, all actions both of ~~men~~ **individuals** and States must be referred,*

We, the people of Éire,

*Humbly acknowledging all our obligations to our Divine Lord, Jesus Christ, Who sustained our ~~fathers~~ **forebears** through centuries of trial,*

Gratefully remembering their heroic and unremitting struggle to regain the rightful independence of our Nation,

And seeking to promote the common good, with due observance of Prudence, Justice and Charity, so that the dignity and freedom of the individual may be assured, true social order attained, the unity of our country restored, and concord established with other nations,

Do hereby adopt, enact, and give to ourselves this Constitution.

THE NATION

Article 1

The Irish nation hereby affirms its inalienable, indefeasible, and sovereign right to choose its own form of Government, to determine its relations with other nations, and to develop its life, political, economic and cultural, in accordance with its own genius and traditions.

Article 2

The national territory consists of the whole island of Ireland, its islands and the territorial seas.

Article 3

Pending the re-integration of the national territory, and without prejudice to the right of the Parliament and Government established by this Constitution to exercise jurisdiction over the whole of that territory, the laws enacted by that Parliament shall have the like area and extent of application as the laws of Saorstát Éireann and the like extra-territorial effect.

THE STATE

Article 4

The name of the State is Éire, or in the English language, *Ireland.*

Article 5

Ireland is a sovereign, independent, democratic state.

Article 6

6.1   All powers of government, legislative, executive and judicial, derive, under God, from the people, whose right it is to designate the rulers of the State and, in final appeal, to decide all questions of national policy, according to the requirements of the common good.

6.2   These powers of government are exercisable only by or on the authority of the organs of State established by this Constitution.

Article 7

The national flag is the tricolour of green, white and orange.

Article 8

8.1   The Irish language as the national language is the first official language.

8.2   The English language is recognised as a second official language.

8.3   Provision may, however, be made by law for the exclusive use of either of the said languages for any one or more official purposes, either throughout the State or in any part thereof.

Article 9

9.1.1°   On the coming into operation of this Constitution any person who was a citizen of Saorstát Éireann immediately before the coming into operation of this Constitution shall become and be a citizen of Ireland.

9.1.2°   The future acquisition and loss of Irish nationality and citizenship shall be determined in accordance with law.

9.1.3°   No person may be excluded from Irish nationality and citizenship by reason of the sex of such person.

9.2   Fidelity to the nation and loyalty to the State are fundamental political duties of all citizens.

Article 10

10.1   All natural resources, including the air and all forms of potential energy, within the jurisdiction of the Parliament and Government established by this Constitution and all royalties and franchises within that jurisdiction belong to the State subject to all estates and interests therein for the time being lawfully vested in any person or body.

10.2   All land and all mines, minerals and waters which belonged to Saorstát Éireann immediately before the coming into operation of this Constitution belong to the State to the same extent as they then belonged to Saorstát Éireann.

10.3   Provision may be made by law for the management of the property which belongs to the State by virtue of this Article and for the control of the alienation, whether temporary or permanent, of that property.

10.4   Provision may also be made by law for the management of land, mines, minerals and waters acquired by the State after the coming into operation of this Constitution and for the control of the alienation, whether temporary or permanent, of the land, mines, minerals and waters so acquired.

Article 11

All revenues of the State from whatever source arising shall, subject to such exception as may be provided by law, form one fund, and shall be appropriated for the purposes and in the manner and subject to the charges and liabilities determined and imposed by law.

THE PRESIDENT

Article 12

12.1   There shall be a President of Ireland (Uachtarán na hÉireann), hereinafter called the President, who shall take precedence over all other persons in the State and who shall exercise and perform the powers and functions conferred on the President by this Constitution and by law.

12.2.1°   The President shall be elected by direct vote of the people.

12.2.2° Every citizen who has the right to vote at an election for members of Dáil Éireann shall have the right to vote at an election for President.

12.2.3° The voting shall be by secret ballot and on the system of proportional representation by means of the single transferable vote.

12.3.1° The President shall hold office for seven years from the date upon which he **or she** enters ~~upon his~~ **into** office, unless before the expiration of that period ~~he~~ **the President** dies, or resigns, or is removed from office, or becomes permanently incapacitated, such incapacity being established to the satisfaction of the Supreme Court consisting of not less than five judges.

12.3.2° A person who holds, or who has held, office as President, shall be eligible for re-election to that office, but only once.

12.3.3° An election for the office of President shall be held not later than, and not earlier than the sixtieth day before, the date of the expiration of the term of office of every President, but in the event of the removal from office of the President or of ~~his~~ **the President's** death, resignation, or permanent incapacity established as aforesaid (whether occurring before or after ~~he~~ **the President** enters upon ~~his~~ office), an election for the office of President shall be held within sixty days after such event.

12.4.1° Every citizen who has completed* his **or her** thirty fifth year of age is eligible for election to the office of President.

12.4.2° Every candidate for election, not a former or retiring President, must be nominated either by:

   i. not less than twenty persons, each of whom is at the time a member of one of the Houses of the Oireachtas, or

   ii. by the Councils of not less than four administrative Counties (including County Boroughs) as defined by law.

12.4.3° No person and no such Council shall be entitled to subscribe to the nomination of more than one candidate in respect of the same election.

12.4.4° Former or retiring Presidents may become candidates on their own nomination.

12.4.5° Where only one candidate is nominated for the office of President it shall not be necessary to proceed to a ballot for ~~his~~ **the** election.

---

* See recommendation at end of page 89.

173

12.5 Subject to the provisions of this Article, elections for the office of President shall be regulated by law.

12.6.1° The President shall not be a member of either House of the Oireachtas.

12.6.2° ~~If~~ A member of either House of the Oireachtas ~~be~~ **who is** elected President~~, he~~ shall be deemed to have vacated his **or her** seat in that House.

12.6.3° The President shall not hold any other office or position of emolument.

12.7 The first President shall enter upon ~~his~~ office as soon as may be after ~~his~~ **the** election, and every subsequent President shall enter upon ~~his~~ office on the day following the expiration of the term of office of his **or her** predecessor or as soon as may be thereafter or, in the event of his **or her** predecessor's removal from office, death, resignation, or permanent incapacity established as provided by section 3 hereof, as soon as may be after the election.

12.8 The President shall enter upon ~~his~~ office by taking and subscribing publicly, in the presence of members of both Houses of the Oireachtas, of Judges of the Supreme Court and of the High Court, and other public personages, the following declaration:-

'In the presence of Almighty God I   , do solemnly and sincerely promise and declare that I will maintain the Constitution of Ireland and uphold its laws, that I will fulfil my duties faithfully and conscientiously in accordance with the Constitution and the law, and that I will dedicate my abilities to the service and welfare of the people of Ireland. May God direct and sustain me.'

12.9 The President shall not leave the State during his **or her** term of office save with the consent of the Government.

12.10.1° The President may be impeached for stated misbehaviour.

12.10.2° The charge shall be preferred by either of the Houses of the Oireachtas, subject to and in accordance with the provisions of this section.

12.10.3° A proposal to either House of the Oireachtas to prefer a charge against the President under this section shall not be entertained unless upon a notice of motion in writing signed by not less than thirty members of that House.

12.10.4° No such proposal shall be adopted by either of the Houses of the Oireachtas save upon a resolution of that House supported by not less than two-thirds of the total membership thereof.

12.10.5° When a charge has been preferred by either House of the Oireachtas, the other House shall investigate the charge, or cause the charge to be investigated.

12.10.6° The President shall have the right to appear and to be represented at the investigation of the charge.

12.10.7° If, as a result of the investigation, a resolution be passed supported by not less than two-thirds of the total membership of the House of the Oireachtas by which the charge was investigated, or caused to be investigated, declaring that the charge preferred against the President has been sustained and that the misbehaviour, the subject of the charge, was such as to render ~~him~~ **the President** unfit to continue in office, such resolution shall operate to remove the President from his **or her** office.

12.11.1° The President shall have an official residence in or near the City of Dublin.

12.11.2° The President shall receive such emoluments and allowances as may be determined by law.

12.11.3° The emoluments and allowances of the President shall not be diminished during his **or her** term of office.

Article 13

13.1.1° The President shall, on the nomination of Dáil Éireann, appoint the Taoiseach, that is, the head of the Government or Prime Minister.

13.1.2° The President shall, on the nomination of the Taoiseach with the previous approval of Dáil Éireann, appoint the other members of the Government.

13.1.3° The President shall, on the advice of the Taoiseach, accept the resignation or terminate the appointment of any member of the Government.

13.2.1° Dáil Éireann shall be summoned and dissolved by the President on the advice of the Taoiseach.

13.2.2° The President may in his **or her** absolute discretion refuse to dissolve Dáil Éireann on the advice of a Taoiseach who has ceased to retain the support of a majority in Dáil Éireann.

13.2.3° The President may at any time, after consultation with the Council of State, convene a meeting of either or both of the Houses of the Oireachtas.

13.3.1°   Every Bill passed or deemed to have been passed by both Houses of the Oireachtas shall require the signature of the President for its enactment into law.

13.3.2°   The President shall promulgate every law made by the Oireachtas.

13.4   The supreme command of the Defence Forces is hereby vested in the President.

13.5.1°   The exercise of the supreme command of the Defence Forces shall be regulated by law.

13.5.2°   All commissioned officers of the Defence Forces shall hold their commissions from the President.

13.6   The right of pardon and the power to commute or remit punishment imposed by any court exercising criminal jurisdiction are hereby vested in the President, but such power of commutation or remission may, except in capital cases, also be conferred by law on other authorities.

13.7.1°   The President may, after consultation with the Council of State, communicate with the Houses of the Oireachtas by message or address on any matter of national or public importance.

13.7.2°   The President may, after consultation with the Council of State, address a message to the Nation at any time on any such matter.

13.7.3°   Every such message or address must, however, have received the approval of the Government.

13.8.1⁰   The President shall not be answerable to either House of the Oireachtas or to any court for the exercise and performance of the powers and functions of ~~his office~~ **the office of the President** or for any act done or purporting to be done by ~~him~~ **the President** in the exercise and performance of these powers and functions.

13.8.2°   The behaviour of the President may, however, be brought under review in either of the Houses of the Oireachtas for the purposes of section 10 of Article 12 of this Constitution, or by any court, tribunal or body appointed or designated by either of the Houses of the Oireachtas for the investigation of a charge under section 10 of the said Article.

13.9   The powers and functions conferred on the President by this Constitution shall be exercisable and performable by ~~him~~ **the President** only on the advice of the Government, save where it is provided by this Constitution that ~~he~~ **the President** shall act in his **or her** absolute discretion or after consultation with or in relation to the Council of State, or on the advice or nomination of, or on receipt of any other communication from, any other person or body.

13.10 Subject to this Constitution, additional powers and functions may be conferred on the President by law.

13.11 No power or function conferred on the President by law shall be exercisable or performable by ~~him~~ **the President** save only on the advice of the Government

Article 14

14.1 In the event of the absence of the President, or ~~his~~ **the** temporary incapacity **of the President**, or ~~his~~ **the** permanent incapacity **of the President** established as provided by section 3 of Article 12 hereof, or in the event of ~~his~~ **the President's** death, resignation, removal from office, or failure to exercise and perform the powers and functions of ~~his office~~ **the office of President** or any of them, or at any time at which the office of President may be vacant, the powers and functions conferred on the President by or under this Constitution shall be exercised and performed by a Commission constituted as provided in section 2 of this Article.

14.2.1⁰ The Commission shall consist of the following persons, namely, the Chief Justice, the **Ceann Comhairle** ~~Chairman of Dáil Éireann (An Ceann Comhairle)~~, and the ~~Chairman~~ **Cathaoirleach** of Seanad Éireann.

14.2.2° The President of the High Court shall act as a member of the Commission in the place of the Chief Justice on any occasion on which the office of Chief Justice is vacant or on which the Chief Justice is unable to act.

14.2.3⁰ The ~~Deputy Chairman~~ **Leas-Ceann Comhairle** ~~of Dáil Éireann~~ shall act as a member of the Commission in the place of the ~~Chairman of Dáil Éireann~~ **Ceann Comhairle** on any occasion on which the office of ~~Chairman of Dáil Éireann~~ **Ceann Comhairle** is vacant or on which the ~~said Chairman~~ **Ceann Comhairle** is unable to act.

14.2.4⁰ The ~~Deputy Chairman~~ **Leas-Chathaoirleach** of Seanad Éireann shall act as a member of the Commission in the place of the ~~Chairman~~ **Cathaoirleach** of Seanad Éireann on any occasion on which the office of ~~Chairman~~ **Cathaoirleach** of Seanad Éireann is vacant or on which the ~~said Chairman~~ **Cathaoirleach** is unable to act.

14.3 The Commission may act by any two of their number and may act notwithstanding a vacancy in their membership.

14.4 The Council of State may by a majority of its members make such provision as to them may seem meet for the exercise and performance of the powers and functions conferred on the President by or under this Constitution in any contingency which is not provided for by the foregoing provisions of this Article.

14.5.1° The provisions of this Constitution which relate to the exercise and performance by the President of the powers and functions conferred on ~~him~~ **the President** by or under this Constitution shall subject to the subsequent provisions of this section apply to the exercise and performance of the said powers and functions under this Article.

14.5.2° In the event of the failure of the President to exercise or perform any power or function which the President is by or under this Constitution required to exercise or perform within a specified time, the said power or function shall be exercised or performed under this Article, as soon as may be after the expiration of the time so specified.

THE NATIONAL PARLIAMENT

Constitution and Powers

Article 15

15.1.1° The National Parliament shall be called and known, and is in this Constitution generally referred to, as the Oireachtas.

15.1.2° The Oireachtas shall consist of the President and two Houses, viz.: a House of Representatives to be called Dáil Éireann and a Senate to be called Seanad Éireann.

15.1.3° The Houses of the Oireachtas shall sit in or near the City of Dublin or in such other place as they may from time to time determine.

15.2.1° The sole and exclusive power of making laws for the State is hereby vested in the Oireachtas: no other legislative authority has power to make laws for the State.

15.2.2° Provision may however be made by law for the creation or recognition of subordinate legislatures and for the powers and functions of these legislatures.

15.3.1° The Oireachtas may provide for the establishment or recognition of functional or vocational councils representing branches of the social and economic life of the people.

15.3.2° A law establishing or recognising any such council shall determine its rights, powers and duties, and its relation to the Oireachtas and to the Government.

15.4.1° The Oireachtas shall not enact any law which is in any respect repugnant to this Constitution or any provision thereof.

15.4.2° Every law enacted by the Oireachtas which is in any respect repugnant to this Constitution or to any provision thereof, shall, but to the extent only of such repugnancy, be invalid.

15.5 The Oireachtas shall not declare acts to be infringements of the law which were not so at the date of their commission.

15.6.1° The right to raise and maintain military or armed forces is vested exclusively in the Oireachtas.

15.6.2° No military or armed force, other than a military or armed force raised and maintained by the Oireachtas, shall be raised or maintained for any purpose whatsoever.

15.7 The Oireachtas shall hold at least one session every year.

15.8.1° Sittings of each House of the Oireachtas shall be public.

15.8.2° In cases of special emergency, however, either House may hold a private sitting with the assent of two-thirds of the members present.

15.9.1° Each House of the Oireachtas shall elect from its members its own ~~Chairman~~ **chair** and deputy ~~Chairman~~ **chair**, and shall prescribe their powers and duties, **the chair of Dáil Éireann to be known as the Ceann Comhairle and the chair of Seanad Éireann to be known as the Cathaoirleach.**

15.9.2° The remuneration of the ~~Chairman~~ **chair** and deputy ~~Chairman~~ **chair** of each House shall be determined by law.

15.10 Each House shall make its own rules and standing orders, with power to attach penalties for their infringement, and shall have power to ensure freedom of debate, to protect its official documents and the private papers of its members, and to protect itself and its members against any person or persons interfering with, molesting or attempting to corrupt its members in the exercise of their duties.

15.11.1° All questions in each House shall, save as otherwise provided by this Constitution, be determined by a majority of the votes of the members present and voting other than the ~~Chairman~~ **chair** or presiding member.

15.11.2° The ~~Chairman~~ **chair** or presiding member shall have and exercise a casting vote in the case of an equality of votes.

15.11.3° The number of members necessary to constitute a meeting of either House for the exercise of its powers shall be determined by its standing orders.

15.12 All official reports and publications of the Oireachtas or of either House thereof and utterances made in either House wherever published shall be privileged.

15.13 The members of each House of the Oireachtas shall, except in case of treason as defined in this Constitution, felony or breach of the peace, be privileged from arrest in going to and returning from, and while within the precincts of, either House, and shall not, in respect of any utterance in either House, be amenable to any court or any authority other than the House itself.

15.14 No person may be at the same time a member of both Houses of the Oireachtas, and, if any person who is already a member of either House becomes a member of the other House, he **or she** shall forthwith be deemed to have vacated his **or her** first seat.

15.15 The Oireachtas may make provision by law for the payment of allowances to the members of each House thereof in respect of their duties as public representatives and for the grant to them of free travelling and such other facilities (if any) in connection with those duties as the Oireachtas may determine.

Dáil Éireann

Article 16

16.1.1° Every citizen ~~without distinction of sex~~ who has reached the age of twenty-one years, and who is not placed under disability or incapacity by this Constitution or by law, shall be eligible for membership of Dáil Éireann.

16.1.2°   i.   All citizens, and

ii. such other persons in the State as may be determined by law,

without distinction of sex who have reached the age of eighteen years who are not disqualified by law and comply with the provisions of the law relating to the election of members of Dáil Éireann, shall have the right to vote at an election for members of Dáil Éireann.

16.1.3° No law shall be enacted placing any citizen under disability or incapacity for membership of Dáil Éireann on the ground of sex or disqualifying any citizen or other person from voting at an election for members of Dáil Éireann on that ground.

16.1.4°   No voter may exercise more than one vote at an election for Dáil Éireann, and the voting shall be by secret ballot.

16.2.1°   Dáil Éireann shall be composed of members who represent constituencies determined by law.

16.2.2°   The number of members shall from time to time be fixed by law, but the total number of members of Dáil Éireann shall not be fixed at less than one member for each thirty thousand of the population, or at more than one member for each twenty thousand of the population.

16.2.3°   The ratio between the number of members to be elected at any time for each constituency and the population of each constituency, as ascertained at the last preceding census, shall, so far as it is practicable, be the same throughout the country.

16.2.4°   The Oireachtas shall revise the constituencies at least once in every twelve years, with due regard to changes in distribution of the population, but any alterations in the constituencies shall not take effect during the life of Dáil Éireann sitting when such revision is made.

16.2.5°   The members shall be elected on the system of proportional representation by means of the single transferable vote.

16.2.6°   No law shall be enacted whereby the number of members to be returned for any constituency shall be less than three.

16.3.1°   Dáil Éireann shall be summoned and dissolved as provided by section 2 of Article 13 of this Constitution.

16.3.2°   A general election for members of Dáil Éireann shall take place not later than thirty days after a dissolution of Dáil Éireann.

16.4.1°   Polling at every general election for Dáil Éireann shall as far as practicable take place on the same day throughout the country.

16.4.2°   Dáil Éireann shall meet within thirty days from that polling day.

16.5   The same Dáil Éireann shall not continue for a longer period than seven years from the date of its first meeting: a shorter period may be fixed by law.

16.6   Provision shall be made by law to enable the member of Dáil Éireann who is ~~the Chairman~~ **Ceann Comhairle** immediately before a dissolution of Dáil Éireann to be deemed without any actual election to be elected a member of Dáil Éireann at the ensuing general election.

16.7 Subject to the foregoing provisions of this Article, elections for membership of Dáil Éireann, including the filling of casual vacancies, shall be regulated in accordance with law.

Article 17

17.1.1° As soon as possible after the presentation to Dáil Éireann under Article 28 of this Constitution of the Estimates of receipts and the Estimates of expenditure of the State for any financial year, Dáil Éireann shall consider such Estimates.

17.1.2° Save in so far as may be provided by specific enactment in each case, the legislation required to give effect to the Financial Resolutions of each year shall be enacted within that year.

17.2 Dáil Éireann shall not pass any vote or resolution, and no law shall be enacted, for the appropriation of revenue or other public moneys unless the purpose of the appropriation shall have been recommended to Dáil Éireann by a message from the Government signed by the Taoiseach.

Seanad Éireann

Article 18

18.1 Seanad Éireann shall be composed of sixty members, of whom eleven shall be nominated members and forty-nine shall be elected members.

18.2 A person to be eligible for membership of Seanad Éireann must be eligible to become a member of Dáil Éireann.

18.3 The nominated members of Seanad Éireann shall be nominated, with their prior consent, by the Taoiseach who is appointed next after the re-assembly of Dáil Éireann following the dissolution thereof which occasions the nomination of the said members.

18.4.1° The elected members of Seanad Éireann shall be elected as follows:-

i. Three shall be elected by the National University of Ireland.

ii. Three shall be elected by the University of Dublin.

iii. Forty-three shall be elected from panels of candidates constituted as hereinafter provided.

18.4.2° Provision may be made by law for the election, on a franchise and in the manner to be provided by law, by one or more of the following institutions, namely:

i.   the universities mentioned in subsection 1° of this section,

ii. any other institutions of higher education in the State,

of so many members of Seanad Éireann as may be fixed by law in substitution for an equal number of the members to be elected pursuant to paragraphs i and ii of the said subsection 1°.

A member or members of Seanad Éireann may be elected under this subsection by institutions grouped together or by a single institution.

18.4.3°   Nothing in this Article shall be invoked to prohibit the dissolution by law of a university mentioned in subsection 1° of this section.

18.5   Every election of the elected members of Seanad Éireann shall be held on the system of proportional representation by means of the single transferable vote, and by secret postal ballot.

18.6   The members of Seanad Éireann to be elected by the Universities shall be elected on a franchise and in the manner to be provided by law.

18.7.1°   Before each general election of the members of Seanad Éireann to be elected from panels of candidates, five panels of candidates shall be formed in the manner provided by law containing respectively the names of persons having knowledge and practical experience of the following interests and services, namely:-

i.   National Language and Culture, Literature, Art, Education and such professional interests as may be defined by law for the purpose of this panel;

ii. Agriculture and allied interests, and Fisheries;

iii. Labour, whether organised or unorganised;

iv. Industry and Commerce, including banking, finance, accountancy, engineering and architecture;

v. Public Administration and social services, including voluntary social activities.

18.7.2°   Not more than eleven and, subject to the provisions of Article 19 hereof, not less than five members of Seanad Éireann shall be elected from any one panel.

18.8   A general election for Seanad Éireann shall take place not later than ninety days after a dissolution of Dáil Éireann, and the first meeting of Seanad Éireann after the general election shall take place on a day to be fixed by the President on the advice of the Taoiseach.

18.9   Every member of Seanad Éireann shall, unless he **or she** previously dies, resigns, or becomes disqualified, continue to hold office until the day before the polling day of the general election for Seanad Éireann next held after his **or her** election or nomination.

18.10.1°   Subject to the foregoing provisions of this Article elections of the elected members of Seanad Éireann shall be regulated by law.

18.10.2°   Casual vacancies in the number of the nominated members of Seanad Éireann shall be filled by nomination by the Taoiseach with the prior consent of persons so nominated.

18.10.3°   Casual vacancies in the number of the elected members of Seanad Éireann shall be filled in the manner provided by law.

Article 19

Provision may be made by law for the direct election by any functional or vocational group or association or council of so many members of Seanad Éireann as may be fixed by such law in substitution for an equal number of the members to be elected from the corresponding panels of candidates constituted under Article 18 of this Constitution.

Legislation

Article 20

20.1   Every Bill initiated in and passed by Dáil Éireann shall be sent to Seanad Éireann and may, unless it be a Money Bill, be amended in Seanad Éireann and Dáil Éireann shall consider any such amendment.

20.2.1°   A Bill other than a Money Bill may be initiated in Seanad Éireann, and if passed by Seanad Éireann, shall be introduced in Dáil Éireann.

20.2.2°   A Bill initiated in Seanad Éireann if amended in Dáil Éireann shall be considered as a Bill initiated in Dáil Éireann.

20.3   A Bill passed by either House and accepted by the other House shall be deemed to have been passed by both Houses.

Money Bills

Article 21

21.1.1° Money Bills shall be initiated in Dáil Éireann only.

21.1.2° Every Money Bill passed by Dáil Éireann shall be sent to Seanad Éireann for its recommendations.

21.2.1° Every Money Bill sent to Seanad Éireann for its recommendations shall, at the expiration of a period not longer than twenty-one days after it shall have been sent to Seanad Éireann, be returned to Dáil Éireann, which may accept or reject all or any of the recommendations of Seanad Éireann.

21.2.2° If such Money Bill is not returned by Seanad Éireann to Dáil Éireann within such twenty-one days or is returned within such twenty-one days with recommendations which Dáil Éireann does not accept, it shall be deemed to have been passed by both Houses at the expiration of the said twenty-one days.

Article 22

22.1.1° A Money Bill means a Bill which contains only provisions dealing with all or any of the following matters, namely, the imposition, repeal, remission, alteration, or regulation of taxation; the imposition for the payment of debt or other financial purposes of charges on public moneys or the variation or repeal of any such charges; supply; the appropriation, receipt, custody, issue or audit of accounts of public money; the raising or guarantee of any loan or the repayment thereof; matters subordinate and incidental to these matters or any of them.

22.1.2° In this definition the expressions "taxation", "public money" and "loan" respectively do not include any taxation, money or loan raised by local authorities or bodies for local purposes.

22.2.1° The ~~Chairman of Dáil Éireann~~ **Ceann Comhairle** shall certify any Bill which, in his **or her** opinion, is a Money Bill to be a Money Bill, and his **or her** certificate shall, subject to the subsequent provisions of this section, be final and conclusive.

22.2.2° Seanad Éireann, by a resolution, passed at a sitting at which not less than thirty members are present, may request the President to refer the question whether the Bill is or is not a Money Bill to a Committee of Privileges.

22.2.3° If the President after consultation with the Council of State decides to accede to the request he **or she** shall appoint a Committee of Privileges consisting of an equal number of members of Dáil Éireann and of Seanad Éireann and a ~~Chairman~~ **chair** who shall be

185

a Judge of the Supreme Court: these appointments shall be made after consultation with the Council of State. In the case of an equality of votes but not otherwise the ~~Chairman~~ **chair** shall be entitled to vote.

22.2.4° The President shall refer the question to the Committee of Privileges so appointed and the Committee shall report its decision thereon to the President within twenty-one days after the day on which the Bill was sent to Seanad Éireann.

22.2.5° The decision of the Committee shall be final and conclusive.

22.2.6° If the President after consultation with the Council of State decides not to accede to the request of Seanad Éireann, or if the Committee of Privileges fails to report within the time hereinbefore specified the certificate of the ~~Chairman of Dáil Éireann~~ **Ceann Comhairle** shall stand confirmed.

Time for consideration of Bills

Article 23

23.1 This Article applies to every Bill passed by Dáil Éireann and sent to Seanad Éireann other than a Money Bill or a Bill the time for the consideration of which by Seanad Éireann shall have been abridged under Article 24 of this Constitution.

23.1.1° Whenever a Bill to which this Article applies is within the stated period defined in the next following sub-section either rejected by Seanad Éireann or passed by Seanad Éireann with amendments to which Dáil Éireann does not agree or is neither passed (with or without amendment) nor rejected by Seanad Éireann within the stated period, the Bill shall, if Dáil Éireann so resolves within one hundred and eighty days after the expiration of the stated period be deemed to have been passed by both Houses of the Oireachtas on the day on which the resolution is passed.

23.1.2° The stated period is the period of ninety days commencing on the day on which the Bill is first sent by Dáil Éireann to Seanad Éireann or any longer period agreed upon in respect of the Bill by both Houses of the Oireachtas.

23.2.1° The preceding section of this Article shall apply to a Bill which is initiated in and passed by Seanad Éireann, amended by Dáil Éireann, and accordingly deemed to have been initiated in Dáil Éireann.

23.2.2° For the purpose of this application the stated period shall in relation to such a Bill commence on the day on which the Bill is first sent to Seanad Éireann after having been amended by Dáil Éireann.

Article 24

24.1 If and whenever on the passage by Dáil Éireann of any Bill, other than a Bill expressed to be a Bill containing a proposal to amend the Constitution, the Taoiseach certifies by messages in writing addressed to the President and to the ~~Chairman~~ **chair** of each House of the Oireachtas that, in the opinion of the Government, the Bill is urgent and immediately necessary for the preservation of the public peace and security, or by reason of the existence of a public emergency, whether domestic or international, the time for the consideration of such Bill by Seanad Éireann shall, if Dáil Éireann so resolves and if the President, after consultation with the Council of State, concurs, be abridged to such period as shall be specified in the resolution.

24.2 Where a Bill, the time for the consideration of which by Seanad Éireann has been abridged under this Article,

(a) is, in the case of a Bill which is not a Money Bill, rejected by Seanad Éireann or passed by Seanad Éireann with amendments to which Dáil Éireann does not agree or neither passed nor rejected by Seanad Éireann, or

(b) is, in the case of a Money Bill, either returned by Seanad Éireann to Dáil Éireann with recommendations which Dáil Éireann does not accept or is not returned by Seanad Éireann to Dáil Éireann,

within the period specified in the resolution, the Bill shall be deemed to have been passed by both Houses of the Oireachtas at the expiration of that period.

24.3 When a Bill the time for the consideration of which by Seanad Éireann has been abridged under this Article becomes law it shall remain in force for a period of ninety days from the date of its enactment and no longer unless, before the expiration of that period, both Houses shall have agreed that such law shall remain in force for a longer period and the longer period so agreed upon shall have been specified in resolutions passed by both Houses.

Signing and Promulgation of Laws

Article 25

25.1 As soon as any Bill, other than a Bill expressed to be a Bill containing a proposal for the amendment of this Constitution, shall have been passed or deemed to have been passed by both Houses of the Oireachtas, the Taoiseach shall present it to the President for his **or her** signature and for promulgation by him **or her** as a law in accordance with the provisions of this Article.

25.2.1° Save as otherwise provided by this Constitution, every Bill so presented to the President for his **or her** signature and for promulgation by him **or her** as a law shall be signed by the President not earlier than the fifth and not later than the seventh day after the date on which the Bill shall have been presented to ~~him~~ **the President.**

25.2.2° At the request of the Government, with the prior concurrence of Seanad Éireann, the President may sign any Bill the subject of such request on a date which is earlier than the fifth day after such date as aforesaid.

25.3 Every Bill the time for the consideration of which by Seanad Éireann shall have been abridged under Article 24 of this Constitution shall be signed by the President on the day on which such Bill is presented to him **or her** for signature and promulgation as a law.

25.4.1° Every Bill shall become and be law as on and from the day on which it is signed by the President under this Constitution, and shall, unless the contrary intention appears, come into operation on that day.

25.4.2° Every Bill signed by the President under this Constitution shall be promulgated by him **or her** as a law by the publication by his direction of a notice in the Iris Oifigiúil stating that the Bill has become law.

25.4.3° Every Bill shall be signed by the President in the text in which it was passed or deemed to have been passed by both Houses of the Oireachtas, and if a Bill is so passed or deemed to have been passed in both the official languages, the President shall sign the text of the Bill in each of those languages.

25.4.4° Where the President signs the text of a Bill in one only of the official languages, an official translation shall be issued in the other official language.

25.4.5° As soon as may be after the signature and promulgation of a Bill as a law, the text of such law which was signed by the President or, where the President has signed the text of such law in each of the official languages, both the signed texts shall be enrolled for record in the office of the Registrar of the Supreme Court, and the text, or both the texts, so enrolled shall be conclusive evidence of the provisions of such law.

25.4.6° In case of conflict between the texts of a law enrolled under this section in both the official languages, the text in the national language shall prevail.

25.5.1°　It shall be lawful for the Taoiseach, from time to time as occasion appears to him **or her** to require, to cause to be prepared under his **or her** supervision a text (in both the official languages) of this Constitution as then in force embodying all amendments theretofore made therein.

25.5.2°　A copy of every text so prepared, when authenticated by the signatures of the Taoiseach and the Chief Justice, shall be signed by the President and shall be enrolled for record in the office of the Registrar of the Supreme Court.

25.5.3°　The copy so signed and enrolled which is for the time being the latest text so prepared shall, upon such enrolment, be conclusive evidence of this Constitution as at the date of such enrolment and shall for that purpose supersede all texts of this Constitution of which copies were previously so enrolled.

25.5.4°　In case of conflict between the texts of any copy of this Constitution enrolled under this section, the text in the national language shall prevail.

Reference of Bills to the Supreme Court

Article 26

This Article applies to any Bill passed or deemed to have been passed by both Houses of the Oireachtas other than a Money Bill, or a Bill expressed to be a Bill containing a proposal to amend the Constitution, or a Bill the time for the consideration of which by Seanad Éireann shall have been abridged under Article 24 of this Constitution.

26.1.1°　The President may, after consultation with the Council of State, refer any Bill to which this Article applies to the Supreme Court for a decision on the question as to whether such Bill or any specified provision or provisions of such Bill is or are repugnant to this Constitution or to any provision thereof.

26.1.2°　Every such reference shall be made not later than the seventh day after the date on which such Bill shall have been presented by the Taoiseach to the President for his **or her** signature.

26.1.3°　The President shall not sign any Bill the subject of a reference to the Supreme Court under this Article pending the pronouncement of the decision of the Court.

26.2.1°　The Supreme Court consisting of not less than five judges shall consider every question referred to it by the President under this Article for a decision, and, having heard arguments by or on behalf of the Attorney General and by counsel assigned by the Court, shall pronounce its decision on such question in open court as soon

26.2.2°   The decision of the majority of the judges of the Supreme Court shall, for the purposes of this Article, be the decision of the Court and shall be pronounced by such one of those judges as the Court shall direct, and no other opinion, whether assenting or dissenting, shall be pronounced nor shall the existence of any such other opinion be disclosed.

as may be, and in any case not later than sixty days after the date of such reference.

26.3.1°   In every case in which the Supreme Court decides that any provision of a Bill the subject of a reference to the Supreme Court under this Article is repugnant to this Constitution or to any provision thereof, the President shall decline to sign such Bill.

26.3.2°   If, in the case of a Bill to which Article 27 of this Constitution applies, a petition has been addressed to the President under that Article, that Article shall be complied with.

26.3.3°   In every other case the President shall sign the Bill as soon as may be after the date on which the decision of the Supreme Court shall have been pronounced.

Reference of Bills to the People

Article 27

This Article applies to any Bill, other than a Bill expressed to be a Bill containing a proposal for the amendment of this Constitution, which shall have been deemed, by virtue of Article 23 hereof, to have been passed by both Houses of the Oireachtas.

27.1   A majority of the members of Seanad Éireann and not less than one-third of the members of Dáil Éireann may by a joint petition addressed to the President by them under this Article request the President to decline to sign and promulgate as a law any Bill to which this Article applies on the ground that the Bill contains a proposal of such national importance that the will of the people thereon ought to be ascertained.

27.2   Every such petition shall be in writing and shall be signed by the petitioners whose signatures shall be verified in the manner prescribed by law.

27.3   Every such petition shall contain a statement of the particular ground or grounds on which the request is based, and shall be presented to the President not later than four days after the date on which the Bill shall have been deemed to have been passed by both Houses of the Oireachtas.

27.4.1°   Upon receipt of a petition addressed to him **or her** under this Article, the President shall forthwith consider such petition and shall, after consultation with the Council of State, pronounce his **or her** decision thereon not later than ten days after the date on which the Bill to which such petition relates shall have been deemed to have been passed by both Houses of the Oireachtas.

27.4.2°   If the Bill or any provision thereof is or has been referred to the Supreme Court under Article 26 of this Constitution, it shall not be obligatory on the President to consider the petition unless or until the Supreme Court has pronounced a decision on such reference to the effect that the said Bill or the said provision thereof is not repugnant to this Constitution or to any provision thereof, and, if a decision to that effect is pronounced by the Supreme Court, it shall not be obligatory on the President to pronounce his **or her** decision on the petition before the expiration of six days after the day on which the decision of the Supreme Court to the effect aforesaid is pronounced.

27.5.1°   In every case in which the President decides that a Bill the subject of a petition under this Article contains a proposal of such national importance that the will of the people thereon ought to be ascertained, he **or she** shall inform the Taoiseach and the ~~Chairman~~ **chair** of each House of the Oireachtas accordingly in writing under his **or her** hand and Seal and shall decline to sign and promulgate such Bill as a law unless and until the proposal shall have been approved either

i. by the people at a Referendum in accordance with the provisions of section 2 of Article 47 of this Constitution within a period of eighteen months from the date of the President's decision, or

ii. by a resolution of Dáil Éireann passed within the said period after a dissolution and re-assembly of Dáil Éireann.

27.5.2°   Whenever a proposal contained in a Bill the subject of a petition under this Article shall have been approved either by the people or by a resolution of Dáil Éireann in accordance with the foregoing provisions of this section, such Bill shall as soon as may be after such approval be presented to the President for his **or her** signature and promulgation by him **or her** as a law and the President shall thereupon sign the Bill and duly promulgate it as a law.

27.6   In every case in which the President decides that a Bill the subject of a petition under this Article does not contain a proposal of such national importance that the will of the people thereon ought to be ascertained, he **or she** shall inform the Taoiseach and the ~~Chairman~~ **chair** of each House of the Oireachtas accordingly in writing under his **or her** hand and Seal, and such Bill shall be signed by the President not later than eleven days after the date on which the Bill shall have been deemed to have been passed by both Houses of the Oireachtas and shall be duly promulgated by him **or her** as a law.

THE GOVERNMENT

Article 28

28.1   The Government shall consist of not less than seven and not more than fifteen members who shall be appointed by the President in accordance with the provisions of this Constitution.

28.2   The executive power of the State shall, subject to the provisions of this Constitution, be exercised by or on the authority of the Government.

28.3.1°   War shall not be declared and the State shall not participate in any war save with the assent of Dáil Éireann.

28.3.2°   In the case of actual invasion, however, the Government may take whatever steps they may consider necessary for the protection of the State, and Dáil Éireann if not sitting shall be summoned to meet at the earliest practicable date.

28.3.3°   Nothing in this Constitution shall be invoked to invalidate any law enacted by the Oireachtas which is expressed to be for the purpose of securing the public safety and the preservation of the State in time of war or armed rebellion, or to nullify any act done or purporting to be done in time of war or armed rebellion in pursuance of any such law. In this sub-section 'time of war' includes a time when there is taking place an armed conflict in which the State is not a participant but in respect of which each of the Houses of the Oireachtas shall have resolved that, arising out of such armed conflict, a national emergency exists affecting the vital interests of the State and 'time of war or armed rebellion' includes such time after the termination of any war, or of any such armed conflict as aforesaid, or of an armed rebellion, as may elapse until each of the Houses of the Oireachtas shall have resolved that the national emergency occasioned by such war, armed conflict, or armed rebellion has ceased to exist.

28.4.1°   The Government shall be responsible to Dáil Éireann.

28.4.2°   The Government shall meet and act as a collective authority, and shall be collectively responsible for the Departments of State administered by the members of the Government.

28.4.3°   The Government shall prepare Estimates of the Receipts and Estimates of the Expenditure of the State for each financial year, and shall present them to Dáil Éireann for consideration.

28.5.1°   The head of the Government, or Prime Minister, shall be called, and is in this Constitution referred to as, the Taoiseach.

28.5.2°   The Taoiseach shall keep the President generally informed on matters of domestic and international policy.

28.6.1°   The Taoiseach shall nominate a member of the Government to be the Tánaiste.

28.6.2°   The Tánaiste shall act for all purposes in the place of the Taoiseach if the Taoiseach should die, or become permanently incapacitated, until a new Taoiseach shall have been appointed.

28.6.3°   The Tánaiste shall also act for or in the place of the Taoiseach during the temporary absence of the Taoiseach.

28.7.1°   The Taoiseach, the Tánaiste and the member of the Government who is in charge of the Department of Finance must be members of Dáil Éireann.

28.7.2°   The other members of the Government must be members of Dáil Éireann or Seanad Éireann, but not more than two may be members of Seanad Éireann.

28.8   Every member of the Government shall have the right to attend and be heard in each House of the Oireachtas.

28.9.1°   The Taoiseach may resign from office at any time by placing his **or her** resignation in the hands of the President.

28.9.2°   Any other member of the Government may resign from office by placing his **or her** resignation in the hands of the Taoiseach for submission to the President.

28.9.3°   The President shall accept the resignation of a member of the Government, other than the Taoiseach, if so advised by the Taoiseach.

28.9.4°   The Taoiseach may at any time, for reasons which to him **or her** seem sufficient, request a member of the Government to resign; should the member concerned fail to comply with the request, his **or her** appointment shall be terminated by the President if the Taoiseach so advises.

28.10   The Taoiseach shall resign from office upon his **or her** ceasing to retain the support of a majority in Dáil Éireann unless on his **or her** advice the President dissolves Dáil Éireann and on the reassembly of Dáil Éireann after the dissolution the Taoiseach secures the support of a majority in Dáil Éireann.

28.11.1° If the Taoiseach at any time resigns from office the other members of the Government shall be deemed also to have resigned from office, but the Taoiseach and the other members of the Government shall continue to carry on their duties until their successors shall have been appointed.

28.11.2° The members of the Government in office at the date of a dissolution of Dáil Éireann shall continue to hold office until their successors shall have been appointed.

28.12 The following matters shall be regulated in accordance with law, namely, the organisation of, and distribution of business amongst, Departments of State, the designation of members of the Government to be the Ministers in charge of the said Departments, the discharge of the functions of the office of a member of the Government during his **or her** temporary absence or incapacity, and the remuneration of the members of the Government.

INTERNATIONAL RELATIONS

Article 29

29.1 Ireland affirms its devotion to the ideal of peace and friendly co-operation amongst nations founded on international justice and morality.

29.2 Ireland affirms its adherence to the principle of the pacific settlement of international disputes by international arbitration or judicial determination.

29.3 Ireland accepts the generally recognised principles of international law as its rule of conduct in its relations with other States.

29.4.1° The executive power of the State in or in connection with its external relations shall in accordance with Article 28 of this Constitution be exercised by or on the authority of the Government.

29.4.2° For the purpose of the exercise of any executive function of the State in or in connection with its external relations, the Government may to such extent and subject to such conditions, if any, as may be determined by law, avail of or adopt any organ, instrument, or method of procedure used or adopted for the like purpose by the members of any group or league of nations with which the State is or becomes associated for the purpose of international co-operation in matters of common concern.

29.4.3° The State may become a member of the European Coal and Steel Community (established by Treaty signed at Paris on the 18th day of April, 1951), the European Economic Community (established by Treaty signed at Rome on the 25th day of March, 1957) and the European Atomic Energy Community (established by Treaty signed at Rome on the 25th day of March, 1957). The State may ratify the Single European Act (signed on behalf of the Member States of the Communities at Luxembourg on the 17th day of February, 1986, and at the Hague on the 28th day of February, 1986).

29.4.4° The State may ratify the Treaty on European Union signed at Maastricht on the 7th day of February, 1992, and may become a member of that Union.

29.4.5° No provision of this Constitution invalidates laws enacted, acts done or measures adopted by the State which are necessitated by the obligations of membership of the European Union or of the Communities, or prevents laws enacted, acts done or measures adopted by the European Union or by the Communities or by institutions thereof, or by bodies competent under the Treaties establishing the Communities, from having the force of law in the State.

29.4.6° The State may ratify the Agreement relating to Community Patents drawn up between the Member States of the Communities and done at Luxembourg on the 15th day of December, 1989.

29.5.1° Every international agreement to which the State becomes a party shall be laid before Dáil Éireann.

29.5 2° The State shall not be bound by any international agreement involving a charge upon public funds unless the terms of the agreement shall have been approved by Dáil Éireann.

29.5.3° This section shall not apply to agreements or conventions of a technical and administrative character.

29.6 No international agreement shall be part of the domestic law of the State save as may be determined by the Oireachtas.

THE ATTORNEY GENERAL

Article 30

30.1 There shall be an Attorney General who shall be the adviser of the Government in matters of law and legal opinion, and shall exercise and perform all such powers, functions and duties as are conferred or imposed on him **or her** by this Constitution or by law.

30.2   The Attorney General shall be appointed by the President on the nomination of the Taoiseach.

30.3   All crimes and offences prosecuted in any court constituted under Article 34 of this Constitution other than a court of summary jurisdiction shall be prosecuted in the name of the People and at the suit of the Attorney General or some other person authorised in accordance with law to act for that purpose.

30.4   The Attorney General shall not be a member of the Government.

30.5.1°   The Attorney General may at any time resign from office by placing his **or her** resignation in the hands of the Taoiseach for submission to the President.

30.5.2°   The Taoiseach may, for reasons which to him **or her** seem sufficient, request the resignation of the Attorney General.

30.5.3°   In the event of failure to comply with the request, the appointment of the Attorney General shall be terminated by the President if the Taoiseach so advises.

30.5.4°   The Attorney General shall retire from office upon the resignation of the Taoiseach, but may continue to carry on his **or her** duties until the successor to the Taoiseach shall have been appointed.

30.6   Subject to the foregoing provisions of this Article, the office of Attorney General, including the remuneration to be paid to the holder of the office, shall be regulated by law.

THE COUNCIL OF STATE

Article 31

31.1   There shall be a Council of State to aid and counsel the President on all matters on which the President may consult the said Council in relation to the exercise and performance by him **or her** of such of his **or her** powers and functions as are by this Constitution expressed to be exercisable and performable after consultation with the Council of State, and to exercise such other functions as are conferred on the said Council by this Constitution.

31.2   The Council of State shall consist of the following members:

  i.   As *ex-officio* members: the Taoiseach, the Tánaiste, the Chief Justice, the President of the High Court, the ~~Chairman of Dáil Éireann~~ **Ceann Comhairle**, the ~~Chairman~~ **Cathaoirleach** of Seanad Éireann, and the Attorney General.

ii. Every person able and willing to act as a member of the Council of State who shall have held the office of President, or the office of Taoiseach, or the office of Chief Justice, or the office of President of the Executive Council of Saorstát Éireann.

iii. Such other persons, if any, as may be appointed by the President under this Article to be members of the Council of State.

31.3 The President may at any time and from time to time by warrant under his **or her** hand and Seal appoint such other persons as, in his **or her** absolute discretion, he **or she** may think fit, to be members of the Council of State, but not more than seven persons so appointed shall be members of the Council of State at the same time.

31.4° Every member of the Council of State shall at the first meeting thereof which he **or she** attends as a member take and subscribe a declaration in the following form:

'In the presence of Almighty God I,   , do solemnly and sincerely promise and declare that I will faithfully and conscientiously fulfil my duties as a member of the Council of State.'

31.5 Every member of the Council of State appointed by the President, unless he **or she** previously dies, resigns, becomes permanently incapacitated, or is removed from office, shall hold office until the successor of the President by whom he **or she** was appointed shall have entered upon his **or her** office.

31.6 Any member of the Council of State appointed by the President may resign from office by placing his **or her** resignation in the hands of the President.

31.7 The President may, for reasons which to him **or her** seem sufficient, by an order under his **or her** hand and Seal, terminate the appointment of any member of the Council of State appointed by him **or her**.

31.8 Meetings of the Council of State may be convened by the President at such times and places as he **or she** shall determine.

Article 32

32 The President shall not exercise or perform any of the powers or functions which are by this Constitution expressed to be exercisable or performable by him **or her** after consultation with the Council of State unless, and on every occasion before so doing, he **or she** shall have convened a meeting of the Council of State and the members present at such meeting shall have been heard by him **or her**.

THE COMPTROLLER AND AUDITOR GENERAL

Article 33

33.1 There shall be a Comptroller and Auditor General to control on behalf of the State all disbursements and to audit all accounts of moneys administered by or under the authority of the Oireachtas.

33.2 The Comptroller and Auditor General shall be appointed by the President on the nomination of Dáil Éireann.

33.3 The Comptroller and Auditor General shall not be a member of either House of the Oireachtas and shall not hold any other office or position of emolument.

33.4 The Comptroller and Auditor General shall report to Dáil Éireann at stated periods as determined by law.

33.5.1° The Comptroller and Auditor General shall not be removed from office except for stated misbehaviour or incapacity, and then only upon resolutions passed by Dáil Éireann and by Seanad Éireann calling for his **or her** removal.

33.5.2° The Taoiseach shall duly notify the President of any such resolutions as aforesaid passed by Dáil Éireann and by Seanad Éireann and shall send ~~him~~ **the President** a copy of each such resolution certified by the ~~Chairman~~ **chair** of the House of the Oireachtas by which it shall have been passed.

33.5.3° Upon receipt of such notification and of copies of such resolutions, the President shall forthwith, by an order under his **or her** hand and Seal, remove the Comptroller and Auditor General from office.

33.6 Subject to the foregoing, the terms and conditions of the office of Comptroller and Auditor General shall be determined by law.

THE COURTS

Article 34

34.1 Justice shall be administered in courts established by law by judges appointed in the manner provided by this Constitution, and, save in such special and limited cases as may be prescribed by law, shall be administered in public.

34.2 The Courts shall comprise Courts of First Instance and a Court of Final Appeal.

34.3.1° The Courts of First Instance shall include a High Court invested with full original jurisdiction in and power to determine all matters and questions whether of law or fact, civil or criminal.

34.3.2° Save as otherwise provided by this Article, the jurisdiction of the High Court shall extend to the question of the validity of any law having regard to the provisions of this Constitution, and no such question shall be raised (whether by pleading, argument or otherwise) in any Court established under this or any other Article of this Constitution other than the High Court or the Supreme Court.

34.3.3° No Court whatever shall have jurisdiction to question the validity of a law, or any provision of a law, the Bill for which shall have been referred to the Supreme Court by the President under Article 26 of this Constitution, or to question the validity of a provision of a law where the corresponding provision in the Bill for such law shall have been referred to the Supreme Court by the President under the said Article 26.

34.3.4° The Courts of First Instance shall also include Courts of local and limited jurisdiction with a right of appeal as determined by law.

34.4.1° The Court of Final Appeal shall be called the Supreme Court.

34.4.2° The president of the Supreme Court shall be called the Chief Justice.

34.4.3° The Supreme Court shall, with such exceptions and subject to such regulations as may be prescribed by law, have appellate jurisdiction from all decisions of the High Court, and shall also have appellate jurisdiction from such decisions of other courts as may be prescribed by law.

34.4.4° No law shall be enacted excepting from the appellate jurisdiction of the Supreme Court cases which involve questions as to the validity of any law having regard to the provisions of this Constitution.

34.4.5° The decision of the Supreme Court on a question as to the validity of a law having regard to the provisions of this Constitution shall be pronounced by such one of the judges of that Court as that Court shall direct, and no other opinion on such question, whether assenting or dissenting, shall be pronounced, nor shall the existence of any such other opinion be disclosed.

34.4.6° The decision of the Supreme Court shall in all cases be final and conclusive.

34.5.1° Every person appointed a judge under this Constitution shall make and subscribe the following declaration:

'In the presence of Almighty God I,⠀⠀⠀⠀⠀⠀⠀ do solemnly and sincerely promise and declare that I will duly and faithfully and to the best of my knowledge and power execute the office of Chief Justice (*or as the case may be*) without fear or favour, affection or ill-will towards any man **or woman**, and that I will uphold the Constitution and the laws. May God direct and sustain me.'

34.5.2° This declaration shall be made and subscribed by the Chief Justice in the presence of the President, and by each of the other judges of the Supreme Court, the judges of the High Court and the judges of every other Court in the presence of the Chief Justice or the senior available judge of the Supreme Court in open court.

34.5.3° The declaration shall be made and subscribed by every judge before entering upon his **or her** duties as such judge, and in any case not later than ten days after the date of his **or her** appointment or such later date as may be determined by the President.

34.5.4° Any judge who declines or neglects to make such declaration as aforesaid shall be deemed to have vacated his **or her** office.

Article 35

35.1 The judges of the Supreme Court, the High Court and all other Courts established in pursuance of Article 34 hereof shall be appointed by the President.

35.2 All judges shall be independent in the exercise of their judicial functions and subject only to this Constitution and the law.

35.3 No judge shall be eligible to be a member of either House of the Oireachtas or to hold any other office or position of emolument.

35.4.1° A judge of the Supreme Court or the High Court shall not be removed from office except for stated misbehaviour or incapacity, and then only upon resolutions passed by Dáil Éireann and by Seanad Éireann calling for his **or her** removal.

35.4.2° The Taoiseach shall duly notify the President of any such resolutions passed by Dáil Éireann and by Seanad Éireann, and shall send him **or her** a copy of every such resolution certified by the ~~Chairman~~ **chair** of the House of the Oireachtas by which it shall have been passed.

35.4.3° Upon receipt of such notification and of copies of such resolutions, the President shall forthwith, by an order under his **or her** hand and Seal, remove from office the judge to whom they relate.

35.5   The remuneration of a judge shall not be reduced during his **or her** continuance in office.

Article 36

36   Subject to the foregoing provisions of this Constitution relating to the Courts, the following matters shall be regulated in accordance with law, that is to say:—

    i.   the number of judges of the Supreme Court, and of the High Court, the remuneration, age of retirement and pensions of such judges,

    ii.   the number of the judges of all other Courts, and their terms of appointment, and

    iii.   the constitution and organization of the said Courts, the distribution of jurisdiction and business among the said Courts and judges, and all matters of procedure.

Article 37

37.1   Nothing in this Constitution shall operate to invalidate the exercise of limited functions and powers of a judicial nature, in matters other than criminal matters, by any person or body of persons duly authorised by law to exercise such functions and powers, notwithstanding that such person or such body of persons is not a judge or a court appointed or established as such under this Constitution.

37.2   No adoption of a person taking effect or expressed to take effect at any time after the coming into operation of this Constitution under laws enacted by the Oireachtas and being an adoption pursuant to an order made or an authorisation given by any person or body of persons designated by those laws to exercise such functions and powers was or shall be invalid by reason only of the fact that such person or body of persons was not a judge or a court appointed or established as such under this Constitution.

TRIAL OF OFFENCES

Article 38

38.1   No person shall be tried on any criminal charge save in due course of law.

38.2   Minor offences may be tried by courts of summary jurisdiction.

38.3.1°   Special courts may be established by law for the trial of offences in cases where it may be determined in accordance with such law that the ordinary courts are inadequate to secure the effective administration of justice, and the preservation of public peace and order.

38.3.2° The constitution, powers, jurisdiction and procedure of such special courts shall be prescribed by law.

38.4.1° Military tribunals may be established for the trial of offences against military law alleged to have been committed by persons while subject to military law and also to deal with a state of war or armed rebellion.

38.4.2° A member of the Defence Forces not on active service shall not be tried by any courtmartial or other military tribunal for an offence cognisable by the civil courts unless such offence is within the jurisdiction of any courtmartial or other military tribunal under any law for the enforcement of military discipline.

38.5 Save in the case of the trial of offences under section 2, section 3 or section 4 of this Article no person shall be tried on any criminal charge without a jury.

38.6 The provisions of Articles 34 and 35 of this Constitution shall not apply to any court or tribunal set up under section 3 or section 4 of this Article.

Article 39

Treason shall consist only in levying war against the State, or assisting any State or person or inciting or conspiring with any person to levy war against the State, or attempting by force of arms or other violent means to overthrow the organs of government established by this Constitution, or taking part or being concerned in or inciting or conspiring with any person to make or to take part or be concerned in any such attempt.

FUNDAMENTAL RIGHTS

Personal Rights

Article 40

40.1 All citizens shall, as human persons, be held equal before the law.

This shall not be held to mean that the State shall not in its enactments have due regard to differences of capacity, physical and moral, and of social function.

40.2.1° Titles of nobility shall not be conferred by the State.

40.2.2° No title of nobility or of honour may be accepted by any citizen except with the prior approval of the Government.

40.3.1° The State guarantees in its laws to respect, and, as far as practicable, by its laws to defend and vindicate the personal rights of the citizen.

40.3.2° The State shall, in particular, by its laws protect as best it may from unjust attack and, in the case of injustice done, vindicate the life, person, good name, and property rights of every citizen.

40.3.3° The State acknowledges the right to life of the unborn and, with due regard to the equal right to life of the mother, guarantees in its laws to respect, and, as far as practicable, by its laws to defend and vindicate that right.

This subsection shall not limit freedom to travel between the State and another state.

This subsection shall not limit freedom to obtain or make available, in the State, subject to such conditions as may be laid down by law, information relating to services lawfully available in another state.

40.4.1° No citizen shall be deprived of his **or her** personal liberty save in accordance with law.

40.4.2° Upon complaint being made by or on behalf of any person to the High Court or any judge thereof alleging that such person is being unlawfully detained, the High Court and any and every judge thereof to whom such complaint is made shall forthwith enquire into the said complaint and may order the person in whose custody such person is detained to produce the body of such person before the High Court on a named day and to certify in writing the grounds of his **or her** detention, and the High Court shall, upon the body of such person being produced before that Court and after giving the person in whose custody he **or she** is detained an opportunity of justifying the detention, order the release of such person from such detention unless satisfied that he **or she** is being detained in accordance with the law.

40.4.3° Where the body of a person alleged to be unlawfully detained is produced before the High Court in pursuance of an order in that behalf made under this section and that Court is satisfied that such person is being detained in accordance with a law but that such law is invalid having regard to the provisions of this Constitution, the High Court shall refer the question of the validity of such law to the Supreme Court by way of case stated and may, at the time of such reference or at any time thereafter, allow the said person to be at liberty on such bail and subject to such conditions as the High Court shall fix until the Supreme Court has determined the question so referred to it.

40.4.4° The High Court before which the body of a person alleged to be unlawfully detained is to be produced in pursuance of an order in that behalf made under this section shall, if the President of the High Court or, if he **or she** is not available, the senior judge of that Court who is available so directs in respect of any particular case, consist of three judges and shall, in every other case, consist of one judge only.

40.4.5° Where an order is made under this section by the High Court or a judge thereof for the production of the body of a person who is under sentence of death, the High Court or such judge thereof shall further order that the execution of the said sentence of death shall be deferred until after the body of such person has been produced before the High Court and the lawfulness of his **or her** detention has been determined and if, after such deferment, the detention of such person is determined to be lawful, the High Court shall appoint a day for the execution of the said sentence of death and that sentence shall have effect with the substitution of the day so appointed for the day originally fixed for the execution thereof.

40.4.6° Nothing in this section, however, shall be invoked to prohibit, control, or interfere with any act of the Defence Forces during the existence of a state of war or armed rebellion.

40.4.7° Provision may be made by law for the refusal of bail by a court to a person charged with a serious offence where it is reasonably considered necessary to prevent the commission of a serious offence by that person.

40.5 The dwelling of every citizen is inviolable and shall not be forcibly entered save in accordance with law.

40.6.1° The State guarantees liberty for the exercise of the following rights, subject to public order and morality:—

    i. The right of the citizens to express freely their convictions and opinions.

    The education of public opinion being, however, a matter of such grave import to the common good, the State shall endeavour to ensure that organs of public opinion, such as the radio, the press, the cinema, while preserving their rightful liberty of expression, including criticism of Government policy, shall not be used to undermine public order or morality or the authority of the State.

    The publication or utterance of blasphemous, seditious, or indecent matter is an offence which shall be punishable in accordance with law.

ii. The right of the citizens to assemble peaceably and without arms.

Provision may be made by law to prevent or control meetings which are determined in accordance with law to be calculated to cause a breach of the peace or to be a danger or nuisance to the general public and to prevent or control meetings in the vicinity of either House of the Oireachtas.

iii. The right of the citizens to form associations and unions.

Laws, however, may be enacted for the regulation and control in the public interest of the exercise of the foregoing right.

40.6.2° Laws regulating the manner in which the right of forming associations and unions and the right of free assembly may be exercised shall contain no political, religious or class discrimination.

The Family

Article 41

41.1.1° The State recognises the Family as the natural primary and fundamental unit group of Society, and as a moral institution possessing inalienable and imprescriptible rights, antecedent and superior to all positive law.

41.1.2° The State, therefore, guarantees to protect the Family in its constitution and authority, as the necessary basis of social order and as indispensable to the welfare of the Nation and the State.

41.2.1° In particular, the State recognises that by her life within the home, woman gives to the State a support without which the common good cannot be achieved.

41.2.2° The State shall, therefore, endeavour to ensure that mothers shall not be obliged by economic necessity to engage in labour to the neglect of their duties in the home.

41.3.1° The State pledges itself to guard with special care the institution of Marriage, on which the Family is founded, and to protect it against attack.

41.3.2° A Court designated by law may grant a dissolution of marriage where, but only where, it is satisfied that:–

i. at the date of the institution of the proceedings, the spouses have lived apart from one another for a period of, or periods amounting to, at least four years during the previous five years,

      ii. there is no reasonable prospect of a reconciliation between the spouses,

     iii. such provision as the Court considers proper having regard to the circumstances, exists, or will be made for the spouses, any children of either or both of them and any other person prescribed by law, and

     iv. any further conditions prescribed by law are complied with.

41.3.3°   No person whose marriage has been dissolved under the civil law of any other State but is a subsisting valid marriage under the law for the time being in force within the jurisdiction of the Government and Parliament established by this Constitution shall be capable of contracting a valid marriage within that jurisdiction during the lifetime of the other party to the marriage so dissolved.

Education

Article 42

42.1   The State acknowledges that the primary and natural educator of the child is the Family and guarantees to respect the inalienable right and duty of parents to provide, according to their means, for the religious and moral, intellectual, physical and social education of their children.

42.2   Parents shall be free to provide this education in their homes or in private schools or in schools recognised or established by the State.

42.3.1°   The State shall not oblige parents in violation of their conscience and lawful preference to send their children to schools established by the State, or to any particular type of school designated by the State.

42.3.2°   The State shall, however, as guardian of the common good, require in view of actual conditions that the children receive a certain minimum education, moral, intellectual and social.

42.4   The State shall provide for free primary education and shall endeavour to supplement and give reasonable aid to private and corporate educational initiative, and, when the public good requires it, provide other educational facilities or institutions with due regard, however, for the rights of parents, especially in the matter of religious and moral formation.

42.5   In exceptional cases, where the parents for physical or moral reasons fail in their duty towards their children, the State as guardian of the common good, by appropriate means shall endeavour to supply the place of the parents, but always with due regard for the natural and imprescriptible rights of the child.

Private Property

Article 43

43.1.1°   The State acknowledges that ~~man~~ **a man or woman**, in virtue of his **or her** rational being, has the natural right, antecedent to positive law, to the private ownership of external goods.

43.1.2°   The State accordingly guarantees to pass no law attempting to abolish the right of private ownership or the general right to transfer, bequeath, and inherit property.

43.2.1°   The State recognises, however, that the exercise of the rights mentioned in the foregoing provisions of this Article ought, in civil society, to be regulated by the principles of social justice.

43.2.2°   The State, accordingly, may as occasion requires delimit by law the exercise of the said rights with a view to reconciling their exercise with the exigencies of the common good.

Religion

Article 44

44.1   The State acknowledges that the homage of public worship is due to Almighty God. It shall hold ~~His~~ **the** Name **of God** in reverence, and shall respect and honour religion.

44.2.1°   Freedom of conscience and the free profession and practice of religion are, subject to public order and morality, guaranteed to every citizen.

44.2.2°   The State guarantees not to endow any religion.

44.2.3°   The State shall not impose any disabilities or make any discrimination on the ground of religious profession, belief or status.

44.2.4°   Legislation providing State aid for schools shall not discriminate between schools under the management of different religious denominations, nor be such as to affect prejudicially the right of any child to attend a school receiving public money without attending religious instruction at that school.

44.2.5°   Every religious denomination shall have the right to manage its own affairs, own, acquire and administer property, movable and immovable, and maintain institutions for religious or charitable purposes.

44.2.6°   The property of any religious denomination or any educational institution shall not be diverted save for necessary works of public utility and on payment of compensation.

DIRECTIVE PRINCIPLES OF SOCIAL POLICY

Article 45

The principles of social policy set forth in this Article are intended for the general guidance of the Oireachtas. The application of those principles in the making of laws shall be the care of the Oireachtas exclusively, and shall not be cognisable by any Court under any of the provisions of this Constitution.

45.1   The State shall strive to promote the welfare of the whole people by securing and protecting as effectively as it may a social order in which justice and charity shall inform all the institutions of the national life.

45.2   The State shall, in particular, direct its policy towards securing:-

i.   That the citizens (all of whom, men and women equally, have the right to an adequate means of livelihood) may through their occupations find the means of making reasonable provision for their domestic needs.

ii.   That the ownership and control of the material resources of the community may be so distributed amongst private individuals and the various classes as best to subserve the common good.

iii. That, especially, the operation of free competition shall not be allowed so to develop as to result in the concentration of the ownership or control of essential commodities in a few individuals to the common detriment.

iv.   That in what pertains to the control of credit the constant and predominant aim shall be the welfare of the people as a whole.

v.   That there may be established on the land in economic security as many families as in the circumstances shall be practicable.

45.3.1°   The State shall favour and, where necessary, supplement private initiative in industry and commerce.

45.3.2°   The State shall endeavour to secure that private enterprise shall be so conducted as to ensure reasonable efficiency in the production and distribution of goods and as to protect the public against unjust exploitation.

45.4.1° The State pledges itself to safeguard with especial care the economic interests of the weaker sections of the community, and, where necessary, to contribute to the support of the infirm, ~~the widow~~ **widows and widowers**, the orphan, and the aged.

45.4.2° The State shall endeavour to ensure that the strength and health of workers, men and women, and the tender age of children shall not be abused and that citizens shall not be forced by economic necessity to enter avocations unsuited to their ~~sex~~, age or strength.

AMENDMENT OF THE CONSTITUTION

Article 46

46.1 Any provision of this Constitution may be amended, whether by way of variation, addition, or repeal, in the manner provided by this Article.

46.2 Every proposal for an amendment of this Constitution shall be initiated in Dáil Éireann as a Bill, and shall upon having been passed or deemed to have been passed by both Houses of the Oireachtas, be submitted by Referendum to the decision of the people in accordance with the law for the time being in force relating to the Referendum.

46.3 Every such Bill shall be expressed to be 'An Act to amend the Constitution'.

46.4 A Bill containing a proposal or proposals for the amendment of this Constitution shall not contain any other proposal.

46.5 A Bill containing a proposal for the amendment of this Constitution shall be signed by the President forthwith upon his **or her** being satisfied that the provisions of this Article have been complied with in respect thereof and that such proposal has been duly approved by the people in accordance with the provisions of section 1 of Article 47 of this Constitution and shall be duly promulgated by the President as a law.

THE REFERENDUM

Article 47

47.1 Every proposal for an amendment of this Constitution which is submitted by Referendum to the decision of the people shall, for the purpose of Article 46 of this Constitution, be held to have been approved by the people, if, upon having been so submitted, a majority of the votes cast at such Referendum shall have been cast in favour of its enactment into law.

47.2.1°   Every proposal, other than a proposal to amend the Constitution, which is submitted by Referendum to the decision of the people shall be held to have been vetoed by the people if a majority of votes cast at such Referendum shall have been cast against its enactment into law and if the votes so cast against its enactment into law shall have amounted to not less than thirty-three and one-third per cent of the voters on the register.

47.2.2°   Every proposal, other than a proposal to amend the Constitution, which is submitted by Referendum to the decision of the people shall for the purposes of Article 27 hereof be held to have been approved by the people unless vetoed by them in accordance with the provisions of the foregoing sub-section of this section.

47.3   Every citizen who has the right to vote at an election for members of Dáil Éireann shall have the right to vote at a Referendum.

47.4   Subject as aforesaid, the Referendum shall be regulated by law.

REPEAL OF CONSTITUTION OF SAORSTÁT ÉIREANN

AND CONTINUANCE OF LAWS

Article 48

The Constitution of Saorstát Éireann in force immediately prior to the date of the coming into operation of this Constitution and the Constitution of the Irish Free State (Saorstát Éireann) Act, 1922, in so far as that Act or any provision thereof is then in force shall be and are hereby repealed as on and from that date.

Article 49

49.1   All powers, functions, rights and prerogatives whatsoever exercisable in or in respect of Saorstát Éireann immediately before the 11th day of December, 1936, whether in virtue of the Constitution then in force or otherwise, by the authority in which the executive power of Saorstát Éireann was then vested are hereby declared to belong to the people.

49.2   It is hereby enacted that, save to the extent to which provision is made by this Constitution or may hereafter be made by law for the exercise of any such power, function, right or prerogative by any of the organs established by this Constitution, the said powers, functions, rights and prerogatives shall not be exercised or be capable of being exercised in or in respect of the State save only by or on the authority of the Government.

49.3   The Government shall be the successors of the Government of Saorstát Éireann as regards all property, assets, rights and liabilities.

Article 50

50.1   Subject to this Constitution and to the extent to which they are not inconsistent therewith, the laws in force in Saorstát Éireann immediately prior to the date of the coming into operation of this Constitution shall continue to be of full force and effect until the same or any of them shall have been repealed or amended by enactment of the Oireachtas.

50.2   Laws enacted before, but expressed to come into force after, the coming into operation of this Constitution, shall, unless otherwise enacted by the Oireachtas, come into force in accordance with the terms thereof.

Dochum Glóire Dé

agus

Onóra na hÉireann

List of Submissions

*(Note: * denotes that an oral presentation was also made)*

FROM GOVERNMENT DEPARTMENTS/OFFICES

Department of the Environment

Department of Transport, Energy and Communications

Office of the Comptroller and Auditor General

Office of the Ombudsman

FROM THE PUBLIC

ACCA

Adoption Review Group

B Ahern

Anonymous

An Bord Pleanála

Association of Irish Humanists*

Mrs M Barry

Patrick F Beisley

Birr Branch of Family Solidarity

James Blaney

Rosaleen Bohan-Long

Bord na Gaeilge

Dr Maureen Boyd

Delma Bourke

M Brennan

Barrie Brooks

John Bustard

Kathleen Cafferky

Campaign to Separate Church and State*

Children's Protection Society

Cobh Pro-Life

Ann Collins

Commission on the Family

Community Standards Association

Gerry Concagh

Dr Mary Condren

Conference of Religious of Ireland Justice Commission*

Archbishop Desmond Connell

Conradh na Gaeilge

Maureen Comer

Coolock Community Law Centre and Free Legal Advice Centres Ltd*

Dermot Cooney

Cork County Council

Cork South West Pro-Life Campaign

Daisy Corrigan

Council for the Status of the Family

The de Borda Institute*

Seámus de Barra

Brigid Di Cuarta

Paddy Doyle

Dundrum Pro-Life Campaign

Paul Durbey

J Egan

Peter I Emerson

Robert Fair

The Fannan Family

Tom Finn

Paddy Fitzgerald

Eamon Fitzpatrick

Focus on Children

Joseph F Foyle

General Council of County Councils*

J W Geoghegan

Grandparents Obliterated

The Green Party*

Dr Eamon G Hall

Frederick Haynes

Julia Heffernan

Mary A Herriott

Dr M C Hickey

M Hunt

Institute of European Affairs

Irish Association of Family Planning Doctors

The Irish Commission for Justice and Peace*

Irish National Organisation of the Unemployed*

Joint Committee for Family Planning

Derek Joyce and Dermot Murray

John R Joyce

Ann Kavanagh

Joseph Keane

Kevin Keely

Peggy Kelleher

Maureen Kelly

Peter and J Kelly

Seán and Joan Kelly

Kerry County Council

Dermot Kiely

215

Kilkenny County Council

Liam Kirwan

Kathleen Lavin

Chris Leahy

Gerard Leahy

Alderman Seán Dublin Bay Rockall Loftus

Eileen McArdle

James McCaffrey

Dr Brian McCarthy

Margaret McCarthy

Maura McCarthy

Patrick McDermott

James McGeever

Rev Canon G McGreevy

Mary McGovern

Teresa McGovern

Dr Maud McKee

Patricia McKenna MEP

Michael McKeown

Dermot J McNulty

Elizabeth McPhillips

Liam Mac Seoirse

Vincent H Madden

The Marine Institute

Rosaleen Molloy

Geraldine Moylan

Richard Muller

Muíntír na hÉireann*

C H Murray

National Association for the Mentally Handicapped of Ireland*

National Newspapers of Ireland

National Rehabilitation Board

National Women's Council of Ireland

National Youth Council of Ireland

North Belfast Justice Group

Dr Ruairí Ó Bléine

Conor Ó Briain

E O'Brien

Donal Ó Brolcháin

Con O'Callaghan and Seán Ó Céilleachair

John O'Connell

Rory O'Connell

Loretta O'Connor

Dr Hugh F O'Donnell

Joseph O'Donnell

P D O'Donnell

Anna O'Donovan

Fergus O'Donovan

Professor Eamon O'Dwyer

Dermot O'Flynn

Andreas Ó Lochlainn

Marian O'Mahony

Frank O'Meara

Dr Emer O'Reilly and Dr Keith Perdue

Jim O'Sullivan

Marie O'Sullivan

Michael J A O'Sullivan

The Office of Public Works

Parental Equality (Tallaght)

Simon Partridge

Diarmuid Rossa Phelan

Physical Education Society of Ireland

Pro-Life Campaign*

Dr Mary M Randles and Nurse D Allen

Dr Anne Rath

Paul Regan

Peter Reilly

Rochestown/Douglas Women's Group

Rosemarie Rowley

Gerard Ryan

Brian Shanley

Simon Community*

SIPTU*

South Eastern Health Board

Southern Health Board

Kathleen Stephens

John Storrs

Dr Áine Sullivan

Dr Clive R Symmons

Joan Thornton

David Thunder

UCC Law Society

Údarás na Gaeltachta

Betty Whelan

Gerry Whyte

Michael J Wilson

Women Against Violence Against Women

Women in Media and Entertainment

John Wood

Youth Defence

Index

(Note: page numbers in italics refer to the text of Bunreacht na hÉireann given passim *in the left-hand margins)*

in regard to woman in the home 85-86, 167-168

CONSTRUCTIVE VOTE OF NO CONFIDENCE 48, 49, 53-56, 136-141. *See also* Dissolution of Dáil Éireann

CONTINUANCE OF LAWS 46, 48

COSGRAVE, LIAM 3, 106

COUNCIL OF STATE *17*, 29, *32*, 32, *59*, 59, *92*

declaration or affirmation 32, 48

minor or technical change 32

COURTS 32-34, 48. *See also* High Court, Special Courts, Supreme Court

date of invalidity of a law 33

declaration taken by judges 34, 48

impeachment of judges 34, 48

judicial conduct 34, 48

minor or technical changes 34

right of appeal from a decsion to acquit 33, 48

structures 32, 48

DÁIL ÉIREANN 3, *15,* 15, *16,* 16, 26, 28, *29,* 31, *32,* 32, *53, 55,* 59, 63, 81, 82, *90,* 90, *91,* 91, 92, 105, 106, 107, 113, 114, 116, 118, 134

casual vacancies in 7

Ceann Comhairle 76, 78, 111, 114, 150, 169

Clerk of 76, 77, 78

complaints about members of 75

dissolution of 49, 53-56, 98, 136-141

elections to 76, 111

fixed term 53, 139, 140

DELEGATED LEGISLATION 28, 47. *See also* National Parliament

DEMOCRATIC LEFT 109

DE VALERA, EAMON 18, 126

DIRECTIVE PRINCIPLES OF SOCIAL POLICY 26, *45,* 45, 48

socioeconomic rights 45

DISSOLUTION OF DÁIL ÉIREANN

power to dissolve 53-56, 98, 136-141

DIVORCE 110

conditions linked in single constitutional proposal 18-19

foreign divorces 42

referendum on 18-19, 21

DOWNING STREET DECLARATION (1993) 4, 5, 108. *See also* Constitutional Reviews

EDUCATION 42-43, 48

equality in 43

extension of right to free second level 42

minimum education 42-43

right applicable to all parents 42

ELECTORAL SYSTEMS 29. *See also* National Parliament

EMIGRANTS

votes for 110

ENVIRONMENT 47, 48

Department of the 70, 76, 78

ELECTORAL AND ETHICS COMMISSION 50, 75-78, 81, 99-100. *See also* Constituency Commission, Referendum

functions of 78

membership of 78

EQUALITY BEFORE THE LAW 36-37, 48

a core norm 36

'affirmative action' 37

between men and women 37

equal access to justice 37